The Soul
of Scotland

Harry Reid

SAINT ANDREW PRESS

Edinburgh

First published in 2016 by
SAINT ANDREW PRESS
121 George Street
Edinburgh EH2 4YN

ISBN 978 0 7152 0973 8

British Library Cataloguing in Publication Data
A catalogue record for this book is available from the British Library.

It is the publisher's policy to only use papers that are natural and
recyclable and that have been manufactured from timber grown in
renewable, properly managed forests. All of the manufacturing
processes of the papers are expected to conform to the environmental
regulations of the country of origin.

Typeset by Manila Typesetting
Printed and bound in the United Kingdom by
CPI Group (UK) Ltd, Croydon

Contents

CONTENTS

CONTENTS

A preface and a warning

This book is doubly partial. It is partial in the sense that it is opinionated and subjective; it is also partial in the sense that it is incomplete because it is not intended to be a thorough and objective examination of Scotland's long and frequently combustible (sometimes literally) relationship with Christianity. Rather, it is a series of meditations and brief essays; some of these are, I trust, gently reflective, while others are pungent – and perhaps rather too pungent for some tastes.

I hope I know my limitations: for example, while I discuss at length and with enthusiasm the controversial, and often exceedingly critical, Scottish literary treatment of the nation's Christian experience, I hardly mention music, and only very briefly mention fine art and architecture. This is because I reckon I'm reasonably well equipped to deal with the literature, but almost totally unequipped to deal with other artistic matters.

I have for long believed that Scotland is an extremely literary country and that its accumulated fictive corpus is quite magnificent. Until very recently (I have not discussed contemporary writers), a surprising amount of this literary creativity dealt directly with religion, and a lot more of it treated the subject tangentially.

So, unlike the other two books on aspects of Scottish Christianity that I have written for Ann Crawford at Saint Andrew Press (both of which have been gratifyingly well received), this one is in a sense experimental. It is certainly not a narrative, although I hope it is a book that could be easily enough read from start to finish. It is also very much a book to be dipped into. There is no doubt some overlapping, though I have of course attempted to keep that to an absolute minimum. I have been enormously helped by the man I regard as the doyen of copy editors, Ivor Normand, who has heroically managed to extract at least some cohesion from an at times disparate and inchoate text.

I really hope that two things in particular shine through: my intense love of Scotland, which gets stronger as I get older; and the committed, very personal Christian slant on all the material.

I was first encouraged to write about Scottish Christianity when the then Moderator of the General Assembly of the Church of Scotland, Dr Andrew McLellan, an exceptional man to whom I owe much, commissioned me to write a candid book on the condition of the national Kirk. This was in 2001; and the resultant book was duly published by Ann Crawford of Saint Andrew Press in 2002. To help with the research, I was given an honorary fellowship by the divinity faculty of Edinburgh University; and this allowed me to tap into some impressive brainpower, as well as to spend a lot of time reading about the history of the Kirk in the splendid New College Library. During this period, I also interviewed many ministers, elders and other members of the national Church, as well as a few critical outsiders and onlookers. I accumulated considerably more material than I could possibly use in the book.

A few years later, I was commissioned by Ann Crawford to write a history of the Reformation, with particular reference to Scotland, for Saint Andrew Press. This time, I did my research at the excellent library of the Highland Theological College in Dingwall. I remain enormously indebted to Martin Cameron, the senior librarian of that young but impressive institution. Once again, I gathered much material; and some of it remained unused, ready to be plundered in aid of some future project. That project turned into this book.

Now an apology. If some of the words that follow appear to be excessively controversial, let me insist that I wish to cause no offence. The Scots are a very disputatious people and, when it comes to religion, their argumentative and combative nature sometimes takes over and utterly vanquishes their gentler qualities.

Scottish Christianity has rarely been meek and mild. Added to that, we can be a very vituperative nation. Contrary to the view sometimes expressed, I believe that most Scots have great cerebral self-confidence. Listen to Glaswegians arguing in a pub, and I defy you not to be impressed by the confidence and fluency with which contentious views are forcefully, loudly – and sometimes very humorously – expressed.

I don't think the minor Scottish aristocrat Catharine Cockburn ever argued in a Glasgow pub; in fact, I'm sure she didn't. But, in her own way, she rather proves the point. In the early eighteenth century, she took it upon herself to defend the celebrated English philosopher John Locke on various very abstruse matters of faith and theology, particularly concerning the Resurrection. She wrote fierce and exceptionally well-argued letters to various journals. In her own way, this obscure woman typified that great Scottish characteristic, the ability to flyte – that is, to take off into robust and ever-accelerating flights of argument.

Then there is a much more recent academic gentleman, William Ferguson. In his rewarding book *The Identity of the Scottish Nation*, he suddenly takes it upon himself to have some sport – over several pages – with a forgotten writer called James Aitken Wylie, a nineteenth-century Scottish cleric who was, among other things, editor of the *Free Church Magazine* and author of an 'excessively pietistic' *History of Protestantism*. Ferguson has enormous fun as he tears the 'wordy reverend historian' to shreds. You begin to feel seriously sorry for this poor, dead and long-ignored figure, now resurrected only to be destroyed – a man who apparently thought that all Scottish history amounted to a long and triumphant march towards the refulgent glories of Presbyterianism.

So, the Scots certainly like disputation. They also appreciate forceful and pugnacious writing. Hugh MacDiarmid, greatest of all the great Scots writers of the twentieth century, who is discussed at length in the pages that follow, could not resist attacking his fellow Scots writers, again and again, often in an excessively vicious ad hominem manner.

MacDiarmid, the son of a Free Church elder, was a committed Christian and Sunday School teacher in his youth, but in his maturity he became a fierce atheist. In this, he was typical of many prominent Scottish figures through the twentieth century. I suggest that his journey in some ways symbolises Scotland's loss of Christianity.

In sum, the conduct of religious and theological debate in Scotland has frequently been ferocious and, at times, completely over the top. Sometimes it has been, literally, a matter of life and death. In this overall context, it would be surprising if this book did not have some pretty robust passages.

Scottish religious disputation has too often been excessive and mired in negativity, but at many other times it has been gentler and authentically numinous, blessed with the quality of life-enriching affirmation, which is surely what Christianity is ultimately all about. And, while not too many Scots take their spiritual life seriously right now, until very recently many of them most certainly did. Scottish Christianity is neither dead nor dying; it may just be having a wee nap before it rises and flourishes once more.

Anyway, I do hope that this book has its kind and thoughtful side; but I accept that it is also, at times, quite assertive. Overall, however, my instinct is that if a choice must be made, it is better to err on the side of what Hugh MacDiarmid would no doubt have condemned as bourgeois gentility.

Above all, I trust that what follows reflects at least something of the very intense Scottish Christian experience – rich, conflicted, confused and occasionally noble as it has been.

Introduction:

Keills

Argyll is a heart-stoppingly gorgeous region of western Scotland, to the south of the Highlands. It has a spectacular coastline of around 3,000 miles, and over 90 islands, some of them of considerable size, all of them of considerable beauty.

Perhaps Argyll's most spectacular geographic feature is its multiplicity of sea lochs, these final slivers of the Atlantic which cut into the fragile edge of this extraordinary landscape where human activity has struggled to assert itself against the constant assault of time and the ocean. How are we to apprehend this wild and wonderful land?

If you look at a map of Scotland, you might imagine it as a face. The left side is pockmarked – or, worse: ravaged, knifed, assaulted, broken – whereas the right, or eastern, side along the North Sea littoral looks more smooth and mellow. This is in fact fanciful, and far from the reality, but it is none the less true that the mighty Atlantic Ocean batters the west of Scotland. There is persistent exposure and erosion.

Yet here are, among many treasures, some of the most beautiful stones in the world. The great Scottish poet Hugh MacDiarmid wrote that there are many ruined buildings in the world, but no ruined stones. There was a time when I thought this was profound; now I'm less sure. Up and down the west littoral of Scotland, there are many stones that are at once ruinous and sublime. They are stone crosses, and carved slabs, and they speak of Christian faith. They may have been eroded, but their message has not been defeated. They assert something strong and everlasting that we can only imperfectly understand. They are the most moving and noble monuments I know of.

Let us go, as an example, to the long, lonely spit of land that lies south of the little community of Tayvallich, in Knapdale. On one side is the beautiful sea loch of Sween; on the other is the Sound of Jura, a superb stretch of deep water that separates the mainland from the fine, large island where George Orwell wrote *1984*. Here is one of the largest natural whirlpools in the world; here is constant natural glory – but also wildness and harshness.

We are on the fringes here, where the Atlantic lashes and roars and bites at the land. On other days, it is quiescent and benign; but this stillness, however beguiling, is false.

The narrow, rough road from Tayvallich ends at the tip of the long peninsula. The geography is, as ever in these parts, complicated: a very small sea loch, Loch na Cille, really more of a modest inlet than a proper sea loch, has now taken the place of Loch Sween. Between it and the promontory is the tidal island of Dana. Loch na Cille, though tiny, is extremely beautiful. Cille means Columba, so the loch was named after the greatest of the Irish evangelists who came to Christianise Scotland.

Just before the road-end (and it must be one of the least travelled roads in all the British Isles), and halfway up a little hill, is a most remarkable place. Here is no soaring cathedral, no towering statue of Christ the Redeemer, no splendid, monumental city of the dead. Instead there is a gaunt, simple chapel, alone in its standfast assertion, exposed to some of the wildest weather in Europe, standing amid the unkempt grass. It looks like some bereft shed.

This is the Chapel of Keills. It dates to the twelfth century and is dedicated to the Irish Saint Abban Cormaic. It served as a parish church for at least 500 years. It is almost brutally undistinguished, without a steeple or a tower or indeed any external ornamentation. There are just four windows. Three of them are at the east end of the little building, to allow as much light as possible to fall on the simple stone altar.

Everything seems plain, lonely and stark. Yet the plainness is deceptive, for there are riches. Early Christian carvers, craftsmen and artists worked here. They used stone from the quarry of Doide, across the sea loch of Sween.

The Chapel of Keills was a kind of sacred sentinel, guarding its wonderful accumulation of crosses and cross-slabs scattered in the ancient graveyard that surrounds it. Several of these crosses, including the magnificent High Cross of Keills, have been moved by Historic Scotland into the chapel, for as I say, the weather here can be fierce, and erosion is constant.

The High Cross, which is just over 8 feet tall, and at least 1,500 years old, is a particularly fine example of early Christian art, very richly carved – although, unlike many of the crosses hereabouts, on one side only. Among the ornamentation is a clear depiction of Daniel in the lions' den. Not all the crosses and slabs in the little chapel possess grandeur. There is a small, simple slab that was made for a smith. His implements – hammer, tongs, anvil – can be seen on the eroded surface.

The wonder is that Keills is by no means unique – far from it. In this obscure part of Scotland, there are several such chapels, many such crosses. And Keills itself was once a relatively busy place. Not only did early Irish missionaries arrive to evangelise Scotland; later, Irish drovers regularly came to land on this spit of land with their cattle, to take them along the trails that eventually led to the staging post at Kilmichael Glassary, about 20 miles to the north-east. From Kilmichael, they would be taken on to the great trysts of Falkirk and Crieff. Today, such activity is hard to invoke.

I stand on the side of the little hill, just above the chapel, listening. All I can hear is the constant soft sough of the wind and the gentle tinkle of a hidden hill stream, its waters running fast to the sea loch, interrupted occasionally by the honking of wild geese on the strand below. A more peaceful, beatific scene you could hardly imagine. Not another human in sight.

There is elemental, time-denying beauty all around; then, as the wind suddenly gathers strength and its new keenness whips at me, I think of the men and women and children who worshipped their Christian God here so many centuries ago. And of how some of them created, from very little, religious art of sublime beauty. Their apprehension of what was far beyond themselves speaks to this day of something enduring and true, something that might break the heart but never the soul.

Christianity came relatively late to Scotland, to a series of places like Whithorn and Keills on the mainland, and to islands like Islay and Iona. The man who is supposed to have introduced it first – no-one can be exactly sure about this – is St Ninian, in the year AD 397. A more celebrated saint, the Irishman Columba (he died exactly 200 years after Ninian allegedly arrived at Whithorn), is the figure most generally associated with very early Christianity in the west of Scotland.

The period between AD 400 and 700 was one of sporadic, at times intensive, evangelisation by missionaries, mainly from Ireland. After AD 700, Viking raids became very frequent; these Norsemen were ferocious folk, and there is little to be said in their favour. They were unremittingly brutal and much given to slaughter and rapine. The missionaries were no match for them, nor were the native people. Yet the missionaries somehow sustained, and slowly Christianity became an integral part of Scotland's life and identity.

The history of Christianity in Scotland is confused, bloody and epic. It is intermingled with Scotland's cultural and social and even economic history to a remarkably intense extent. And, in Scotland, politics and Christianity were never far apart.

This most powerful of legacies is in our possession. Only in the late twentieth century did the fervour of Christianity, and its influence on so many aspects of national life, start to fall into severe decline. So, now it can be hard to regard Scotland as an actively Christian country. And yet this complex residue is still with us, in all its controversial richness, all its confused intermingling of grace and strife; but what of the future?

There are still hundreds of thousands of committed Christians living and working in Scotland, a compact country of around five million souls. The main difference with the past is that their Christianity is now often discreet and even furtive. I sometimes think of contemporary Christianity in Scotland as being like a strong, fast-flowing subterranean river under a city, often forgotten or ignored, but always there, always moving on, and always with the potential to find a spectacular new course.

Considerable, possibly dramatic, Christian revival is feasible in Scotland. I shall touch on that in The Elie declaration chapter. But this book is more about the past and the present than the future.

A romp through Scottish religious history

If the English toy with religion, the Scots are obsessed with it.
The Revd Campbell Maclean

The stormy saga of Scottish Christianity commenced shortly before AD 400 when St Ninian arrived in the far south-west of Scotland on his mission of evangelisation, allegedly having been sent by St Martin of Tours. This was the very time when the Western Roman Empire was in acute crisis; indeed it was breaking apart. Three generations or so earlier, the then emperor, Constantine, had officially endorsed Christianity, although not necessarily for reasons of personal faith.

This had obviously given Christianity, if not the Empire itself, a considerable boost. But Scotland had been largely ignored by the Romans, although there was – and is – a rather implausible legend that the father of Pontius Pilate briefly commanded a Roman out-station near Fortingall, and that the man who condemned Christ to death was actually born in Scotland.

Christianity was a religion in which there was a strong emphasis on succour for the poor, the sick and the downtrodden. Christians also evinced notable bravery and determination in the face of adversity, and a very clear understanding that they owed allegiance to an authority other than, and higher than, the temporal power. The second two characteristics were very much to the fore in the history of Christianity in Scotland; the first a little less so.

Ninian built a church, the famed Candida Casa, which was probably the first settled Christian site north of Hadrian's Wall. After Ninian, more evangelists arrived from Ireland, notably Columba in the sixth century. This most energetic and adventurous man had founded monasteries in Ireland; the one he founded in Scotland, on the little island of Iona, just west of the much bigger island of Mull, will forever be associated with him. So, Ninian and Columba and their colleagues spread the word in a rugged, remote country that had been very different, culturally, from the Empire in which early Christianity had grown and eventually flourished.

It is important to realise how far removed, and not only in the physical sense, were both Ireland and Scotland from Rome. Christianity, of course, has always been brilliant at adapting to local customs and cultures; it was, and remains, a religion that is pluralistic, with many different forms and churches, and indeed churches within churches. At the same time, it is also very much a religion for the individual, with its great emphasis on personal salvation. All this certainly suited the Scots, whose embracing of Christianity has constantly been marked by division and dispute (and too often by strife). There was a time, in the centuries leading up to the Reformation, when Rome did establish some kind of control over Scotland, but it was very patchy. Scots liked to do their own thing.

None of this is to diminish the valour, devotion and the sheer assertion of the early Scottish Christians. Their Christianity tended to be Celtic, not Roman. Scottish Christians were attacked, often with extreme violence, by raiders from Scandinavia. But they prevailed.

✠

A unified Scottish Kingdom very slowly and painfully emerged between the ninth and eleventh centuries. The outstanding religious figure in Scotland in this period was not Scottish, but English/Hungarian. This was St Margaret, Queen of Scotland. She transformed the Scottish court and had a very benign influence on the Scottish people. She is undoubtedly one of the four or five key figures in Scottish history.

Gradually, a strong sense of Scottish nationhood developed. Religion had played a key part in the process, and the papacy was important in validating the nationhood. The most important document of this period was the Declaration of Arbroath (1320), the language of which is noble. As a public statement of patriotism fused with religious zeal, it is unsurpassed. The declaration is a numinous document, written by Abbot Bernard de Linton of

Arbroath, Keeper of the Monymusk Reliquary which supposedly contains the relics of St Columba, and as such was an important symbolic link with Scotland's early non-Roman Christianity. The reliquary became a key totemic artefact of Scottish independence, and it neatly indicates how Scottish nationhood was a religious as much as a political concept.

The declaration reminds the Scottish king to do what he is told – that is, not to make Scots subject to the English. If the king should dare to make this dreadful mistake, he will be driven out 'as our enemy'. Further, 'as long as but 100 of us remain alive, we shall never on any conditions be subjected to English rule'. This is superb, if chippy, stuff: the monarch is being told he is a conditional monarch, the condition being that he does what his subjects want, which is basically to keep the English out.

This is the core message in the document; we arrive at it after a religious preamble about the conversion of Scots to Christianity. Significantly, the declaration also notes that the Scots are free, and nobody, not Picts or Vikings or English, could subjugate them. Edward I of England comes in for some eloquent stick: he is accused of cruelty, massacre, violence, pillage, arson, the imprisonment of clergy, the burning of monasteries, the robbing of monks, the killing of nuns. At this point in the catalogue of extreme misdemeanours, Bernard presumably became a little tired, so he just adds, with a slightly jaded sense of anticlimax: 'and other outrages without number'.

☒

The Scottish Reformation, about which very many people, including myself, have written very many words, was a remarkable movement in which modern Scotland was undoubtedly born, although there was a paradox: Protestantism was established in Scotland through the direct help of the English Queen Elizabeth and her army; and the leader of the Scottish Reformation, John Knox, was a great Anglophile. England, rather than France, was now Scotland's best ally. But the national Scottish Presbyterian Church and the Anglican Church were to be very different.

That so many words have been written about Scotland's Reformation is in a way fair enough, as Scottish Christianity increasingly became a religion of the Word. Bible study, preaching and verbal debate were all to be crucial components in the nation's official religion. There was far less emphasis on – and in some cases downright contempt for – visual art: an unfortunate downside of the zeal of the early reformers was a wanton destruction of many artefacts and some fine buildings. And, in a sense, the emphasis on the Word also rebounded on Scotland. Scottish literature, which is much discussed in this book, is rich and splendid, but much of it is downright hostile to the Scottish Christian experience.

Whatever its flaws – and there were many – the Reformation was the movement that engendered the very strong Scottish commitment to democracy, education and social welfare. The local kirk sessions played a pivotal part in their communities. Most ordinary Scots were of course much more concerned with their families, and their local kirk, than with distant affairs of state. The kirk sessions were sometimes repressive, but on the whole they were positive forces in the local communities, providing a kind of fusion of practical caring Christianity and hardline Presbyterian instruction.

The Reformation was dominant in the Lowlands. In the Highlands and Islands, both Roman Catholicism and Episcopalianism remained strong – if not in actual numbers, then certainly in terms of commitment and devotion.

At this time, also, Calvinism came to dominate the Scottish mindset. I have been an apologist for Calvinism, and to some extent I still am; yet there was again a downside, namely the distorted version of Calvinism that became prevalent for a time in the seventeenth century, although that unfortunate doctrine-twisting has been pretty well expunged. The most crisp, intelligent and effective intellectual demolition of this perverted Calvinism was, surprisingly, not produced until the twentieth century, when the perhaps unlikely figure of John Buchan, in by far his finest novel, *Witch Wood*, wrote a devastating fictive account of hypocrisy and viciousness besmirching the Scottish Presbyterian Kirk in the Scottish Borders.

Altogether, the seventeenth century – bloody, confused and epic – was a most intense and difficult time for Scottish Christianity. James VI of Scotland became, in 1603, the first British king. The new model of 'One king, Two kingdoms' was to be a disaster for Scottish Presbyterianism. Almost immediately, the settled achievements of the Reformation period, and the Presbyterian polity of Scotland, were under threat; but it was not until the succession of James's crass son Charles, who was a disastrous monarch for both Scotland and England, that the full assault began. It was led by the king's ecclesiastical henchman Archbishop William Laud, whose insistence on Anglican forms of worship in Scotland provoked resentment that sometimes spilled over into fury.

Unsurprisingly, this insensitive – and, for many, downright treacherous – meddling led to a determined fightback. The great Scottish National Covenant of 1638 is a wonderful document, and one that greatly influenced the authors of the American Declaration of Independence in 1776. While it is nothing like as eloquent or as moving as the Declaration of Arbroath, and indeed is somewhat disfigured by a tedious legalism, it nonetheless manages to achieve a magnificent assertion of national liberty.

It was enormously popular; its vigorous and deep acceptance by the Scottish people came about through an intensive and almost orgiastic national endorsement, something that is unique in British history. For a time, the Scottish people were impassioned with a glorious fervour that combined profound religious conviction, political ardour and a noble desire for freedom. When the Marquess of Hamilton, the leading Scot at the court of King Charles in England, arrived at Leith with the impossible task of trying to persuade the Scottish people to reject the Covenant, he found, in effect, a nation lined up to make him think again.

This was perhaps the most moving and splendid set-piece in the entire tableau of Scottish history. The assembled Scottish nobility were the first to meet him; then the gentry, almost like an army ready for battle, standing in their ranks for almost 2 miles. Then, at the far end of Leith Links, stood more than 600 kirk ministers. And all the way up the hill to Edinburgh were the ordinary folk – more than 20,000 of them. At least half the parishes in Scotland were directly represented.

The Covenant created something very special – the belief that an entire nation was directly covenanted with God. This notion of the covenanted godly nation, of the Scottish people being united in a unique Christian commonwealth, remained a potent idea for many years. It made the national Presbyterian Church more important than the nation's Parliament. At the same time, the practical consequences of the idea of the Covenant should not be exaggerated, for – as so often in Scotland's Christian history – the bond was soon fractured.

The last great Anglo-Scottish war was waged in 1650–2, when Oliver Cromwell, a puritan English Christian of excessive zeal, a military genius, and a brilliant if at times crazed politician, rampaged around Scotland, subjugating the Scots and Scotland with a thoroughness that rankles, for many, to this day. The end came with the fall of the great castle of Dunnottar, near Stonehaven.

Within two generations, the few remaining Covenanters were a tiny and valiant, if somewhat fanatical, rump who were brutally hunted down like animals by the vicious, hate-filled forces of the state. These later Covenanters were extraordinary people, and for many in Scotland to this day they remain extremely divisive; some revere them, not least for their quite amazing courage; others, probably far more, detest them. They are remembered in some very simple but extraordinarily beautiful poems.

But the idea of the covenanted nation (now without the Covenanters) struggled on for several generations. It was finally smashed when the national Kirk broke in two at the time of the Disruption in 1843.

✠

Meanwhile, the Act of Union in 1707, a matter of controversy then and ever since, was very problematic for Christianity in Scotland, not least because Scotland's preferred version of Christianity had to become yet more politicised. The Union was deeply unpopular in Scotland, but the people of Scotland could not muster sufficient political will to resist it. They looked to their national Church to resist the proposed Union. Some unlikely alliances were formed at this time, Covenanters finding common cause with Jacobites. It was religion that divided the two nations more than anything else: Scottish Presbyterianism was set against English Episcopalianism. The Union was opposed bitterly by the Scottish Kirk.

To placate Scotland's religious fury, protection was granted to the Scottish Kirk in the provisions of the Union legislation; but, even so, many Scots feared that their beloved Church would not, or indeed could not, be protected by an essentially English Parliament. And their fears were justified, for within five years the Union was breached, on the controversial and sensitive issue of church patronage. So, although 'the Protestant religion and the Presbyterian government' had allegedly been safeguarded in 1707, more and more Scots came to realise that their national religion had not in fact been protected at all.

The Kirk had led the opposition to the Union, but had proved to be politically impotent. The new British state was duly created, but it was not wanted by many, probably most, in Scotland, including the majority of clerics. There was a specific fear within the national Kirk that the Union would lead to the reimposition of bishops, but there was also a more generalised fear of religious interference from London. The General Assembly objected very strongly to the proposed Union, while Scottish Catholics saw it as a blow to their hopes that the Stuarts would one day rule Scotland again. (At this divisive and wretched time, one Scottish aristocrat actually suggested that, after the Union, English armies would be able to move freely into Scotland without opposition in order to put down any Catholic insurrection.)

The Kirk had done its best to mobilise Scottish public opinion against the Union, but it failed; the Scottish Parliament, probably at that stage in Scottish history less representative than the Kirk, proved happy to go against the clear grain of Scottish opinion, and it voted to abolish itself by 110 votes to 47. So, when the first real breach of the terms of the Union proved to be on a religious matter, this was hardly surprising. The Kirk was now seen to be enfeebled and unable to speak and act for Scotland. In the absence of a Scottish Parliament, the General Assembly of the national Kirk did for a time become the nearest thing the Scottish people had to a proper parliament of their own, but it was hardly a proper Parliament.

Meanwhile, the divisive tendency in Scotland continued through the decades. In the mid-nineteenth century, the most spectacular division occurred, the result of a splendidly dramatic walkout from the General Assembly. This was of course the highly significant – and tragic – Disruption of 1843, when the national Church in effect split into two parts in the course of a few hours. This resulted in the energy of Scottish Protestant Christians – and how energetic these Scottish Victorian Christians tended to be – being grievously wasted. For instance, there was an enormous effort to build new churches and to raise funds for these buildings. The speed and scale of building was phenomenal; but Scotland became seriously, and eventually embarrassingly, over-churched.

The split had materialised over the ever-controversial issue of patronage, but there was a social split too. The Kirk had become far too worldly. It was slack and soft. That eloquent minister Campbell Maclean, a notable Presbyterian cleric in late twentieth-century Scotland, much later characterised its diminished state perfectly when he noted that the Kirk's ministers had become dressy; they dined and wined with the laird, they played cards (heaven forfend) and, worst of all, they actually read their sermons! By contrast, the new Church was for upstarts and querulous busybodies devoid of all good taste, uncultured pulpiteers who purveyed fear-ridden religious emotionalism. This pastiche was Campbell Maclean at his mischievous best, but there is reality lurking there too.

Meanwhile, there was nothing like enough practical Christian work among the new, urbanised, exploited and largely unchurched Scottish proletariat. In this context, the building of so many grand new churches for the middle classes could be regarded as a sick-making affront, a shamefully misdirected effort.

☒

Today, the most obvious physical manifestation of the decline of organised Christianity in Scotland, and the rise of secularism, is the multiplicity of redundant churches, many of them very fine monuments of ecclesiastical architecture, which are now used for a variety of non-religious purposes.

The Disruption had confirmed, in the most melodramatic fashion, the propensity of organised Scottish Christianity to split, split and split again. As an example of the fracturing tendency, it was well-nigh perfect. The legacy, however, was anything but perfect. Protestant Scotland was both energised and enfeebled; at the very time when it needed to be strong, far too much energy was misdirected to what amounted to petty inter-church competition. This was when Scotland was undergoing problematic social and industrial change that desperately required a committed and coherent Christian response. That response never came.

Thus, in the second half of the nineteenth century, as Scotland was almost overwhelmed by the process of industrialisation, Scottish Christianity took a spectacular wrong turning. The nation's industrial output was amazing: at one point, Glasgow, a prodigiously productive industrial city, was building more than half the ships that were launched in the entire world. But it brought with it a tremendous social cost; and Christianity in Scotland shamefully stood on the sidelines.

In Scotland, far too much time and energy was dissipated after the Disruption in the competitive, showy building of new churches and schools and manses. What was really required, as the visionary socialist Keir Hardie came to understand, was a fusion of practical politics and Christianity. As it was, Scotland welcomed a huge number of immigrants from Ireland, partly because Scotland itself was not able to find enough workers to cope with the demands of over-rapid industrialisation, and partly because conditions in Ireland were particularly desperate. 'Welcomed' is in some ways an insensitive and inaccurate word, for sadly some of these immigrants were treated abominably.

Indeed, the Revd Campbell Maclean, who was not without personal sympathy for the mainly Catholic Irish immigrants, claimed that they had made their 'alien God' a symbol of their very will to survive. And so, industrial Scotland became the battleground for what he termed a 'holy war'. The national Church in Scotland became mired in a disgraceful anti-Irish campaign, producing scarring tensions, some of which linger to this day.

There was a great cleansing – and something of a revival – in the mid-twentieth century, led by a clever and saintly man called John Baillie. Eventually, the Roman Catholic Church in Scotland, which had become somewhat battered and cowed, revived significantly, mainly due to the efforts of an exceptional cleric, Cardinal Tom Winning.

But any revival of Christianity was superficial and short-lived. Indeed, the 1960s and 1970s were decades of grievous, even catastrophic, decline for Scottish Christianity. At this time, a clear but largely unheeded voice was that of the eminent Dominican, Father Anthony Ross, Roman Catholic chaplain to Edinburgh University, a friend and counsellor to many students, Catholic or not, and a very significant figure in the capital's intellectual and cultural scene in the early 1970s. He was a keen student of Scottish history, and he insisted that Christianity had helped to give Scotland unity long before there was any significant political unity. But he felt that this historic Christian legacy had been betrayed.

When he surveyed the condition of contemporary Christianity in 1960s Scotland, he feared for the future. He insisted that Scotland had had various opportunities to become a truly Christian nation, but these opportunities had been thrown away. Scotland had become essentially secular and had completely lost confidence in the gospel of Christ and the authority of the Holy Spirit.

Now, 45 years on, Scottish Christianity is finding it even more difficult to respond to the prevailing and confident secularism of our times. I suspect, however, that this is just a passing phase; and at the close of this book I shall sketch out some notions that may just offer a possible renewal.

PART I

Travelogue

Listen to the stones

Part 1 of this book, the Travelogue, is dedicated to the Revd Henry Thorold. I first met Henry in 1977, when he was 56, although he looked much older. On a journalistic assignment in deepest England, I'd been interviewing the Duke of Rutland at Belvoir Castle. As I drove away from the beautiful Vale of Belvoir, I passed through a large village called Sedgebrook. There was a throng of folk at the entrance to the grounds of the village school. I stopped to see what was going on – and just then an ancient grey Bentley swept by, rather too fast, into the school grounds.

As people scattered, the car stopped right in front of the temporary podium, and out stepped a tall, imposing, somewhat shambling figure. This turned out to be the Revd Henry Thorold, who was to open the fête. Apart from his dog collar and elaborate buttonhole, he was dressed entirely in black. He accomplished his official chore with great style, taking the opportunity to plug his latest booklet on Lincolnshire's redundant churches. When he had finished his speech, I approached him and asked what the Church thought of the local controversies I'd been discussing with the duke. 'Don't you ask me about the Church, my man,' he boomed. 'I may be in holy orders, but I have nothing, absolutely nothing, to do with the Church.' At this, I noticed, the local vicar nodded vigorously. Later, I learned that his words were not entirely true. He was a distinguished if unhappy Anglican, and an eminent authority on church buildings.

Despite the unfortunate start, we became friends. He invited me to his splendid house, the fourteenth-century Marston Hall. Marston is a small village situated just north of Grantham – you can just see it from the east-coast mainline. Not far away is Southwell Cathedral, one of Henry's favourite buildings. He was 'squarson' of Marston – that is, both squire and parson. The Thorolds went

3

back, he once told me, very many centuries. One Thorold was sheriff of Lincoln in 1052. Henry dedicated one of his books to Dame Eugenia Thorold, the abbess of Pontoise, who died in 1667.

He was a doughty campaigner for the preservation of very old churches, of which there were many in surrounding Lincolnshire and Nottinghamshire, but he was also a general champion of the ruined churches, abbeys and priories of England, Wales and Scotland. He wrote many distinguished and erudite guide books. He was a good friend of John Betjeman and Peter Burton, and an entertaining if very opinionated conversationalist. When his *Collins Guide to the Ruined Abbeys of England, Wales and Scotland* was published in 1993, he sent me a copy, simply inscribed: 'Harry – your Scottish abbeys are wonderful'. And he meant it. Although he was the quintessential Englishman, he had a genuine love for Scotland.

After studying at Christ Church, Oxford, where – as he was fond of reminding people – the college chapel was in fact a cathedral, he moved north and was ordained in Scotland, where he served as an Episcopalian priest at Gilbert Scott's fine St Paul's Cathedral in the heart of Dundee, becoming personal chaplain to the Bishop of Brechin. But he soon returned to England.

Although an authentic authority on church history and church architecture, he told me I must not worry if I mixed up my squints with my squinches, or despair if I confused the Cistercians with the Premonstratensians. What really mattered, he insisted, was *atmosphere*, the feel of a place, the thrill of discovery and – above all – 'what the stones say'. By this last phrase he meant not only the (frequently hard to decipher) inscriptions on the actual stones, but – more importantly and more mysteriously – how the ancient buildings spoke to you. He believed that you could learn far more about Christianity by pottering around old churches and abbeys than by heeding what contemporary Christian clerics had to say.

Pilgrimage

Addressing the Kirk's General Assembly in 2011, the Lord High Commissioner, Lord Wilson of Tillyorn, commended the revival of pilgrimage. He said: 'The idea of pilgrimage, travelling preferably by foot, is of course a very old one. It is very good to know that old practice is being revived.'

I could not agree more. Tourism is the world's biggest industry; and faith tourism is making a rapidly growing contribution to the industry, right across the globe. But of course we are talking here about something that is far more than commercial; we are talking about spiritual quest, often combined with considerable physical effort. And I would not discount the vast potential that there is in the development of faith tourism for Scotland's economy. Scotland is a relatively small country, but its geography is very varied and its physicality is complicated. It is wonderfully rich in religious sites and destinations. In this chapter, I present an admittedly very selective but, I hope, enthusiastic and realistic guide to some of Scotland's most special places. There are literally thousands of important religious sites in Scotland, so this chapter is necessarily eclectic.

I think Whithorn, and its fine environs in the Machars peninsula, must be the primary focus. Not only is this where Christianity first came to Scotland; Whithorn was also the destination of King Robert the Bruce, Scotland's most celebrated monarch, as he struggled slowly southwards on his great pilgrimage shortly before he died in 1329. This was, I believe, the most moving journey in Scotland's history.

If I were to choose some special places for faith tourism in Scotland, my list would no doubt be disputed by just about everybody who studies it. But, apart from Whithorn, I would certainly wish to make a special case for Keills Chapel in Argyll, the Ukrainian prisoner of war chapel near Lockerbie, the secret hidden seminary at Scalan in the Braes of Glenlivet, and Carfin Grotto.

It's also important to note that Scotland has more than 30 cathedrals, some of which are indubitably very special indeed. Some are ruined; others still maintain flourishing congregations. I have visited most, but not quite all of them.

Glasgow has four splendid and very different cathedrals; the Greek Orthodox one in the Dowanhill area was formerly a Victorian Presbyterian church. The Roman Catholic one by the River Clyde is relatively small and, after its recent makeover, exceptionally bright and airy; it is notable for the utterly magnificent portrait of Saint John Ogilvie by Peter Howson. The Episcopal cathedral of St Mary in the West End is a fine Gothic church by Sir George Gilbert Scott.

It is not demeaning to these three to suggest that they cannot equal the magnificence – admittedly the somewhat dark and brooding magnificence – of the cathedral of St Mungo, dedicated in 1136. It is the largest and most complete of Scotland's medieval cathedrals that are still used for regular worship; its minister is known as the Minister of Glasgow.

This cathedral, and the superb northern cathedral of St Magnus in Orkney, are without doubt among the most special religious buildings in the entire British Isles. I was privileged to be shown round St Magnus Cathedral by the Revd Ron Ferguson when he was minister there; he had many insights about the ongoing life of the church, and these smashed any notions that ancient and venerable cathedrals have to be fusty and arid places.

I was equally privileged to be guided round St Mungo's Cathedral, Glasgow, including some secret and rarely visited places, by the scholar Dr James Macaulay, who is one of its distinguished elders; that was also an unforgettable experience. He made this somewhat mysterious but very special building a place of living history and living faith.

Some of Scotland's cathedrals are to be found in unlikely places. There is one on the small island of Iona and another on the even smaller island of Lismore. The fine small town of Oban in Argyll – surprisingly, the largest community on Scotland's Atlantic coast – boasts two cathedrals; again surprisingly, neither has anything to do with the Church of Scotland. The Episcopal cathedral is a most unusual place, a bit like three separate buildings squeezed into one cramped site. This reflects its erratic stop-start construction over more than a century. So, while it is distinctly higgledy-piggledy, with a confusion of different styles, it possesses a pleasing eccentricity and intimacy. The Roman Catholic cathedral on the Corran Esplanade is, for a Catholic church, quite plain, even austere; it is splendidly situated so near the sea that, if the wind is blowing from the right direction, it is full of sea smells and sea sounds.

Having written that, my personal preference is for smaller and more intimate churches, some of which are discreet almost to the point of secrecy. I am particularly fond of the tiny community of Anwoth, near Gatehouse in the gorgeous Galloway countryside. Here are not one but two churches. The old parish church was built in the 1620s and is thus an early post-Reformation church. It is famed for its association with Samuel Rutherford, the great scholar and hero of the Covenanting movement, who ministered here for a decade. Nearby is the parish church, built 200 years later, which sadly ended its life as a working church in the early twenty-first century and is now privately, and well, maintained.

Anwoth was a favourite place of Dorothy L. Sayers, the (somewhat controversial) Christian apologist who gave very popular, if eccentric, Christian talks on the radio during the Second World War as part of the effort to boost morale on the home front. She is now remembered mainly for her rather snooty detective tales featuring Lord Peter Wimsey.

I wish to mention just one other church in this section: St Conan's Kirk, on a magnificent site above Loch Awe. The A85 trunk road curves round the northern end of this deep and brooding loch; somehow, on the very steep wooded slope between the road and the loch, there is room for both the Glasgow–Oban railway and this gem of a church, a hotchpotch of different architectural styles, built in stages between 1881 and 1930.

It looks small from the outside, but its interior is surprisingly grand and spacious, almost like a small cathedral. There are no fewer than three separate chapels within the kirk, as well as the long nave and a lovely cloistered area. There are gargoyles and other pieces of distinctly eccentric stonework, and a magnificent sundial. The situation is squeezed; you can be standing just outside the kirk, and a train can rush by just yards beneath you while huge lorries are roaring past just above you. Despite this, it somehow contrives to be a place of tranquillity and unusual beauty.

Smithton and Scalan

On a weekday morning in the spring of 2013, I found myself in Inverness with a couple of hours to kill. I had read a couple of very positive articles about the architecture of the Roman Catholic church at nearby Culloden, opened in 2009 after an appeal had raised over £750,000, so I decided to drive over and have a look at it. Needless to say, it was shut. It was impressive enough from the outside, but its modernity and freshness seemed slightly diminished because it was so adamantly shut against the quotidian world.

As I returned to my car, I noticed, diagonally across the road, a stream of people going into a long, low building, equally modern if less striking in its external appearance. I thought it must be a primary school, but then I noticed that there were plenty of old people and several middle-aged folk going in as well as toddlers and children and their parents or minders. I decided to wander in myself; to my genuine astonishment, I discovered it was a church. How often on a Scottish weekday morning do you find so many folk of all ages going into a church?

Standing in the entrance lobby was the minister, David Meredith. He wasn't wearing a dog collar, but he introduced himself at once, and then said: 'You are Harry Reid. Welcome!' I'm not at all famous, so this surprised me. Mr Meredith told me I was in Smithton-Culloden Free Church of Scotland, and that he knew all about my writings on Scottish religious matters. He offered to show me round, and suggested that we could then have coffee and a chat.

This was one of the most positive moments I had as I toured round Scotland. I emphasise: I was only there by accident. No-one, not David or any of his congregation, could have had the faintest idea that I was in the area. The first surprise was that the church was actually open on a weekday; the second was that it was so busy. The feeling of positivity grew as I was shown round by David.

He was, by a considerable margin, by far the most upbeat cleric I met on my travels. And he was showing me round an evangelical Presbyterian Free Church – the sort of place that is still all too often characterised in popular culture as being hardline, dour and unwelcoming.

The place was teeming, and everyone was friendly. The kitchen was busy; people were having coffee here and there in various recreation areas. There were toddlers' groups, study groups and old folk's groups. There was a sense of much semi-organised activity, plus quite a few people just sitting around blethering. Even so, there was a sense of social purpose, a kind of benign bustle. The only quiet spaces were the sanctuary and David's study.

The sanctuary, where worship takes place, sits 450 comfortably. It appeared contemporary and comfortable – but a bit bland, like a convention centre. No cross was on view anywhere, which surprised me and irritated me just slightly. There was nothing like a traditional altar or pulpit; the ambience was functional and slightly aseptic. The space was light and airy but not at all frivolous.

There was a utilitarian, softly austere feel to it all, producing a definite sense that anything ceremonial, any direct appeal to the emotions, would be out of place. The blandness was not so much blandness as a stripping-away of any flimflammery that might detract from the purposes of God.

At the services each Sunday, in the morning and again in the evening, David preaches for about 40 minutes. He told me he sought to offer the very best of contemporary Calvinism. He understood that fundamentalist Calvinism could be sectarian, and insisted that he and his church were not sectarian. David also said his church was attracting a steady flow of new members (in what, admittedly, is an area enjoying a spectacular population boom) and was doing particularly well in the 20–30 age group. Morning service each Sunday was attended by about 400 (about twice as many as the nearest Church of Scotland), and evening service by about 250.

David firmly put his success down to one simple tenet: respect for the authority of the Bible. The church was built in 1990; it was so successful that an extension had to be built 20 years later, at a cost of £1.6 million.

There were more women than men in David's busy church that morning, but of course the Free Church does not ordain women ministers. 'Our ministers and our elders are all male', David confirmed. 'The old chauvinism of the past has gone, but female elders or ministers will never happen. We have two women on our church staff: one deals with our families, the other with our young people. Neither has a preaching role.'

I sensed that some things would be changing – perhaps softening is a better word – in his church in the years to come. He did not demur. When I asked for a specific example, he said: 'Music. We used to have no music at all. About two years ago, we decided to have some. We use a piano and the occasional praise band.' I left realising that I'd chanced on something that was completely counter to the prevailing pessimism and insecurity that undermines so much of contemporary Scottish Christianity.

⚔

Some 45 miles from David's church as the crow flies, but rather more if you travel by road, is another place of strong spirituality. This place, however, is remote, lonely, abandoned and – almost – bereft. What gives it life and strength is its history.

If that proverbial crow flew to it in a straight line from Culloden, it would fly over some of the most beautiful and varied country in all Scotland: across the lovely valley of the River Findhorn, surely Scotland's finest and most intriguing river, then the bleak bare moor by Lochindorb, then the douce hills of Cromdale, and finally the grim heights between Upper Glenlivet and the wind-blasted Ladder Hills. This last area is, supremely, whisky country, with a rich history of illicit distilling and general derring-do; today it is a hard-worked high country, parts of which are punctuated with famous (and legal) distilleries, most of them spruce and trig, boasting slick visitor centres and shopping halls. The area is criss-crossed by some of the highest roads in Scotland. Even in May, the weather can be bitterly cold.

I experienced this myself as I sought my lonely destination, the remote house of Scalan, high in the Upper Braes of Glenlivet.

Admittedly the weather was freakish: the nearby Lecht road – the second-highest public road in Scotland – was covered with 3 inches of snow. As I got out of my car at an obscure road-end, I was battered and whipped not so much by snow, although there were intermittent fierce flurries, as by persistent hail and some of the most vicious winds I've ever experienced in Scotland – and this was in *late* May.

But, in a way, the fierce and bitter weather was appropriate, because it made me approach my destination in a mood that better allowed me to understand things such as privation, perseverance and a general battling against the odds and the elements. As I struggled along a (thankfully) well-defined track, a thin sun broke the gloom. Suddenly I could see, a few hundred yards away, an old grim house standing almost furtively in its amphitheatre of hills that were being battered by gusting winds and powdered with snow. This was once the 'forbidden seminary' of Scalan, a gaunt building that housed a clandestine school where Catholic priests were, illegally, trained.

I pushed open the door and found the inside just as cold as the outside, though there was welcome respite from the wind. I glanced at the visitors' book: a group who had visited a month earlier noted that they had found it hard to gain access because the doorway was blocked by snow. They had to dig hard for several minutes before getting in.

As I looked round the empty building, there was a pervasive sense of loss. Downstairs, the study/refectory, the library and 'bishop's room'; upstairs, the tiny chapel, the Master's room and the dormitory – all of them were stripped bare. Slowly, I understood that this historic 'nursery of faith' was a place worthy of veneration and deep respect.

The story of Scalan has been told thoroughly and exceptionally well by Dr John Watts, the distinguished historian-headmaster. What follows is a brief account of the seminary in that troubled century, the eighteenth.

The authorities were intent on expunging Catholicism from Scotland, but they never quite succeeded. One of the areas where Catholicism had flourished, and continued to be practised covertly, was the area around Buckie and Huntly. The great family hereabouts was that of the Gordons, who remained Catholic. Scalan lies in harsher high country, somewhat to the south and the west but still within the territory the Gordons protected. Even though Catholic worship was banned and attendance at mass was punishable by deportation, plenty of people were prepared to break the law; they were sustained by the Gordons. But they needed priests.

So, it was decided to train Scottish priests locally. Here, high among the Upper Braes of Glenlivet, a small group of priest/teachers prepared students, most of them local, and defied proscription and persecution for over 80 years. The first two Scalan students raised to the priesthood were George Gordon and Hugh Macdonald, who was the son of the laird of Morar in the West Highlands.

In the early years, the college was kept safe by the Gordon family, but in the late 1720s soldiers were sent to 'molest' it several times. The building was not directly assaulted, but the students had to flee. There followed a period of constant harassment for the students and their teachers, already suffering privation in 'as cold and stormy a place as there is in all Scotland', as one of the trainee priests put it. Only at the very end of the century was the little illicit seminary finally closed. Just over 100 priests had been trained there. This was testament to strong faith, unremitting resolution and considerable physical bravery.

The worst period for Scalan came, inevitably, during the reprisals that followed the Battle of Culloden. The students, anticipating serious trouble, took from the seminary almost everything that could be moved, including the vestments, the books and the documents, and placed them carefully in various hiding places. A detachment of troops was indeed sent to Glenlivet. Among much other destruction, the soldiers demolished the supposedly secret seminary, smashing it and then burning it. The heather roof went first. As the students and their teachers had anticipated this wanton attack, they were safe, having disappeared into the various high glens surrounding the site. Eventually, a temporary replacement building was erected; there were still some soldiers in the area, but they proved susceptible to bribes.

Then the Kirk's General Assembly sent a couple of commissioners to report on what was going on in Glenlivet. Their visit was cursory. They claimed, absurdly, that there were thirty boys and three priests in the little house, but this was just exaggerated local hearsay. The reality at this particular time was that there were only five boys – and no priest/instructor.

The boys who studied at Scalan endured a very tough life, not least because of the constant fear of attack; they had to be ready to move into the surrounding hills, which were hardly hospitable even in high summer, at any time of day or night. Their daily routine was austere: it began at 6am, when they washed in the Crombie Burn by the house – how bitterly cold that must have been in winter – and then they faced a breakfast of porridge. Indeed, porridge was often served three times a day. Meat was served two or three times a week.

Among the teachers were various men who went on to serve the Roman Catholic Church well in various capacities. Perhaps the most notable was John Geddes, who became a bishop and revived the Scots College in Spain. Of the pupils, the most notable was probably Paul McPherson, who became a well-regarded priest and eventually had a distinguished and long career, not in Scotland but in Rome.

What is now the house of Scalan, the one I describe above, was built in the late 1760s, which were slightly safer times. The thick outer walls have protected the interior ever since. At the beginning of the nineteenth century, times became more propitious for Scottish Catholics. A new, larger seminary was safely established near Inverurie in Aberdeenshire. It may seem contrived to link the modern story of the Free Church at Smithton-Culloden and the eighteenth-century saga of the Roman Catholic Church defying proscription at Scalan. But both, in admittedly very different ways, tell of the necessity of going against the odds and determinedly countering the prevailing culture. Of course, the Free Church, in early twenty-first-century Scotland, is not banned, and its adherents do not face the physical dangers that Roman Catholics faced all those years ago. But it is a Church that has endured many crises, splits, secessions and reinventions since it was born at the Disruption of 1843. 'Freedom' can easily descend to near-anarchy. For a long time in modern Scotland, the Free Church was mocked and even vilified as a Church for bigots and prudes, killjoys and hypocrites.

Some of the media were partly responsible for the caricature, which sometimes verged on the cruel.

Possibly because Scotland is now so much more secular, there is both more indifference and more respect for the Free Church. It is seen to be standing by its beliefs rather than trimming; at the same time, it is seen to be willing to embrace change. This may be paradoxical, but the Free Church is managing to attract new members. Attendances at its services are rising, albeit modestly. In 2013, an average total of 12,839 people attended Free Church services every week. This is a modest number compared to that of the Church of Scotland; but at least the Free Church can point to a trend in the right direction, and particularly among 20- to 30-year-olds. And the trend may well be strengthened as more congregations leave the national Kirk, annoyed by its tolerance of gay clergy and by other issues.

So, the Free Church is somehow managing not just to survive but to grow, amid a wider moral and social context that remains hostile: one in which traditional Presbyterianism is even now routinely mocked and even despised. I'm sure one of the reasons for the Free Church success is that it has some exceptional ministers, such as David Meredith, and David Robertson in Dundee. It also maintains its own small but impressive seminary in Edinburgh, where the academic standards are consistently high.

Obviously, David Meredith and his congregation can assert their faith more openly and in a far less hostile environment than the teachers and scholars of Scalan. But, even so, their success is being achieved amid something that can still be akin to sociological intimidation.

☒

Meanwhile, if the secret seminary at Scalan represents one kind of Catholic defiance, another is represented at the remarkable Roman Catholic church at Tynet, a few miles inland from the North Sea coast. Built to deceive, and to look like a sheep cot – if a rather grandiose one – it was built when the celebration of mass was still an offence. It has nothing of the gaunt defiance of Scalan, and is beautifully maintained; inside, it is almost plush. It is used regularly for worship.

Nearby is the splendid coastal town of Buckie, which has a large harbour area and an attractive upper town. Christianity seems to be doing rather better here than in most Scottish communities. Buckie has a population of around 10,000 and has plenty of active churches. At one time a very prosperous fishing port, famous for its huge fleet of drifters, it has had to reinvent itself as a town servicing the oil industry. Many of the population now work offshore.

In this area of north-east Scotland, the Roman Catholic Church survived the immediate post-Reformation era better than anywhere else in Scotland. The most dominant church, of the eight that still have thriving congregations, is St Peter's Roman Catholic church towards the west of the upper town. A splendid Gothic church with two tall towers, which is sometimes described as 'Buckie Cathedral', it was built in the mid-nineteenth century, and it still speaks of confidence, even assertion.

Even here, the story is one of decline. St Peter's used to have two priests; now it struggles to maintain one. The large garden area immediately to the south of the church was once a considerable vegetable and fruit garden; now it is wasteland. 'No-one wants to know about gardening now; it's too much like hard work', I was told.

Yet the church is by no means moribund. Around 250 attend mass every Sunday. Its high exterior, which makes it a notable landmark, catching the eye from miles around, is forbidding – and defiant? Inside, it is gracious, airy and very attractive, with a lot of fine modern artwork. The low marble wall around the altar was at one point to be taken down to make the area more 'open', but thankfully sensible advice prevailed after a parishioners' revolt.

⊠

A smaller gem of a church is to be found in the little town of Fochabers, a few miles inland. This is the Gordon Chapel, which is adorned with gorgeous pre-Raphaelite stained-glass windows by Sir Edward Burne Jones. Much later, Petra Anderston completed an exceptional stained-glass window depicting the feeding of the 5,000 in a Banffshire setting. This was to acknowledge more recent benefactors, the Baxter family.

The chapel was built in the 1830s following a benefaction from a member of the Gordon family – most of whom were Catholics – who sold all her jewellery to pay for it. The chapel has survived several vicissitudes. At one time, it actually belonged not to the Episcopal Church but to the Crown Estate. Troops were billeted here during the Second World War, and later it was proposed that it be converted into a cinema. Luckily, this philistinism was thwarted after a local revolt, and the chapel was returned to the Scottish Episcopal Church.

This area of Scotland is home to probably more beautiful and special churches – many of them modest in size – than any other part of Scotland. Along the splendid, craggy coastline, there are some particularly lovely little white churches, generally high above the sea. The most spectacular is the one at Findochty, a simple white box perched above the eastern of the community's two little harbours. The hill on which it stands is not high, but very steep; beneath it, the community of lower Findochty nestles around its little harbour. This church can be seen from many miles away. Inside, it is spare and perfectly maintained.

Three caves

Of the two great early evangelisers of Scotland, St Columba is far more celebrated than Ninian. Yet, when it comes to their caves, it's the other way round. St Ninian's Cave is much visited, while St Columba's Cave, at the north end of Loch Caolisport, is discreet to the point of neglect.

To get to the rather obscure St Columba's Cave, you can drive south from Ardrishaig on Loch Fyne, and after a mile or so turn right on to the narrow road that traverses the main Knapdale peninsula.

When you come to the small community of Achahoish on the west side of the peninsula, you turn on to the even narrower road that twists down to the head of Loch Caolisport, perhaps the loveliest of all the many sea lochs on Scotland's west coast.

The little road appears to be meandering to nowhere in particular. It's actually heading for the local 'big hoose', a splendid and unlikely Victorian pile designed by the great architect David Bryce in the late 1860s, called Ellary House. (A few years later, a calamitous fire almost destroyed it, and it was rebuilt, on an even grander scale, by Robert Lorimer.) After a mile or so, as you drive round the head of the loch, you can see its impressive bulk, peeking through the trees on the western shore.

Shortly before you reach the house, a discreet sign indicates that you have arrived at St Columba's Cave. You can park by the lochside and walk through ancient woodland past a derelict twelfth-century chapel – the ruins are in a pretty sorry state, and in truth don't amount to much. Most of the stone was probably quarried by local folk; this has been the fate of many monuments throughout Scotland.

A few yards further into the woods, there is a little drama. Even though you are looking for the cave, there is a shock as not one but two caves suddenly appear. Both are deep and impressive, and somehow unexpected and thrilling. The caves were, as archaeologists have proved, used as long ago as 9000–8000 BC, but are mainly now of interest because Christian ceremonies were held here in the sixth and seventh centuries.

The specific association with Columba may be spurious; some say he landed here before he went on to Iona. In a way, this would have made sense, for he would probably have required the permission of the ruler of Dalriada, King Conall, to take over Iona, which is in effect what he was about to do.

King Conall lived in a fort, now disappeared, atop a hill near Loch Caolisport; and Columba, who was a kinsman of Conall, may well have come to visit him. But, if so, why did he not stay at Conall's fort? Perhaps his use of the cave was to indicate his humility and his holiness.

A Christian service is still held in the larger right-hand cave every Good Friday; there is an altar slab, and a little basin for the holy water, and various improvised crosses. More crosses are scratched on to the walls.

The agile may climb the crags above the caves and join an old track that leads south-west towards the Point of Knap. Nearby stands St Maelrubha's Knap Chapel. Here, there is a renowned collection of carved stones. The Chapel of Keills, described in the introduction to this book, is not far away across Loch Sween. Altogether, this part of Argyll is a treasure house. There are many ancient crosses that mark churchyards, various places of sanctuary and old pilgrims' routes.

✖

Back down at the roadside, by Loch Caolisport, there is hardly any traffic. Along the lochside are lovely deciduous woods, wild flowers and rhododendrons. You can glance down to the bulk of Ellary House, towering above the water, a monument to Victorian assurance and assertion; and then look back in the direction of the caves, and think of all the privations and trials that the early evangelists must have endured. Meanwhile, the loch is almost too picturesque. Not far from the shore, there is an exquisite little islet called Eilean na h-Uamhaidh (isle of the cave). This a place of almost sublime peace.

Yet, even quite recently, there were some very bad times in this apparently paradisiacal vicinity. A mile or so up behind the twin caves, in the direction of Kilmory Knap, there were terrible skirmishes and even battles in the early nineteenth century, when absentee landowners tried to evict their tenants. Of course, the crofting folk fought those who came to evict them; but eventually their homes were broken and burned.

Culloden, near Inverness, may be the site of the last major pitched battle fought on Scottish soil (in 1746); but, in the years since then, there have been localised battles that have been just as harrowing, if much smaller in scale.

Amid all the gorgeous beauty, there is a lingering sense of struggle and even desolation in this part of Argyll, a place of harshly juxtaposed moods. The fair days are fine, but the ferocious winds and the blasts of rain from the Atlantic are never that far away.

✠

St Ninian's Cave, on the shore of Luce Bay, a mile or so north-west of Burrow Head, is much busier than St Columba's Cave, and more popular as a place of pilgrimage, although rather less impressive as an actual cave. It is usually approached via a popular pathway through the pleasant Physgill Woods. As you emerge from the trees, you see the sea, and suddenly everything opens up. You join the stony foreshore, turn right – and the cave is just three or four minutes' walk away.

I have visited the cave three times, and on each occasion there have been a lot of folk around. There are many improvised crosses, made with sticks, driftwood and flotsam, and a lot of messages carved and scratched on to the walls of the cave and on to some large stones on the shore in front of it. Some, but by no means all, of these messages are religious.

Right at the back of the cave, which is not that large, there is a stone with the single word 'papa' carved on it. Most of the scratchings are recent; some of the crosses carved inside the cave apparently date from the eighth century.

St Ninian is supposed to have used the cave for both refuge and worship, and it remains a place of authentic pilgrimage, though most of the visitors are simply tourists enjoying a walk. The messages indicate that people have apparently come here from all over the world.

The last time I visited the cave, I didn't linger long: I walked north along the shore, away from the folk crowding round. Soon, all was peaceful: no human voices, no dogs barking; even the seagulls had disappeared. The only sound was the gentle lap of the water.

I walked on, turned and looked back. There was a human figure about 80 yards away, black in the sunlight. It stood stock still, like a sculpture. Was there a Gormley sculpture here? Had I walked blindly past it?

Then the figure stirred and moved. The man looked round, turned back, and resumed his stare across the sea – directly to Ireland, an island that was Christian well before Scotland was.

Dunnottar Castle

Scotland is blessed with a multiplicity of fine castles great and small, ancient and modern, many of them in settings that are melodramatic. Some of them have very dark histories, full of cruelty, treachery and horror. Some, such as Hermitage Castle in Liddesdale, are extraordinarily grim and bleak, while others, mainly along the west coast, are particularly picturesque and romantic. Some are seriously underrated, like Carnasserie Castle in Argyll.

I think the two most spectacular of them all are both sea-girt, on the east coast: Tantallon Castle near North Berwick, and the splendid ruins of Dunnottar Castle, a little south of Stonehaven, which is my personal favourite – not least because I visited it several times as an awe-struck child.

Its situation, on a high promontory, pounded by the North Sea on three sides, utterly takes the breath away. The castle was once huge and rambling; now its ruins brood in a Gothic kind of way. The promontory housed an early Christian church; then the great castle was built. It has an appropriately stormy history: there is a long saga of brutality, imprisonment, escape and so on. It was taken by the English in the late thirteenth century; the great Scottish patriot William Wallace then stormed it, reclaimed it, and burned some of the English garrison to death.

When we visited Dunnottar, my mother would tell me – and I never tired of the story – of a very brave and resourceful woman, Mrs Christian Granger, the wife of the minister at the local parish kirk of Kinneff. During the Cromwellian wars of the mid-seventeenth century, the Scottish regalia – the crown jewels – were removed to the fastness of the castle for supposed safety. The castle was soon under siege by Cromwell's invaders.

Mrs Granger managed to secure a permitted visit to Mrs Ogilvy, the wife of the governor of the castle. Somehow, when deep in the castle,

Mrs Granger was able to appropriate the treasures. She concealed the crown and sceptre under her own apron. The rest of the regalia and jewels were wrapped in flax and lowered by rope over the high cliff at the edge of the castle, where they were retrieved by her accomplice, a young girl who was supposedly gathering seaweed. The Honours were temporarily hidden and then taken to the nearby Kinneff manse by dead of night and placed under the Grangers' marital bed. Then they were more securely stored under a huge slab beside a pew in the kirk.

Soon afterwards, Dunnottar Castle was thoroughly ransacked by the troops of Oliver Cromwell, but of course no trace of the regalia was found. Both couples, the Ogilvys and the Grangers, were threatened with torture, but they disclosed nothing. After the restoration of King Charles II, almost a decade later, the jewels were taken, in triumph, the long way south from Kinneff Kirk to Edinburgh Castle, where they remain today.

There may be some embellishment in this account, passed on down the generations, but the basic story is true. There is a neat symbolism in the removal of Scotland's symbolic treasure from the huge castle to the little kirk a mile or so inland: Scotland's most precious worldly goods were safer in God's little house than in the huge castle built by human hands.

※

There is a car park near the castle, but it is possible to visit it from the nearby coastal town of Stonehaven. A fine round walk goes through Dunnottar Woods (broad-leaved and very lovely), across some open agricultural country, down to the promontory with the fierce, roaring seas far beneath, and then back to Stonehaven via a clifftop path. The round trip is about 6 miles.

The castle is mentioned in the great Scottish politician Tom Johnston's intemperate book *Our Scots Noble Families*, a gloriously outspoken blast of anger which he wrote as a young man. (Johnston was, among many other things, a fine journalist and distinguished statesman; Churchill asked him to serve as Secretary of State for Scotland during the Second World War.) Johnston's theme was that many, maybe most, of Scotland's noble families were thieves, scoundrels, ruffians, cheats, rogues and much else that was even worse. They were godless folk who were much given to thieving from the Church – mainly by appropriating its lands. They also, according to Johnston, routinely exploited and oppressed the poor. It is not a balanced book, but there is enough truth in it to render it disturbing. As a left-wing polemic it is unsurpassed.

In his onslaught on the Keith family, Johnston mentions that at Dunnottar they 'kept a castle where torture was a common occurrence' – and where, in 1685 (a little later than the episode of the regalia), 167 Covenanters were incarcerated for an entire summer in a dark underground chamber, ankle-deep in mire. Johnston concludes: 'There was only standing room; the Covenanters were subjected to horrible tortures, and many died'.

To be fair to the maligned Keith family, I should mention that their Lord Keith, who became the 10th Earl Marischal, employed a relative, James Keith, as his adviser. This man was to become the leader of Edinburgh's Episcopalians in the early eighteenth century, and his life seems to have proceeded serenely even after the savage anti-Episcopalian legislation following the 1715 rebellion. When his *History of the Affairs of Church and State in Scotland* was published in 1734, one of the 350 subscribers was the famed freebooter Rob Roy Macgregor. Possibly this sustained blast of clerical wisdom was too much for Rob Roy's wayward soul, for he died before the year was out.

Incidentally, Dunnottar Castle features in one of the happiest scenes in Lewis Grassic Gibbon's novel *Sunset Song*.

Carfin

Carfin, a couple of miles north-east of Motherwell, is situated in a part of central Scotland where pastoral farmland lies side by side with bleak areas of scarred post-industrial blight. It has become famous for its grotto, which is now one of the key religious sites in all Scotland.

In 1934, the Scottish writer Edwin Muir undertook a journey through his country and then wrote it up in a book called, somewhat unimaginatively, *Scottish Journey*. It was an unhappy journey, and it is an unhappy book. Muir was a distinguished poet and critic, rather than a journalist, and he was too fastidious for some tastes. But his book is bleak rather than precious. At times he is withering, perhaps unduly so – as when he visited Walter Scott's house at Abbotsford. Often he is repelled by what he sees in his own country. For the most part, he observes rather than engages with people. The tone is somewhat aloof, but the book is charged with Muir's deep indignation about the state of Scotland. He is constantly concerned about Scotland's lack of coherent identity and its political and social barrenness.

By far the happiest and most surprising passage in the book comes towards the end, when Muir visits Carfin Grotto on a very hot summer's day. He decided that the grotto was the 'only palpable assertion of humanity' in a 'blasted region'. He was delighted by 'this lovely place' with its green lawns, its flowers, its little streams winding through their rock mazes, its shrines and statues. He found in the grotto a peace that was 'exceedingly rare in the modern world'. Carfin itself he found bleak and ugly, but it was redeemed by the recently created grotto.

Conscious, as so many Scottish writers are, of religious tensions, he felt the need to explain why he had praised the grotto rather than treated it 'with sarcasm'. The grotto, he stated, was the 'creation of a sincere faith'.

Muir came to the grotto only a few years after it was created. Now, considerably expanded, it is a well-established place of pilgrimage; and it also attracts many tourists, some of whom are secular in disposition. It is easy to find, being directly across the road from Carfin railway station, which had been closed but was reopened because of the growing popularity of the grotto, which now attracts around 75,000 visitors each year.

✠

The inspirational figure who created this special place came from Greenock – ironically a town where Muir spent the unhappiest years of his life. Thomas Taylor was the son of a Greenock head teacher. He studied in the 1890s at Blairs College, near Aberdeen, and later at the St Sulpice seminary in Paris. After teaching at St Peter's College in Bearsden near Glasgow, he became parish priest of Carfin during the First World War.

In 1893, he had undertaken a pilgrimage to Lourdes which made a huge impression on him. He seems to have become almost obsessed with the famous place of pilgrimage. He wrote a book about Lourdes and organised many visits there.

In the early 1920s – a time of social despair, mass unemployment and industrial strife – he planned and supervised the creation of the Carfin Grotto as a kind of testament to Lourdes, rather than a copy of it. He was assisted by the voluntary labour of many men, most of whom were unemployed. So, this was a project of social and economic renewal as well as a spiritual one.

The grotto has been enhanced in various ways over the years. There are now two car parks, a shop and a café. But entrance is free, and there is little sense of commercial exploitation. There are various chapels, regularly used for worship, within the grounds; open-air services are also held. There is an indisputable sense of peace; this is clearly a sanctuary set apart for prayer and spiritual renewal. Pilgrims come from all over the world. It is a green place, with immaculately maintained lawns and tiny, carefully constructed hills.

Statues abound; it has to be said that they are of varying quality. The most notable are a statue of St Andrew, holding his large diagonal cross, and a very powerful representation of Pope John Paul II by Tom Allan. The latter manages to convey both physical weakness and spiritual strength. The old Pope's body is stooped, his crozier is held against his head, his vestments are blowing in the wind.

There are also various shrines and memorials. For me, the most moving and rewarding area is the sunken garden, where seven beautiful bas-reliefs reflecting the life of Jesus are built into the curved retaining wall. I understand, however, that this part of the grotto has been designated for significant restoration (I'm not sure that it needs it).

When I visited, lunchtime mass was being celebrated in one of the chapels. Over 100 folk were taking part, and some of them had spilled out on to the surrounding grass. As I inspected the more obscure parts of the grotto, their singing wafted towards me, sometimes faintly, sometimes quite loudly. This added to the sense of gentle reverence. Yet I was surprised, in this apparently peaceful place, to see stern notices in the shop and the café warning that the staff must on no account be abused.

There is without doubt a marginally mawkish feel to some of the adornments in the grotto. The overall atmosphere is very far removed from the cheerless austerity that has characterised much of Scottish Presbyterianism.

I found the grotto a serene and special place, rendered all the more remarkable by its situation in the heartlands of post-industrial Scotland. (The famous Ravenscraig steelworks, which became a symbol of Scotland's industrial past when it was controversially closed by one of Mrs Thatcher's governments in the mid-1980s, was situated only a mile or so to the south.)

Some friends have suggested that I should compile a personal list of Scotland's top ten, or top twenty, religious sites. I have resisted the temptation; but let me say that Carfin Grotto would certainly be in my top ten.

Snobbery and deference

Scotland's capital, Edinburgh, is situated on the southern littoral of the broad estuary of the Forth. On either side of the city are the very characterful counties of East and West Lothian. Much of the former is characterised by a douce, gentle landscape, notable for splendid golf courses, substantial farms and glorious long beaches. There is an industrial heritage, but it is meagre. West Lothian, on the other hand, is much more gritty. It is largely an industrial and post-industrial landscape, although two large and very fine estates – Hopetoun and Dalmeny – straggle along the Forth estuary. And here we find two of the most beautiful and characterful small churches in all Scotland.

Dalmeny Church, in the model village of the same name, is a masterpiece in miniature. It is by far the best-preserved Norman church in Scotland. Dating from the mid-twelfth century, it stands in an exceptionally well-kept open graveyard. Its most splendid – indeed spectacular – feature is the main south door, which gives direct access to the long, narrow nave. The door is surmounted by rounded arches which feature a profusion of intricate sutures and delicate carvings, mainly of beasts both mythical and real. There are some neatly insinuated local references. Whoever the anonymous sculptor was, all these years ago, he created a masterpiece of early medieval art.

The church is still the local parish church, regularly used for worship, as it has been for more than eight centuries. There is a congregation of around 100 communicants. Although Dalmeny is in West Lothian, the congregation is regarded as part of the Presbytery of Edinburgh. Inside the building, there is a sense of a well-used 'working' church, though there are many other interesting medieval features. But, in the apse, right at the east end of the building, there are three small but very striking modern stained-glass windows.

These were created by the artist Lalia Dickson and funded by a Polish officer, Colonel Stanisław Sokołowski, who was stationed near Dalmeny during the Second World War. The windows depict the Madonna and Child; St Theresa of Poland and the national arms of that country; and, very beautifully, St Margaret of Scotland. Margaret had, of course, local associations; Queensferry, named after her, is just a mile away. Dalmeny Church is generally closed during the week, but it is easy to gain access; you simply cross the road to a cottage where a helpful lady provides the key. Would that more Scottish parish churches could make similar arrangements!

⊠

Dalmeny Church is easy to find, being situated in the heart of its village. Abercorn Kirk is much more obscurely situated, on the edge of the deer park of the great Hopetoun Estate, a few miles to the west. It is plainer and less richly adorned than the kirk at Dalmeny, but it too is an old and venerable church still used for weekly worship. And it is – commendably – always open. It dates back to the twelfth century but has been much altered and renovated, and few of the original features remain. A very extensive restoration took place in 1893.

Its fine, large graveyard has a remarkable number of stones featuring the skull and crossbones. In a corner of the yard, the old session house has been converted into a very small but interesting museum where some of the graveyard's more ancient stones and relics have been placed for safe keeping – an imaginative and constructive use of a redundant building. The graveyard is surrounded by lovely woodland; altogether this is a place of real peace and tranquillity.

Abercorn parish, which has around 75 communicants, is now 'linked' with the parish of Pardovan, Kingscavil and Winchburgh, which has around 300. By such measure does the national Church of Scotland manage its decline in numbers.

⊠

There is one aspect of both Abercorn and Dalmeny that disturbs me. The churches feature grandiose additions which were created by the local lairds and landowners for their comfort, and indeed to keep landowners and hoi polloi apart. I have always been impressed by the essentially democratic nature of the Scottish Reformation; but this quality was grievously vitiated, later on, by the showy building of various aisles, lofts and special galleries where local bigwigs, rich and aloof, could make all too clear the chasm that separated them from the ordinary parishioners. This kind of showing off, I'd suggest, has no place in a Presbyterian house of God. It is supposed to be just that, the house of God – not the House of the Laird.

At Abercorn, the 'Hopetoun Aisle' by the chancel is undoubtedly splendid, but is it in keeping with the spirit of the rest of the church? Other aisles were created by the eminent local Dundas and Dalyell families. There is also a 'laird's loft'. These various appendages distort the original clarity of the church building; and I reckon they vitiate its purity.

The Earl of Hopetoun's 'loft' is in truth a grandiose piece of ostentation, including a large retiring room. There is also a more furtive 'squint' from which the pulpit can be discreetly viewed. In all this, there is a sense that the local grandees were prepared to attend worship – but only if they could do so in considerable comfort and style, and be kept well apart from the ordinary folk.

At Dalmeny, too, the local landowners paid for their privacy and luxury. In the late seventeenth century, Sir Archibald Primrose built an aisle on to the north side of the church so that he and his entourage could worship in aloof style, separate from the commonality. Sir Archibald's son became the Earl of Rosebery, and for years the Roseberys maintained an undemocratic right of patronage over the kirk, even selecting the minister.

In this context, it is important to note that Abercorn and Dalmeny were by no means unique; quite the opposite, in fact. To complain about this is not, I trust, to show any ungracious disrespect to the Hopetoun and Rosebery families; it is simply to note that the idea of luxurious and expensive appendages to perfectly adequate churches seems to me to be very much at odds with the idea of the reformed national Scottish Church being any kind of exemplar of democracy and egalitarianism.

But then, even the greatest Scottish reformer of them all, John Knox, realised at various stages of his turbulent career that he needed the support of the Scottish aristocracy – or at least some of them; and it is pretty certain that the Scottish Reformation would not have been secured without the crucial, and for the most part positive, role played by the Lords of the Congregation. These nobles and lords supported Knox in his revolutionary struggle against France (and Rome) – and indeed it was Scottish nobles who invited Knox to return to Scotland from Geneva in the first place, thus paving the way for the most remarkable two or three years in Scottish history.

☒

Meanwhile, I have no wish to write as some chippy correspondent on the fringes of the class war; but it is surely important that this issue of snobbery and deference – for that is what it basically is – should be confronted head on. It is sad that too many Scottish churches still reek of feudalism. In the reformed era, we should have moved far beyond that. And anyway, back in feudal times when there were strictly hierarchical societies, it was often, paradoxically enough, the role of the clergy to temper and limit the powers of the feudal lords.

Of course, in just about any human society, there are inequalities of wealth, power, privilege and influence. It ought to be the role of a democratic church to fight these inequalities, rather than to flaunt them. The very obvious physical presence in many Scottish kirks of laird's lofts and the like indicates all too clearly that the notions of class and social status were accepted, indeed ostentatiously endorsed, by Scotland's national Church.

Yet I'd have thought that one of the compensations – and indeed one of the basic functions – of religion is to render the existing, and often oppressive, social order more tolerable by promoting the excellent notion of the equality of all believers. But perhaps that is ingenuous. Human beings, unfortunately, too often find it hard to resist snobbery and deference, even in the house of God.

The related issue – of patronage – is one that bedevilled Scotland's national Kirk. It simply wouldn't go away. One of the intentions of John Knox and his colleagues, in their blueprint for the new Church in 1560, was to end patronage once and for all. The theory was that ministers should be elected by the parishioners, the people. But landowners retained much power; they sometimes supplied the buildings and provided the stipends for the ministers. The national Church, not the national network of lairds and landowners, was supposed to control the appointment of ministers; but this was too often theory rather than reality.

The issue burned quietly away until it eventually flared up into a continuing conflagration that could not be put out, right through the seventeenth century. General Assemblies asserted the right of kirk sessions to choose and appoint ministers, only for this to be challenged by Acts of the London Parliament.

Patronage was not finally abolished until 1690. The Treaty of Union of 1707 endorsed this, only to be blatantly breached five years later by the new UK Parliament. Successive General Assemblies kept tilting at this law, but they could not prevail. Then the issue flared up yet again in the early Victorian era – and it was of course at the heart of the Disruption of 1843.

Abernethy

South and east of Perth, there is a special pocket of Scottish countryside which I always think of as the land of three rivers, for here
the small but very characterful River Flag flows into the winding and
beautiful River Earn which duly, a little to the east, debouches into the
magnificent, majestic Tay just before it broadens into its wide firth.

In the heart of this attractive area is a community with a population of about 1,000 and a very rich, if not always edifying,
Christian history. This is the village of Abernethy. In its centre is a
tall (75 feet) and slim round tower, which tapers to a circumference
of only 30 feet at its top. It dates from the tenth century, and served
as a lookout, particularly across the north, over the valley of the
Tay, and also as a (very cramped) place of safety for the clergy of
Abernethy's Culdee monastery, which was once significant enough
to be described as a 'university', but weak enough to be frequently
attacked and plundered.

The Culdees (Friends of God) were an eccentric sect. It is sometimes claimed that they were the first properly organised preachers
of Christianity in Scotland. They had hereditary priests, who established various centres across much of Scotland in the ninth and thirteenth centuries. They were criticised for slackness; they certainly
became more and more secular, and some of their monasteries were
eventually taken over by the Augustinians.

Abernethy was the site of a famous – for most Scots, infamous –
encounter between two kings: Malcolm III of Scotland, known as
'the Bighead', and William the Conqueror of England. William
had invaded Scotland – the first full-scale invasion of Scotland by
a substantial, well-disciplined and well-led English army, although
William was intent on a show of superior power rather than an
attempt to achieve permanent subjugation. To gain peace, Malcolm

apparently humiliated himself and his country; or was he merely trying to buy time?

His demeanour was reputedly supine and submissive. He was forced to accept William as his overlord. William also took Malcolm's young son Duncan back to England as a hostage; he was to remain there for 15 years. So, for some, Abernethy was, and still is, a place of shame. By far the best thing Malcolm did was to marry Margaret, an authentic saint.

Much later, Abernethy had a flourishing religious life. There was the parish church, the Secession church (which became the United Presbyterian Kirk), the Free Church (obviously established after the Disruption, and eventually merged with the Secession church), and a small but flourishing gospel hall. This last was established when a certain trio of local worthies, dissatisfied with the religion purveyed in the various churches, decided to organise independent worship in the hall. In the early twentieth century, as many as 70 or 80 attended services there. Later, the building was sold, and the remaining worshippers transferred to the gospel hall in nearby Perth.

There is a splendid museum in Abernethy, opened in 2000, that provides many insights into the relatively recent religious life of the community. Among the concerns to the kirk session of the parish church in the early 1800s was 'antenuptial fornication' (i.e. pre-marital sex), of which there was apparently a great deal in the village. It was not until 1902 that the punishment for this alleged sin ceased.

The museum records how rapidly the nature of religious observance has changed. The parish kirk session rejected calls for Christmas Day services as recently as 1935, and for the appointment of female elders ten years later. (In 1932, there were an amazing 48 applicants for the post of parish minister.) Some thought that the introduction of women ministers would halt the decline – but it has got worse, not better, and major new initiatives are now under way to try to address this.

Abernethy is one of those Scottish communities that is replete with traditions, legends and quirky anecdotes from the past. The young UK home secretary, Winston Churchill, once arrived in

Abernethy to address a great open-air rally. It was attended by more than 2,000 people but was badly disrupted by militant suffragettes.

Much earlier, there was Nechtan, a contender to be king of the Picts, who in exile met and fell in love with St Brigid of Kildare. Despairing of his infatuation, he returned to Scotland and granted Abernethy to God. (Should it not have been the other way round?)

✖

The history of Scotland's national Church, as frequently noted in this book, abounds with splits and secession. At the time of the first really significant post-Reformation split, in 1733, the minister of Abernethy, Alex Moncrieff, was removed from his charge. Although descended from a family of notable Covenanters, and heir to the substantial local estate of Calfargie (indeed, he was known as Calfargie), his association with the leading secessionist Ebenezer Erskine led to his dismissal. He was evidently a powerful preacher – and the story goes that a woman listening to him getting somewhat carried away in the middle of a sermon shouted: 'See – Calfargie is off to heaven, and the rest of us are sitting here'.

At the time of writing, the well-maintained and characterful parish church of St Bride (now linked with the parishes of Dron and Arngask) has more than 300 communicants. The church is notable for its beautiful stained glass, for a particularly beautiful pulpit and for its three-sided gallery.

Nearby is the similarly sized community of Newburgh, which was once a royal burgh – a status it achieved because of the abbey at Lindores, just to the east. A parish school was established here, shortly after the Scottish Reformation, on the lines advocated by John Knox. Newburgh has links with Clan Macduff, although the Macduffs are generally associated with north-east Scotland. There was a famous cross near Lindores. Any member of the Macduff clan guilty of murder was supposed to achieve full atonement if he touched the cross and presented a 'fine' of nine cows, each of which had to be tied to the cross. The story goes that the cross was eventually smashed to pieces by followers of John Knox, the great reformer – a man associated with both wanton destruction and progressive, enlightened developments in education and social welfare.

The abbey ruins are picturesque, but they are meagre, spread about pleasantly enough on a large site. The abbey was founded in 1191. At the time of the Reformation, John Knox arrived here to supervise in person the burning of all the monks' mass books. The Revd Henry Thorold, that enthusiastic English laureate of the vanished worlds of British Christianity, captured the mood of the place thus: 'Unselfconscious and half-forgotten'.

Abbeys

The Scottish Borders is a region of Scotland with a turbulent and often ferocious past. The area was subjected to long periods of bitter Anglo-Scottish warfare, and some of its fine religious buildings suffered terribly from regular, vicious attacks.

Through this very rich landscape – rich in beauty, and rich in history – flows the magnificent River Tweed. It runs through the thoughts of just about everyone who has written about the Borders. Close to its banks are three of the great Border abbeys – Melrose, Kelso and, the ultimate jewel, the exquisite Dryburgh. These sites comprise a particularly precious cluster of monastic ruins.

Melrose and Kelso are small towns. Melrose is a little twee for my taste; Kelso, while equally characterful, has a more workaday feel. The fragments of Kelso Abbey are impressive, the fragments of Melrose perhaps more so. 'Was never scene so sad and fair!' wrote Sir Walter Scott, the great laureate of these parts. Little remains of the early church and its monastic accoutrements; they were attacked and nearly destroyed by the English during various raids in the fourteenth century. The abbey was rebuilt in the fifteenth century; and enough remains for the visitor to, just about, appreciate what must have been its considerable splendour.

But nearby Dryburgh is the real gem. The Revd Henry Thorold opined that the situation of Dryburgh Abbey is 'as beautiful as that of any monastic ruin anywhere' – and who am I to disagree?

Dryburgh itself is a tiny hamlet, notable only for a large hotel – a fine baronial building also located by the river – and of course the abbey ruins, which occupy a large and perfectly maintained site, possibly the most evocative in all Scotland. It consists of beautifully wooded parkland along the Tweed – here broad and fast-flowing – and is well-nigh perfect and quite unforgettable. Sir Walter Scott is buried here, along with his wife Charlotte and his son-in-law, his biographer J. G. Lockhart.

The ruins these days are tranquil and almost ethereal, but the history of the abbey was violent and chaotic. Indeed, its grisly past serves as an antidote to those who think that the destructive zeal of the Scottish reformers in the later fifteenth century was responsible for the sad condition of so many of our great abbeys and cathedrals. This wanton vandalism was inexcusable, but English raiders visited much grievous damage on the Border abbeys well before the Reformation.

Dryburgh Abbey was founded in the twelfth century by Hugh de Morville. Its greatest monastic leader was one of the early abbots, Adam of Dryburgh, whose life straddled the late twelfth and early thirteenth centuries. A pious and modest man himself, he rather naïvely believed that Scotland had been particularly blessed with saintly monarchs. He was a prolific writer of sermons, tracts and spiritual treatises, and was something of a spiritual philosopher. He attempted a 'dialogue' between reason and the soul. He was a modest, much-respected man, and I am told that he was once proposed for sainthood.

The abbey was attacked by the English many times, most violently in 1322, 1385 and then in 1544, the time of Henry VIII's 'rough wooing'. On several other occasions, the abbey was torched as the English tried to destroy it by fire. Several centuries on, the ruins of the abbey are peaceful and dignified. Not much survives of the actual church; but the monastic buildings are in better shape and give a useful insight to the rhythms of the monastic life.

But, in truth, the location, on a particularly lovely curve of the Tweed, is probably even more special than the ruins themselves. The river provided more than beauty; it was also, as more than one historian has noted, a very important source of free food for the monks.

Dryburgh's situation, while extraordinarily lovely, is rather obscure; that only adds to the loveliness.

While the abbey ruins are extensive, a much smaller and rather eerie monument is to be found a little further north, a few hundred yards beyond the hamlet, and again by the side of the Tweed.

This is an extraordinary 'Temple of the Muses' built by the Earl of Buchan in the eighteenth century as a shrine to his favourite poet, James Thomson.

The temple is spectacularly if rather furtively situated on a wooded knoll directly above the Tweed. The dome, which is capped by a fanciful bust of Thomson, perilously resting on a lyre, cannot be viewed from the temple itself; you have to see it as best you can as you approach up the steep path through the woods. You can, however, inspect, close up, the 5-feet-high bronze figures, created as recently as 2002 by Siobhan O'Hehir, and placed on the circular plinth under the dome.

For some, the most pleasing Borders town is Jedburgh – and it has a fine abbey right in its heart. Although the setting is less beautiful than that of Dryburgh, the actual building is in a less ruinous state. It was originally founded in the early twelfth century as an Augustinian priory. Jedburgh is a less romantic place than Kelso, Melrose or Dryburgh, and it has a no-nonsense workaday feel, but it is not an industrial town.

The biggest and most overtly urban of the Border towns is Hawick, a town that is definitely industrial in character but has a certain charm. Situated around the confluence of the River Teviot and the Slitrig Water, it lacks an abbey but boasts several fine churches. Unusually for modern Scotland, most of them are still in use – I counted ten that are still operating as churches; and there may be more. On a working weekday, I visited eight of these churches – including the parish church of St Mary's, which is built on a splendid site, on a mound at the south end of the high street, and the small but lovely (the exterior, that is) Episcopal church by the Slitrig Water, designed by G. Gilbert Scott. At least I visited the exteriors; I could not find one that was open. The eighth, the Teviot Kirk just off the High Street, was only open by chance because the temporary organist was inside, rehearsing. It is warmly decorated, with a splendid gallery on three sides.

It seemed peculiar that a community of around 16,000 souls with so many working churches – including a relatively new one, high on a housing estate on the northern edge of town – should not be able to arrange for at least one of them to be open for a visitor seeking the opportunity for prayer or meditation, a little spiritual peace and quiet – and/or to have a chat with a local volunteer. There is also legitimate curiosity about churches, their interiors and their fitments and decorations, for these are generally of considerable interest and have their individual quirks, and stories to tell. Of course, I understand the problems with security and the provision of volunteers; but surely an ecumenical rota could be maintained to ensure that at least one or two of the town's churches are always open for well-disposed visitors at any particular time?

It is perhaps unfair to single out Hawick: too many Scottish towns have groups and clusters of very fine churches that are not yet redundant – that is, they are still used as churches – but they are only used seven or eight, nine or ten hours a week. This is a grievous under-use of buildings which, as I say, are often of considerable merit, and often dominate their immediate vicinity. To have so many of them shuttered and closed for long periods each week creates a most unfortunate spiritual blight, as well as contributing a sense of shut-out dullness, even downright rejection, to the wider community.

Two unlikely chapels

During the Second World War, it was necessary to provide extra protection for the huge and strategically invaluable harbour of Scapa Flow, Orkney. This took the form of the so-called Churchill Causeways, barriers that were constructed quickly and without any thought, understandably enough, of aesthetics. Italian prisoners of war were transported from other parts of Scotland to help to build them. There was, however, an unexpected offshoot from this mundane if crucial work, which was to have huge aesthetic – and indeed spiritual – significance.

A few of the Italians asked if they could construct and adorn their own chapel. Permission was given; and two redundant, adjoining Nissen huts on the isle of Lamb Holm were provided as the shell of the building. The only stipulation was that the Italians should continue to work their assigned (long) hours on the construction of the causeways. The creation of the chapel had to be accomplished in their relatively meagre spare time.

The prisoners of war, inspired by an exceptional man called Domenico Chiochetti, created, in a remarkably short time, a chapel of considerable beauty, particularly inside. The men had to scrounge and scavenge to get the necessary materials, but they were ingenious, inventive and resourceful. It helped that they were given paint, brushes and tools by an enlightened camp commander.

The result was one of the most extraordinary religious buildings in all Scotland. I have visited it on three separate occasions, and each time I've been more impressed. It was, and remains, very beautiful, if in a marginally mawkish way. It is, above all, a testament to the ability of men far from home, in difficult circumstances, to assert their creativity and their spirituality – and to leave behind them something special and lasting.

The chapel received an unexpected endorsement in May 2014 when Pope Francis sent a special blessing to mark the seventi-eth anniversary of its completion. A special mass was held in it, celebrated by the papal nuncio to the UK, Archbishop Antonio Mennini. Far away in Rome, the Pope himself prayed that the chapel, built in wartime, should long continue to be a place of peace and reconciliation.

⚔

There is another chapel – at the other end of Scotland, near Lockerbie – that was built in similar circumstances. While it is cruder and less sophisticated, for me it has greater spiritual reson-ance. This is the Ukrainian prisoner of war chapel at Hallmuir, a little to the west of Lockerbie. This modest but beguiling little place of worship, at once homely and numinous, has an interesting back story.

I once had a long conversation with a fine Scottish minister, Stuart McWilliam, about his experiences as a British Army padre in Italy at the end of the Second World War. Earlier, Stuart had been on the beaches of Anzio, where he had experienced something close to hell; but he told me that his most demanding task came a year or so later, when he had to help to separate the Ukrainian and German prisoners of war – many thousands of them – who were held in detention at vast camps in north-west Italy. Once they were separated, he had to find whether any of the German prisoners of war were ordained (for various reasons, the German chaplains often pretended to be laymen).

As for the Ukrainians, it became clear that the main task was to try to safeguard them after the war ended. Our Soviet allies were insisting that they were technically Soviet citizens; but, if they were sent back east, they would almost certainly suffer from severe reprisals, including execution. The Ukrainians had been forced into the Nazi army, and had fought against the Russians in 1944; the Nazis had insisted that they were to fight only Russians, not the British or Americans. After the war ended, many of the Ukrainians managed to stay on in Italy, although often in conditions of near-destitution. Then there was a belated move to transport at least some of them to the UK.

Early in 1947, the *Glasgow Herald* reported that around 1,500 Ukrainians were being transported to Glasgow from ports on the Adriatic coast of Italy. They arrived at the Broomielaw on two troop ships. Hundreds more were transported to Liverpool on a third ship. Over the next few weeks, several thousand more arrived in Glasgow. If they had been repatriated to their homeland, they would have been unlikely to survive.

A large contingent of Ukrainians was sent to a camp near Lockerbie, where they were to work in the local forests and farms. They marched to the site at Hallmuir, led by a man carrying a large cross. They quickly gained a reputation as conscientious and very industrious workers. They were housed in about 50 temporary huts, one of which was requisitioned as a chapel. There ensued a transformation similar to what had occurred hundreds of miles to the north a few years earlier.

The Ukrainian chapel is still open to visitors. It is not as beautifully adorned as the Italian chapel; it has a much more homespun feel, and is less sophisticated aesthetically. Some of the decoration might seem somewhat kitsch for Scottish tastes. But it's colourful and very atmospheric. By the altar is a beautifully lit model of Kiev Cathedral, which was badly bombed during the war. This was exquisitely carved, with a mere penknife, by a prisoner of war called Stefan Leski. On the lower altar, there are three special candelabras, again beautifully carved.

The chapel is carefully maintained. Services are held at least 12 times a year, and it is occasionally used for marriages. The UU (Ukraine Uniate) Church maintains allegiance to the Roman Catholic Church, and recognises the primacy of the Vatican, but it is clearly a separate church; for example, it allows its clergy to marry.

Both chapels are very much worth a visit. The Italian one is more celebrated, but I find the Ukrainian one more moving.

PART 2

Recent History

R. F. Mackenzie

It has become a commonplace that the greatest piece of public oratory in the second half of the twentieth century was Martin Luther King's 'I have a dream' speech on Capitol Hill, Washington DC, in 1963. Every time I hear this impassioned passage of oratory, it moves me deeply. But I sincerely believe that I have heard a public speech that was every bit as great, if not greater. It was delivered 11 years later in – of all places – the chambers of Aberdeen City Council, or Aberdeen Corporation as it was then known.

In 1973, the editor of the *Scotsman* asked me to become the paper's first full-time education correspondent. I was greatly enjoying the job I had on the paper at the time, and I was not too pleased. In an extended pep-talk, the editor told me how important the new job would be, not just for the paper but for me too. He did not tell me – how could he? – that it would allow me to witness, just a few months later, a speech of progressive rhetoric, Biblical fervour and authentic prophecy that has lived with me ever since.

I went up to Aberdeen from Edinburgh on a pleasant early spring morning in 1974 expecting to report on what I then regarded as no more than a fierce dispute that was more about the mechanics of educational bureaucracy than the very soul of the nation. Aberdeen Education Committee had, six years previously, appointed to the headship of one of the city's biggest secondary schools – it had over 100 teachers, and class sizes were much bigger then than they are now – a very radical and special man. He was certainly not an orthodox educationist; the council had taken a chance, and a bold one at that.

The new head was born deep in the heart of the vast county of Aberdeenshire, the son of a rural stationmaster. He never lost his soft Aberdeenshire accent. His parents made considerable sacrifices so that he could receive a traditional Scottish education. He went to the leading private school in Aberdeen – Robert Gordon's College – of which he became dux, and went on to Aberdeen University. He came to regard his education as something pitiful and utterly worthless, and the sacrifices his parents made as futile. He was an intelligent, observant man, and he looked at the world through his own eyes. He often saw what others did not want him to see.

He travelled around Europe. He had varied experiences. He was not some vague, unworldly dreamer. He moved through many European countries during the fraught decade of the 1930s, mostly on an extended bicycle trip of thousands of miles. He was staying with a Jewish family in Germany when their house was violently attacked by Nazis in 1938. During the war, he saw active service with Bomber Command. He witnessed at first hand, and understood, the horrors that led to the war, and the horrors of war itself – first as an innocent observer and then as an airman flying as a navigator in bombers.

He then taught at an independent, pioneering, progressive school in the south of England, and after that in state schools in the Scottish Borders and Fife. When he was appointed to Summerhill Academy as its new head, Aberdeen Education Committee knew exactly what they were doing. He had written several books outlining his very progressive views. He regarded the care and nourishment of children as far more important than any concept of formal education. He was certain that many children endured extreme turmoil in their lives – and in their souls. He was a deeply religious man, although he had rejected orthodox Christianity.

The case against him, that spring afternoon in Aberdeen, was that Summerhill Academy had become anarchic. Discipline was non-existent. Older teachers found it impossible to teach; and the younger teachers whom he had appointed and encouraged were not teaching in any conventional sense. The head had an open contempt for examinations; the academy's exam results were, to traditionalists, appalling. This man, this very special man, was called Robert Mackenzie. But he was always known as R. F. Mackenzie.

His staff became deeply divided; Mackenzie himself accepted this. The director of education – who, incidentally, was a most reasonable man and a close friend of my parents – came to regard

Mackenzie's position as untenable. The majority of the Education Committee agreed with him. Some of them had not wanted Mackenzie in the first place. Now a majority decided that he had to go. On that memorable afternoon, the proceedings of the Education Committee were open to the public, and the large committee room was full. Plenty of folk witnessed what happened, but not enough.

The early proceedings were bureaucratic and tedious; there was much discussion about memos, complaints, replies. The education convener, a prominent Labour figure in Aberdeen, Councillor Roy Pirie, summed up the case against the head well and, I thought, fairly. He stated his conclusion: Mackenzie was unwilling or unable to exercise authoritative control over his staff. He could not or would not secure the effective implementation of his own policies. He showed disregard for the need to win the confidence and co-operation of all his staff.

Most of the other speeches were against Mackenzie, although the two most eloquent, by Bob Middleton and Andrew Walls, were fervently in his favour.

Robert Mackenzie heard none of this. He was sitting outside in an ante-room. But he was allowed to address the meeting before the fateful vote was taken. He spoke with enormous emotion and passion. He talked not about the minutiae of the dispute, the memos and the counter-memos, but about the children at the school. He spoke of children, many children, who had 'wounds in their souls'. He said, with a passion and a fervour that reminded me directly of Jesus Christ: 'We could cure these wounds, we would have cured them, but we were not allowed to, Mr Chairman, because you gave us a divided staff'. He also claimed, with credible eloquence, that it was not he who was on trial, but the very concept of comprehensive education.

His deeply moving oratory was to no avail. The decision to suspend him was taken by 16 votes to six. (Technically it was a suspension, but everyone present was certain that Mackenzie would never get his job back.)

As the meeting broke up, and Mackenzie and his family left, there was a minor ruckus. Some of his supporters were trying to protect him from the media, but the reporters present were restrained. The people who were rowdy were among those who were there to support him. A few of the school staff were there. They were very angry with the committee for reneging on their earlier commitments to Mackenzie. One of them was screaming that Mackenzie had been betrayed. I suspected that they too now feared for their jobs.

I tried to get an interview with Mackenzie, even just a few words. In those circumstances of extreme stress, he was understandably flustered and emotional. He managed to tell me, through the din, that he wanted to gather his thoughts. He suggested that I should visit him that evening in his little farmhouse by the River Dee, just outside of town, where everything would be quiet and calm. One of his supporters told me how to get there.

So, I went and filed my report – as did my colleague John Pirie, education correspondent of Scotland's leading tabloid, who started his report with the words: 'I accuse Aberdeen Education Committee of treachery'. It had indeed been an emotive, highly charged occasion.

Then, in the early evening, I headed for the meeting with Mackenzie. He gave me the best interview I ever had as a journalist. Some of the others were much more newsworthy, but none of them was as profound. None of them could match the extraordinary mixture of eloquence, despair, soul-searching and prophecy that Mackenzie articulated in that soft, gentle and very Scottish voice; I still hear it as I write this. None of them was infused with such noble concern about the state of Scotland. None of them was charged with such Biblical intensity.

We drank a lot of whisky. Mackenzie spoke fluently – about his own children, his love for them and for his own parents, and his general love for young people. He spoke again and again in Biblical terms, particularly referring to the parable of the lost sheep. He became angry when he spoke about examiners and educational bureaucrats. He spoke with enthusiasm and deep compassion about youngsters who were miscreants and rebels, who were disruptive and antisocial. He continually called them 'the salt of the earth'.

There was in some of what he said confusion and naïvety, and possibly excessive idealism. There was also vision, nobility, hope and a deeply Christian siding with the losers, or those who, according to

Mackenzie, the education system and society in general decided to make losers. I remember thinking that Mackenzie might have rejected the Christianity of his youth, yet what he was saying seemed to me more directly Christian than almost all the sermons I had ever heard. Indeed, his talk was wonderful and unforgettable. So, it has lasted with me, although it has perhaps not influenced my own subsequent behaviour and attitudes as much as it should have.

More mundanely, it was great copy. The next day, I wrote it up in a long feature for the *Scotsman*, called 'The Unbowed Head'. I mentioned among other things that Mackenzie was intending to write a book about his rejection. I noted that city councillors could suspend a head, but they could not suspend a book. The book was published the following year, duly called *The Unbowed Head*. I felt privileged and proud when Mackenzie asked me to write the introduction. In truth, it was not his best book. Some of it was rambling and repetitive. Perhaps the principal theme was that those entrusted with the education of children in Scotland had little understanding of the turmoil in the children's souls. They thought that education was about transmitting information, pure and simple.

That night, in a comfortable, modest room in a farmhouse by the River Dee, down the hill from the douce community of Cults, Mackenzie spoke as a prophet. It was clear that he was not a practising Christian; but he had clearly imbibed much of the Bible, and the New Testament in particular. He had been brought up in Christ; at the age of 8 he was already 'born again', standing up in public and acknowledging Christ as his saviour. But he didn't really want to talk about that. He was more interested in reflecting that the Church of Scotland, his church, Scotland's national Church, had become totally irrelevant to the lives of almost all the pupils he had tried to help.

He confessed that, as a young man, he had decided that what had been earlier, and what was to become again, his favourite parable – that of the lost sheep – was nonsense. Now, publicly humiliated and rejected, but older and wiser, he reckoned that Christ was a revolutionary, and that the parable was profound. (The thought occurred to me then, and still does, that Mackenzie himself clearly thought that far more than 1 out of 100 sheep were lost. But perhaps I've always been too literal.)

I talked to Mackenzie quite a lot over the next few years. He was, I recall, insistent that few things he had come across in a busy, full life were quite as un-Christian as Scotland generally and the Scottish education system in particular. This was not so much bitterness as a kind of – almost divine – despair. Increasingly, I understood that he saw Scotland as a deeply un-Christian country. He would say something along these lines: 'OK, it has all these churches and cathedrals, manses and ministers, priests and seminaries, all its wonderful old Christian monuments, but . . .'

And then he would ask, simply: 'Is it Christian?' For him, much of his native country's past remained dark, suspicious and violent; it had been more the devil's place than Christ's. He sometimes talked about Carlo Levi's classic work, *Christ Stopped at Eboli*. He reckoned that, as far as Scotland was concerned, Christ stopped at Iona.

And yet, there was another side to him. He candidly confessed that he could not wholly reject Calvinism. He certainly felt that he could not shake himself totally free of his religious upbringing, long after he had quit the Kirk. In a wonderful phrase he used more than once, he said that the religious ideas of his childhood had seeped into him when he wasn't even looking. Later, when travelling in South Africa, he had felt much more comfortable among hard-line Dutch Boers than he had when visiting a church manse in the Aberdeenshire of his youth.

He also understood that many good Scots somehow merged their Christianity with their sense of national identity; they saw their nation's journey as a kind of pilgrimage through the wilderness. But he was sceptical about the Kirk's hold on the people. He talked with affection about ordinary people's 'tolerance' of the Church of Scotland in rural Aberdeenshire. By this, he meant that it was not completely rejected. It was even supported, if in a half-hearted kind of way.

Yet, in this intensively farmed part of Scotland, the call of the Kirk had often come a poor second to the call of the land. Many farmers insisted, at certain times of the year, that their labourers should toil long hours on the Sabbath day, which was much less sacrosanct than it was in, say, the far north-west. And many other country folk preferred to use the Sabbath for a long lie-in rather than kirk attendance. They would, however, still stir themselves to go to communion a couple of times a year. They didn't want to sever the connection.

And I'm pretty certain that Mackenzie himself never completely severed the connection. For him, always, the key was to be found in the souls of the young. He believed that young folk had a greater capacity for understanding than was often allowed. In this respect, he did not want to reject what had been very important to him in his own childhood. He said ministers should not preach at young people but instead reach out to them, explaining carefully and clearly what they believed – while admitting that other adults and seniors believed other things – and then allow them to make up their own minds.

In this, there was the usual Mackenzie mix of simplicity, wisdom, gentleness – and no doubt some ingenuousness too. You always felt it was not quite as straightforward as he made it sound. But then, one of Mackenzie's creeds was that the powerful, the manipulators, the influential, the writers, the well educated, the articulate and the bosses were not at all good at keeping things simple. For them, obfuscation was a means of social control.

So, when you write it, he would tell me, always try to keep it clear.

※

I was very surprised indeed that, in the months and years following his suspension, relatively few of Scotland's religious or intellectual elite appeared to show any sign of supporting Mackenzie. He did have one or two high-profile champions, notably the eminent historians T. C. Smout and James D. Young. Professor Smout called him 'a prophet almost without honour'.

His many critics pointed out, with gusto and, I accept, some validity, that he was certain that he knew what was wrong with Scottish society, but he could not formulate a cohesive, structured set of ideas in response. He talked with fervour about the goodness of young people and the need to revive the idea of community, but he always seemed more comfortable and fluent in talking about what was wrong than how things might get better.

I occasionally wondered if he could not have fused some of his notions with a renewal of his Christian faith; that might have led to something more meaningful. I also wondered if he could not have become a major Scottish Christian prophet, similar to George MacLeod but more of an outsider. But, like so many twentieth-century Scots who were brought up as Christians, he had jettisoned his faith.

He remained an outspoken scourge of authoritarianism and control. Mackenzie genuinely, passionately, believed in a better society, a better Scotland. If, like Martin Luther King, he was a dreamer, he was a noble one. He was a very good man.

The Church reborn

Andrew McGowan, Murdo Ewen Macdonald,
Beechgrove Church and Campbell Maclean

Andrew McGowan

One of the most distinguished figures in modern Scottish Christianity, the Revd Professor Andrew McGowan, has written of the time he was born again in the 1960s. He was an adolescent in a committed Church of Scotland family. A pupil at Uddingston Grammar School, he was active in both the Boys' Brigade and the Band of Hope. His father was an elder, his mother was in the Women's Guild. Andrew went to church each Sunday with his parents. He also attended the youth fellowship and a Bible class before the Sunday service. So, he was typical of many young folk in the Church of Scotland in that important decade. Churchgoing was a regular part of the weekly routine for many families. The congregational youth fellowships were often very well attended. Charismatic star preachers could attract huge audiences.

The important point is that, despite all this activity, something was missing. Andrew himself realised this when he attended a meeting in the gospel hall in Uddingston to hear the Baptist evangelist Hedley Murphy. That night, his life changed. He was born again.

Yet Andrew was already, in the context of the times, an exemplary Christian. He studied the Bible carefully, he attended church regularly and he had already had thoughts of becoming a minister. Yet it was not enough. It was not until the night that he listened to an inspirational lay evangelist that he experienced new birth as a Christian.

Andrew has since excelled in many roles: as a parish minister, as an academic theologian and, perhaps most importantly, as co-founder of the Highland Theological College. It was only much later, as he looked back on his life, that he realised how, on that night in Uddingston in 1968, something had happened that was more profound and significant than even he realised at the time.

Murdo Ewen Macdonald

I think it is reasonable to extrapolate from this something about the nature of organised Christianity in the 1960s in Scotland. Superficially, the national Church was flourishing. There were still too many clusters of churches in prosperous areas and too few churches in more deprived areas, but an ambitious church extension scheme was under way to rectify that.

Looking back, it is easy to see that, despite the superficial success, something was not quite right. There were some great preachers, yet that was not sufficient. One of the greatest of them was Murdo Ewen Macdonald.

I can still remember, very clearly, one particular day: Sunday, 6 October 1968, when I attended not one but two services in Aberdeen. The guest preacher at each of them – at Queen's Cross in the morning, St Ninian's in the evening – was Murdo Ewen Macdonald. It was the day before I was due to return to university in England, but I would undoubtedly have delayed my departure to hear this special man speak twice in the same day. Many others obviously felt the same way: both churches were full. Murdo Ewen must have addressed more than 1,500 people that day.

I confess that I can recall little of what he actually said, but I do remember that in one of the sermons there was a particularly powerful passage – even by his standards – about the Highland Clearances. He was not scared to assail his own Church and its lack of practical help for people who had suffered a great wrong.

Even in an era of fine preachers, Macdonald was exceptional. Brought up as a Gaelic-speaker on Harris, he was a very clever man. He studied divinity at St Andrews and eventually became

Professor of Practical Theology at Glasgow University. He was also an authentic hero, having had many adventures as a paratrooper in the Second World War. He certainly had his pugnacious side; he was a successful boxer. Before he embarked on his academic career, he was a distinguished parish minister in Partick in Glasgow, and then in the West End of Edinburgh.

But although his preaching moved and stirred me, I was slightly uncomfortable: I did sense that there was, in both the services I attended that October day in 1968, an excess of the theatrical. There was an undoubted element of the sermon as box office.

This is in no way whatsoever a criticism of Murdo Ewen Macdonald himself. It is, rather, a criticism of those who listened to him; perhaps they did not listen well enough. At his congregation in Shandwick Place, Edinburgh, he was regarded as a charismatic crowd-puller. Often, the pews were filled well before the service started; many more folk were allowed in to stand at the sides and the back. Then the doors were shut, and more people were excluded. In their hundreds, people had queued round the corner from Shandwick Place, along Stafford Street and into Alva Street, before the church doors opened for the morning service.

Fewer than ten years after his death, this congregation merged with another in central Edinburgh, and Murdo Ewen's old church was taken over by another denomination. Two admittedly hackneyed words spring to mind: changed days.

Murdo Ewen was a very fiery preacher, a committed socialist who thought that Christianity and politics could and should be mixed. He frequently attacked private education. And yet, many of the members of his Edinburgh congregation, and others who listened to him so avidly, week after week, continued to send their children to private, fee-paying schools, of which there are many in Edinburgh. There was a disconnect here, and in such disconnects the precipitate decline of the Kirk really began in earnest. The complacency was not punctured, no matter how fierce the preacher. There was too much that was routine, and there was smugness. Firebrand preachers were (wrongly) regarded as entertainers and crowd-pullers rather than as evangelists.

Maybe there was a certain ambivalence towards firebrand preachers; looking back, it seems extraordinary that Murdo Ewen Macdonald never became Moderator of the General Assembly. Another very fine preacher who missed out on that honour was Stuart McWilliam, a minister I first knew as a boy in Aberdeen. I kept in touch with him as he moved to Wellington in Glasgow and then, in the evening of his life, to Killearn. Less of a firebrand than Macdonald, he could still be very powerful in the pulpit. As a pastor, he was relaxed and easy-going. One of his parishioners once told me that Stuart had admitted to him that he was more diligent in visiting homes where he knew he would be offered some whisky.

Beechgrove Church

Elsewhere I discuss the congregation I belonged to as a boy and a youth: Beechgrove in Aberdeen. After Stuart McWilliam left, a considerable amount of money was spent in the early 1960s on the building of a new 'church centre', a few hundred yards down Midstocket Road from the church itself. This was despite the fact that the church already had its own very large hall, situated right behind the nave; you did not even have to go outside to gain access to it.

In that vast hall, many group activities went on each week. Yet, even with all that, there was felt to be the need for a more 'upmarket' facility. This was nothing to do with outreach; it had more to do, I'm afraid, with smugness and self-delight. The new church centre was very well fitted out; some of it was like the lounge area of a big, posh hotel.

Adolescents can of course be chippy and truculent; and I remember asking my father, who was the congregational treasurer, if the money for this ambitious project could not have been much more pertinently spent elsewhere. He duly gave me the party line; but I did sense that he was, deep down, uneasy about the entire project.

In retrospect, I reckon that my adolescent uneasiness was very much justified. It is hard not to regard the creation of the new Beechgrove Church centre as a frivolous, indulgent, inward-looking vanity project on behalf of a congregation that was prosperous, even if nothing like the wealthiest in Aberdeen. Here, then, we have an excellent pointer to what was going wrong in the 1960s. The kirk of Beechgrove had its very well-supported structures and organisations, it enjoyed regular positive attention in the local media, and it was blessed with a series of charismatic ministers: Stuart McWilliam, Bill Cattanach and Ernie Sangster, all fine men and eloquent preachers. Attendances at the two Sunday services were always good, and almost unthinkable by today's standards. At Beechgrove, the main Sunday morning service was hardly ever attended by fewer than 500 people, and often a couple of hundred more, week in, week out.

✖

But there was too much comfort, too much complacency. Church of Scotland attendances actually peaked in the mid-1950s. In the year 1955, there was a record number of new communicants: over 45,000. These were very fat years for the national Church; attendances were as high as they had been for several generations.

But, from the late 1950s, an insidious decline set in. At first gentle and hardly noticed, it was to become critical from the late 1960s onwards, though I think it took a long time for many people in the Kirk to accept that the decline was more than a passing phase. Despite the presence of such distinguished and concerned figures as George MacLeod, Murdo Ewen Macdonald and Hugh Anderson, the national Kirk seemed to lack a truly prophetic figure.

There was anguished discussion about growing secularisation and the multiplicity of other available activities on Sundays. (For many years in Scotland, golfing on a Sunday had been frowned on as inappropriate. Professional football matches were hardly ever played on Sundays. When they were, there was considerable anger.)

In 1971, Aberdeen Football Club had to play Celtic in a crucial league game at Pittodrie – billed as the league decider – on Saturday, 17 April. The ground capacity then was 36,000, but the demand for tickets was so high that the Pittodrie ticket office was specially opened the previous Sunday, which happened to be Easter Sunday.

There were very long queues; my brother and I were in one of them. Some local Christians, and I don't think they were hardline Sabbatarians, made a big fuss about this sale of tickets on Easter Sunday morning: they claimed it was an affront to the Lord's Day. I knew at least two Dons supporters who decided to do without tickets and boycott the match because of what they thought was a seriously misguided decision. A Church of Scotland minister in the city advised the members of his congregation on no account to attend the game. The Sabbath had been, and to some extent still was, sacrosanct.

There was also at this time a vague concern about declining standards of personal morality; yet the secular people who best articulated this, such as the journalist Malcolm Muggeridge and the campaigner Mary Whitehouse, tended to be derided. Some bourgeois figures, who had been brought up in very conventional, restrictive households, seemed happy to engage in an eager breaking of all the old conventions.

And then, for the people who still took their faith seriously, the publication of a very controversial theological work by the Anglican Bishop of Woolwich, John Robinson, proved exceptionally unsettling, in Scotland as well as in England. Essentially a reworking of some of the ideas of the great theologian Paul Tillich, the book – called *Honest to God* – became an unlikely bestseller; for many earnest Christians, it produced at best confusion, at worst despair.

In retrospect, it is no exaggeration to claim that the period from the early 1960s onwards was catastrophic for the Church of Scotland. The catastrophe was compounded by complacency, and to some extent by fear. There was certainly no concerted attempt to present the Kirk as a leading agency of counter-culturalism. For many senior folk in the Church, the idea seemed to be to accommodate the times.

Meanwhile, some – probably most – of the Kirk's greatest preachers were left-leaning, but they were not allowed to be especially influential at General Assemblies or Presbyteries.

Campbell Maclean

A very special parish minister, and yet another brilliant preacher, was Campbell Maclean at Cramond, in north-west Edinburgh. He first came to my attention when I was no doubt a somewhat truculent adolescent. At the age of 13, in 1961, I had been packed off to a boarding school in Edinburgh; this displeased me, as I had been very happy in Aberdeen in the 1950s. For some of us at the school, the Sunday evening chapel service proved to be a perhaps unlikely shaft of light in the pervasive gloom.

There was a succession of guest preachers, and some of them proved to be both entertaining and inspirational. Campbell Maclean certainly was. He could appeal to the rebellious streak in adolescent boys. He gave me something new: a Presbyterianism that was mischievous and slightly subversive, and also gently mystical. This man had enormous charisma. His sermons were beautifully crafted, and delivered in a lovely West Highland voice (Campbell was also an accomplished religious broadcaster).

I made it my business to find out more about him. He had a Sutherland background, and he could talk softly but realistically about all the hard chores of the crofting life: the peat-digging, the sheep-shearing and so on. But he had been brought up in Dennistoun in the East End of Glasgow, which, even by Glasgow's standards, was a teeming industrial district, noted for tough living conditions and a gallus, aggressive *joie de vivre*. This resonated with me, because it was here that my own mother had spent her early years – as she never tired of telling me and my brother. (Her father and her grandfather were both doctors in Dennistoun.)

I decided that Campbell's 'man of the people' style – albeit very elegantly expressed – had a lot to do with his Dennistoun upbringing. I also learned that he had been reared in a very literary home and that he cherished the Bible, not just because of its divine revelations but also because it was magnificent literature. Indeed, I don't think I've ever come across a cleric of any denomination who loved words more than Campbell Maclean did. Deep in his faith, there was enormous aesthetic joy – and this was, and is, very unusual for a prominent Scots Presbyterian.

After naval service in the Second World War, he studied for the ministry. His first charge was in Campbeltown in the far west; and then he arrived at Cramond, a pretty plush Edinburgh suburb. (Indeed, the beautiful manse at Cramond, set in an equally beautiful garden, is often cited by those, including myself, who believe that the Church of Scotland could raise a huge amount of money by selling all its manses.)

After hearing Campbell preach at the school chapel, a group of us were so impressed by his style that we asked if we could attend his services at Cramond, which was not very far away. The school chaplain, a good man called George Buchanan-Smith, happily sanctioned this; and, though the experiment lasted for only a few weeks, I was privileged to hear some really wonderful sermons. Looking back, the key thing about Campbell was that he was *not* counter-cultural in this time of acute – and, for some, alarming – social change. He went with the flow, and he seemed to accept the incipient permissive society as few other clerics did. But that acceptance came with crucial caveats.

Later, as a young journalist on the *Scotsman*, I heard him address a group of Edinburgh businessmen. His message was both nuanced and controversial: the permissive society, he said, should be welcomed by Christians. People could take from it what they wished. In some ways, this new society would help us to build a kinder, more inclusive, gentler Scotland. And, where we rightly demurred or objected to excessive licence, or to the selfish abuse of new freedoms, we could as Christians stand out all the more because society was losing its old restraints. When anything goes, those who don't always go stand out.

That, of course, is a brief summary of what he said, recalled over a distance of many years; but I think it gets his core theme across. I don't know if it impressed the businessmen, but it certainly impressed me. Campbell was a romantic realist; one of his tenets was that people inevitably create a God, or a version of

God, to suit themselves. He was also, in his rather laconic and elegantly cerebral way, a very committed Christian.

Looking back, I think that he, more than anyone else I came across, could have cracked the 1960s and the 1970s for the Church of Scotland. But, like so many of the Kirk's outstanding figures, he was not properly used. He was a prophet with honour. At the same time, he was probably too sophisticated and too subtle a man to emerge as the leader to haul the national Church out of its growing travails. What was needed was something crude and blunt.

⊠

As a postscript to all this, I should note that, in the autumn of 2012, I was walking along Midstocket Road in Aberdeen when, to my genuine horror, I saw that Beechgrove Church was being demolished. As I approached, I realised that it was a partial demolition; some of the venerable building, where I had spent so many hours as a child and a youth, was being converted into flats. I stood on the pavement for a few minutes, watching the organised violence of the demolition of the now redundant church, and pondering on this destruction, at once real and symbolic, the consequence of a sorry sequence of lost opportunities and misdirected effort.

And so we return to where we started: the experience of the young Andrew McGowan in 1968. He could not have been more fully involved in the life of his local kirk; and yet it took a visiting Baptist evangelist to lead him to the light.

Charisma

Tom Winning, George MacLeod and Margaret Thatcher

Tom Winning

Cardinal Tom Winning was a robust and highly political church leader whose main achievement was to return the Catholic Church, after centuries of absence, to the centre of public affairs in Scotland. He propelled both his church and himself to the forefront of Scottish public life. Before him, there was a sense that Catholics in Scotland were expected to take, if not the back seat, then a seat that was a row or so from the front. Tom Winning himself, surveying the Scotland he had grown up in, said: 'Our Church did not count . . . we kept our heads below the parapet'. But Winning was never a man to keep his head bowed. As his clerical career progressed, he became determined that his church should speak out boldly and prophetically.

With his effective campaigning, Tom Winning was often regarded as a politician first and a cleric second. He almost singlehandedly changed perceptions of Catholicism in Scotland; he gained for his church a new-found public status that he personally relished. Towards the end of his life, he was openly sympathetic to the Scottish National Party; and it would have been fascinating to see how his enthusiasm for nationalism and, by implication, Scottish independence would have developed in the new century. Alas, that was not to be, as he died in 2001.

When I was deputy editor and then editor of the *Herald* in Glasgow, I got to know Tom quite well, and I was certainly one of those who regarded him as a political figure every bit as much as a religious figure. He had the first edition of the *Herald* delivered to his house in Newlands in south Glasgow every night; he perused it with interest. If something upset him, he would ring the paper; if he was really angry, he'd ring that very night, but usually he waited until the next day. I sometimes fielded these calls; and his language was robust, to put it mildly: many in his flock would have been surprised and even appalled. He reminded me more than once of some very irate football managers I'd encountered earlier in my career.

But he was simply doing his job – as he saw it. He had been the Archbishop of Glasgow since 1974, and the *Herald* was the most influential paper in his archbishopric. (He made fewer calls after he was appointed cardinal in 1994. His main media adviser, Father Tom Connelly, had by then finally convinced him that tabloids and the electronic media were more important in the wider Scotland than the broadsheet press.)

Tom Winning wasn't a bully, but he did believe that the Roman Catholic Church had been cowed and subservient for far too long, and kept from its rightful place at the forefront of Scottish society. He was not an admirer of his predecessor, Archbishop James Scanlan. He wanted to be much more proactive. (I never knew Scanlan personally; but some of the Catholics whom I knew and respected did not hold him in high regard. He was often seen being driven round Glasgow in a sleek Mercedes, staring out grumpily. He was regarded as stiff and aloof, and not taken very seriously. The journalist Colm Brogan thought that he was a risible figure. Indeed, Brogan claimed that Scanlan was most famous for a conversation he had had with Pope Paul VI about the Loch Ness Monster.)

Winning's much more assertive style was no accident. He had been brought up in a devout Catholic home in industrial Lanarkshire, amid poverty, in the 1920s and 1930s when the Church of Scotland's campaigns against Irish immigrants and Catholics were at their worst. His father, a miner, was frequently unemployed, and Winning was certain he was often denied work because he was a Catholic. (Between the wars, employers were able to be much more selective in their choice of employees than had been the case in the nineteenth century.) The young Tom Winning was on the receiving end of regular, low-grade sectarian spite and discrimination. If this did not scar him for life, there was undoubtedly a slightly chippy side to his persona – and I can hardly blame him.

Yet he had charm too, and he could be exceptionally good company. He once asked me to spend a day at the Scottish Bishops' Conference when it was meeting at a 'retreat' near Girvan. I was to give a talk and lead a discussion on the media, but I've long since forgotten that part of the occasion. What I do recall is how Winning controlled everything, the social side as well as the formal parts, with immense style; a very Scottish blend of quiet authority and folksy couthiness.

He was a well-kent and welcome customer in several of Glasgow's more old-fashioned Italian restaurants. (Partly, this reflected the fact that he had served in Rome in several different roles, not least as director of the Scots College at the time of the Second Vatican Council. My good friend Arnold Kemp and I had some memorable lunches with him and Tom Connelly. When it was their turn to pay, Tom Winning was careful to ensure that it was the other Tom who paid for the food and, more importantly, the wine.)

Tom Winning did sometimes express what I think was genuine concern about his undoubtedly comfortable lifestyle; I heard him say occasionally that he wished he could be a little more disciplined. He was unfair on himself; in truth he was a workaholic. He talked freely and well at informal social occasions, and he made it clear that he saw ensuring that his church played a leading role in all aspects of Scottish life as a key part of his job. Indeed, during the (sometimes very long) lunches between the two Protestants and the two Catholics, religion was rarely discussed. Our chat was mainly about politics.

At a time when the public influence of organised religion was diminishing in Scotland, Winning conducted a one-man campaign to turn the tide. And I believe he succeeded, through his high profile, his constant interventions in controversial public debates, and his forceful personality, which combined charisma with something close to menace. There were two flaws. The first was that it was all down to him. He was, in many respects, a one-off. The other flaw is that he was often quite narrow in his outlook. As far as he was concerned, organised religion meant the Roman Catholic Church, first and foremost; anything else, even the national Church of Scotland, was secondary.

His political skills were very much to the fore at the time of the controversial Falklands war, which Winning disapproved of; but he had to subsume his genuine personal anger about the war to save Pope John Paul II's visit to Britain in 1982. When the final preparations were being made, Britain was at war with Argentina, a very Catholic country. Winning showed considerable – and, for some, unlikely – diplomatic skill behind the scenes; and the visit went ahead. The Scottish section of the Pope's visit was an undoubted success, with the spectacular highlights being a youth rally at Murrayfield Stadium in Edinburgh and a huge mass in Bellahouston Park, Glasgow.

When Winning was appointed cardinal in 1994, I mentioned to several Catholics I knew that this successful visit of Pope John Paul II must have been the high point in his career thus far. I guessed that his elevation owed much to the facts that the visit had actually taken place against all expectations, and that it had been such a popular triumph. To my surprise, they disagreed. Some claimed that his most important achievement was his ongoing Pro-Life initiative, which undoubtedly saved many lives that would otherwise have been aborted; others mentioned his efforts in the long saga of the sainthood of John Ogilvie. (The story of Ogilvie's canonisation is told elsewhere in this book.)

Tom Winning was not a good administrator, he had difficult relations with some of his priests, and indeed he nearly bankrupted his archbishopric. Nor was he a natural communicator; but he could hold an audience. Once, I heard him deliver a Town and Gown lecture at Strathclyde University. After the address, an early question concerned the vexed issue of denominational schools. Winning defended them strongly. But what was masterly was the way he prefaced his answer. He said he wanted to speak only to the Protestants in the audience. The Catholics could ignore him. Needless to say, this ensured that the entire, large audience was hanging on his every word. He went on to claim that the Protestants, if they were parents, were probably envious of Catholic schools.

A week or so before he died in 2001, I met him for the last time, ironically at a party in Edinburgh hosted by the then Moderator of the Kirk's General Assembly, the Right Revd Dr Andrew McLellan.

Winning was on cracking form, chatting and joshing – but, as always, there was a political edge to his comments.

He had capitalised on the fact that he enjoyed continuity of office, whereas the Moderator is appointed for one year only. Indeed, Tom Winning saw himself as a man for the long haul; and, for many years, he was, more than any other individual, the public face of religion in Scotland. He did not use this carefully achieved and lofty status in a conciliatory way. Without doubt, Winning was divisive. Some of his campaigns verged on bitterness, particularly when it came to matters such as abortion and homosexuality. And yet he was also a sincere, if cautious and realistic, ecumenicist. He had been delighted when he was invited to address the Kirk's General Assembly as a relatively untried archbishop back in 1975, though the invitation caused considerable controversy within the Kirk.

Winning's speech was magnificent. I was then working on the *Scotsman* in Edinburgh; I did not hear the address myself, but I encountered many people who had heard it – journalists and commissioners alike – describing it as a 'triumph'. I think this was the moment when Winning began to be noticed throughout Scotland. In his address, he referred to 'centuries of estranged silence' and went on to 'humbly beg' God's forgiveness. He endorsed ecumenism but admitted that his own church could still prove to be 'a stumbling block'.

It was the tone of the speech – humble, realistic, conciliatory – as much as its content that produced genuine enthusiasm among the commissioners, who stamped their feet loudly in support of the archbishop. Of course, Winning was not always as humble and placatory; but that day he won many new friends.

Apparently, his address was rather less well received in Rome, where a senior Vatican cardinal, a Tuscan called Giovanni Benelli, who was close to the then Pope and who was known as 'the Berlin Wall' because it was so hard to get radical or innovatory ideas past him, let it be known that he was distinctly unimpressed by the contents.

That was Rome. But, even in Scotland, this fine speech, while undoubtedly making a considerable impact (my father, who was a commissioner at the next General Assembly in 1976, told me then that Winning's address was still being discussed enthusiastically a year on), left little long-term residue. Winning himself, I reckon, was never really committed to taking bold ecumenist initiatives that might bear fruit. He was honest when he said his own church might be the stumbling block. And, while he was always ready to 'make waves' during the next 25 years, as far as I can recall he never again made a really significant intervention in the cause of ecumenical progress. Indeed, he sometimes appeared to be moving in the opposite direction. He once lost his political canniness and let slip publicly that he thought Roman Catholicism would eventually be the only Christian faith in Scotland.

When Winning spoke, people listened and paid careful attention. Politicians respected him; some, particularly Tories, feared him. Many Unionist politicians were alarmed when he began to flirt with Scottish nationalism. In a notable speech – in Brussels, of all places, in 1998 – he outlined his vague, but politically potent, sympathy for Scottish nationalism. (He had previously discussed his ideas on at least two occasions with the leader of the Scottish National Party, Alex Salmond.) He announced that a 'nation both old and new' was now taking its place once more on the world stage, and this he described as 'a rebirth of ancient nationhood aided by modern democracy'. He looked ahead to the possibility of full independence for Scotland, probably in about ten years' time.

About this time (I don't think the two things were connected), it was suggested that he might be an outside candidate for the papacy. The rumours certainly did not emanate from Tom himself. Probably there was little in them; yet he had made himself a figure of strong standing, a man to whom attention had to be paid. His legacy was to some extent frittered away by his successor as the senior Roman Catholic cleric in Scotland, Keith O'Brien.

Cardinal O'Brien was even more outspoken than Winning, but I felt that politicians tended to take him less seriously. O'Brien was gracious, courteous and gentle, but his career shuddered to an unfortunate stop in 2013 when he had to step down in disgrace, having been implicated in what was officially described as 'inappropriate sexual activity with various priests'. He was ordered by the Pope to quit Scotland as an act of penitence.

George MacLeod

George MacLeod, like Tom Winning, had charisma, oodles of it; but there most of the similarities end. For a start, MacLeod was born to wealth and an assured sense of social safety. The context in which he grew up was one of a gentle but nonetheless pervasive Protestant ascendancy. High bourgeois members of the Church of Scotland in Glasgow in the early twentieth century could look to the fact that British prime ministers such as Bonar Law and Henry Campbell-Bannerman (both of them educated at Glasgow High School) came from solid Presbyterian stock.

MacLeod's own father was a prosperous accountant and a Conservative MP. Tom Winning was born the son of a miner who was unemployed for long periods and was the grandson of an illegitimate Irish immigrant; George MacLeod was born into a well-established Scottish dynasty of clerics and public figures. He was brought up in considerable comfort and style in the West End of Glasgow, well insulated from the horrors of mass industrialisation nearby. There was, to use the superb later phrase of the novelist Alan Sharp, 'a paralysis of insulation'. There was scant apprehension of the fact that much of the city of Glasgow was ripe for revolt, even revolution. Indeed, the hard left, led by articulate agitators such as James Connolly and the charismatic Govan schoolteacher John Maclean, were already preparing for cataclysmic change. Maclean regularly preached revolution before ever larger and more enthusiastic audiences.

Meanwhile, the young MacLeod lived in another world. He was packed off to a prep school in west Edinburgh, thence to Winchester, one of England's most prominent public schools, and from there to Oriel College, Oxford: a classic progression for someone who was born into a context of settled entitlement and considerable prosperity.

Yet George MacLeod very soon learned that, for many, perhaps most human beings, life was something of a struggle. His world of comfortable certainties was first shattered by the First World War, in which he served with distinction, winning both the MC and the Croix de Guerre. He was a hero, but a thinking hero; appalled by what he had witnessed, he became a pacifist and an exceptionally committed Christian, though his Christianity was never conventional.

He honed his considerable preaching skills as a junior minister at a fashionable church, St Cuthbert's in West Princes Street Gardens, Edinburgh. Then, in a dramatic turning away from the assured path he seemed to be on, he switched to Govan in Glasgow. This was the time of the Depression. While Tom Winning's family were suffering a few miles to the south in Clydeside, MacLeod saw for himself the grisly downside of industrial Scotland. Glasgow may have been the workshop of the world, building an astounding number of loco-motives and great ships, but the human cost was appallingly high, particularly as unemployment ravaged close-knit working commu-nities such as Govan.

George MacLeod, a brave and energetic man, worked hard among the poor of Govan, a part of Glasgow that had special indus-trial resonance. Physically, it is defined by the Clyde; it straggles along the south bank, a little to the west of the city centre, and in the 1930s it was still imbued with the clang and clamour of the building of great ships.

MacLeod did not only preach in his church; Sir Alex Ferguson, the great football manager, recalled much later, in a piece for the *Glasgow Herald*, that when he was a wee boy he and his pals used to wander around Govan on Sunday evenings looking for some-thing to do. Sometimes they would go to Govan Cross, where there was a speaker's corner. He heard MacLeod preaching there, but could not get near the great man; often hundreds were listening. He asked his dad who this man was, and was told: 'That's the minister, son'. And this greatly impressed the young Alex – that the parish minister was out there among the people. 'He had a huge impact on Govan' was Ferguson's verdict.

But MacLeod worked too hard, campaigned too rigorously and empathised too wholeheartedly. He burned himself out. The break-down that came seemed, in retrospect, inevitable. He went to the Holy Land to convalesce. He returned, and threw himself back into his work. He now believed that renewal could best be found by recon-necting with the early Christian Church in Scotland, the Celtic Church of Columba. His idea was not just to revive the values of the early

Celtic Church, but also – just as important – to reconnect with the key democratic values of the Scottish Reformation.

He had flirted with Russian Orthodoxy; he was essentially a romantic, even perhaps a mystic. And, crucially, he had taken his summer holidays on the small island of Iona, just west of Mull – an island forever associated with the early mission of Columba.

So, he formed a big, but specific, idea: men preparing for the ministry in the Church of Scotland could go to Iona, form a community there, and also restore the monastic buildings of the ancient abbey. Thus the Iona Community, which was in time to become Scotland's most important ecumenical body in the later twentieth century, was born. It was a place not just for trainee male ministers in the Kirk, but for lay people as well, men and women, Protestants and Roman Catholics. They could rebuild the ancient abbey and its precincts, and live on site.

George MacLeod was an impatient, impetuous man, never one for orthodox politics – or indeed for conventional Protestant Christianity. Yet he did serve as Moderator of the Kirk's General Assembly in 1957. When he was called to the Assembly Hall as the new Moderator, one of the commissioners, a missionary from Ghana, objected. This man, one Revd Malloch, said that MacLeod's nomination was untimely and unfortunate. This was unprecedented, but some suspected that MacLeod was quite pleased. He relished controversy; and, when the restoration of Iona Abbey was finally completed, he accepted a peerage as Lord MacLeod of Fuinary, which caused many eyebrows to be raised.

Back to where he had started, to safe upper-middle-class certainties and even to complacency? I don't think so. Although I have my doubts about what he achieved in Iona, I could never deny that he was a prophetic figure; there can be no questioning his compassion, his eloquence and his ecumenism, which was particularly important.

At the same time, he was too much of an outsider to achieve orthodox political impact – or even lasting ecumenical impact. And his 'star turns' at successive General Assemblies became cabaret acts: he was entertaining and diverting, and he was a passionate advocate of pacifism and, latterly, ecology; but did anyone take him seriously? Certainly, Tom Winning sometimes doubted if MacLeod was a figure of real substance. And he felt that MacLeod's ecumenism had made scant impact in alleviating the sectarian tensions that carried right through into the twenty-first century.

In 1990, I was able to secure pre-publication rights for the *Glasgow Herald* of Ron Ferguson's excellent biography of MacLeod. We went to town on the project, not just with extensive extracts; we started a debate on MacLeod's significance, his impact on Scotland. Tom Winning was fascinated by this, and I remember him telling me that, while MacLeod was in many ways a genuinely great man, he had not really helped to sort Scotland's residual bigotry problem. Indeed, I was told later that he rather disliked MacLeod, though he never said that to me.

Winning also told me, on another occasion, that the Church of Rome was good at dealing with its 'troublemakers'. The implication was that the Kirk wasn't. I think of George MacLeod as a world-class troublemaker, and a frequently inspirational one. His legacy may be slightly misty (as Iona often is), but I suspect that it may become more important in time.

✕

Despite their charisma, their personal force as men of the left, their enormous potential for joint leadership and their growing unease with Thatcherism – the predominant political ideology of the 1980s – despite all these, neither Winning nor MacLeod did anything really significant to attack the controversial Tory prime minister and her – to them – egregious and deeply offensive policies. Together, I'm sure they could have stirred Scotland into a state of authentic Christian revolt. But it was not to be.

I am certain that Winning and MacLeod could have come together, had they wanted to, and launched various powerful ecumenical initiatives that might have stirred Scotland – and, at the same time, shaken the London government – and produced results. They were both outstanding men, blessed with charisma and the power to communicate powerfully, although the latter came rather more easily to MacLeod. But then perhaps MacLeod was a little too eccentric, while Winning was perhaps too narrow: his main priority, understandably enough, was his own church, which had been battered and bruised, not least by the Church of Scotland, in the early years of the twentieth century.

They were both towering figures, but they never found a common cause.

Margaret Thatcher

As for Mrs Thatcher, she boldly came to Edinburgh to address – some would say harangue – the national Kirk's General Assembly of 1988. Her so-called 'Sermon on the Mound' (the Assembly Hall is near to a street called The Mound) was received somewhat frostily, though there was no blatant discourtesy. But the speech was regarded as provocative, not just by many of the commissioners who heard it – some of them were genuinely outraged – but also by most of the Scottish commentariat, who could hardly contain their collective displeasure.

A quarter of a century later, the full text of the 'Sermon on the Mound' reads like a well-constructed attempt to fuse her undoubtedly sincere Christianity with her stern right-wing economic views. She was courteous about Scotland's national Church and indeed about the Scottish people, referring first to the 'independence of mind and rigour of thought' which had always been powerful Scottish characteristics. She also praised the 'extensive caring services' provided by Scotland's national Church. Then she moved into more challenging mode, indicating that Christianity was about spiritual redemption, not social reform. She told the Assembly that Christians should not go to church simply for social reforms and benefits (this was no doubt a sly retrospective dig at the authors of *Faith in the City*).

She also told the commissioners to work and to use their talents to create wealth, and quoted Paul: 'If a man will not work, he shall not eat'. The creation of wealth was not wrong; what was wrong was the love of money for its own sake. The 'spiritual dimension' came in deciding what to do with the wealth.

The exercise of mercy and generosity could not be delegated to other people. She quoted Paul again: anyone who neglected to provide for his own house had disowned the faith. Further, intervention by the state must never become so great that it removed personal responsibility.

She delved into overtly theological interpretation when she discussed the second of Jesus Christ's two key commandments – to love your neighbour as yourself. She confessed (I reckon with humility, not arrogance) that she had always had difficulty interpreting this command. But she called in aid C. S. Lewis, who had pointed out that we don't love ourselves when we fall below the standards and beliefs we have accepted.

Now, I have personally always thought that the difficulty with this command is the assumption that people do love themselves. Many, probably most, do – but then there are those who hate or loathe themselves; and I think a huge amount of the unhappiness and indeed crime in the world begins with people who seriously dislike themselves.

Anyway, Mrs Thatcher was at this point, I believe, wilfully misinterpreted by people who criticised her speech as a justification for condemning others when they had failed to achieve the standards that 'we' (i.e. Mrs Thatcher) had set for them. I did not then, and do not now, place this construction on her words; but there we are. What is undeniable is that many Scots regarded her address as a deeply offensive affront.

Without doubt it was strong stuff, though it was delivered in a dignified, even staid, context, and very respectfully at that. Many in Scotland did not bother to analyse it; they just reacted with glib fury. Some politicians and journalists chose to brand it as a callous perversion of Christianity (despite the careful references to St Paul). The then Moderator, James Whyte, responded to the prime minister's lecture with a certain amount of bathos by handing her two Kirk reports on social issues. He advised her to read them carefully.

A year later, her government introduced the hated 'community charge' (poll tax) to Scotland, a good year ahead of its introduction south of the Border. That finally confirmed the virulent antipathy that much of the Scottish nation seemed to have for her. No sermon, no speechifying, would ever be able to reverse it. Not that the 'Sermon on the Mound' had done her much good anyway. And yet the two main Christian Churches in Scotland still remained muted and impotent, utterly unable to mobilise against her.

✄

The most significant political action taken by a Scottish cleric around this period was by Canon Kenyon Wright, a hitherto obscure scion of the Episcopal Church in Scotland. He became the very high-profile leader of the Scottish Constitutional Convention, which was a considerable force in the national campaign for Scottish devolution, eventually to be delivered by Tony Blair's government over a decade later. It is perhaps ironic that a man who for most of his career had been a little-known Liberal-Democrat Episcopalian was to play a leading role in the push for a Scottish Parliament, while so many senior clergy in both the national Church and the Roman Catholic Church did so little.

'Doing God'

Douglas Alexander and David Cameron, Frank McElhone,
The press, Scottish broadcasting, The Kirk's publications,
The BBC, William Barclay and Richard Holloway

Many modern Scottish politicians have been brought up in deeply
Christian homes; but there has not been too much obvious residue
from this important aspect of their upbringing.

Gordon Brown, who in 2007 became the first Scottish prime minister of the UK for 43 years, was raised in a pious, God-fearing and
very happy home; his father was a highly regarded kirk minister.
When he was student rector of Edinburgh University in the early
1970s, Gordon told me that his political career – he was clearly
very ambitious even then – would be based on the values he had
soaked up in his Christian home.

Yet Gordon became a senior member – at times an uneasy one – of
Tony Blair's three administrations; this was the very Tony Blair who,
according to one of his leading aides, did not 'do God', although
soon after he quit the premiership he became a Roman Catholic.
When Brown succeeded Blair as prime minister, he showed no sign
at all of pushing God, or at least pushing Christianity, back on to
the political forum. Indeed, it was left to another Labour son of
the manse, Douglas Alexander, to revive the old Socialist notion of
directly fusing Christianity and politics.

Douglas Alexander and David Cameron

Alexander, a high-minded, cerebral MP and former Cabinet minister who was at one time Gordon Brown's lead speechwriter, made a
dramatic intervention into the overall UK political debate towards
the end of 2013. He announced, to a somewhat bemused British

public, that there was a misplaced sense of embarrassment at 'doing God' – that unfortunate phrase once again. Some interpreted this as a sly dig at his boss, the Labour leader Ed Miliband, who is an atheist. But I think this interpretation missed the point. Douglas Alexander's intention was to make it clear that senior British politicians, in general, had become afraid to discuss matters of faith. He also insisted that there was a pressing need for political leaders to do something about the growing persecution of Christians right across the world.

Alexander's forthright remarks prompted little response until several months later, at Easter 2014 to be precise, when the UK prime minister, David Cameron, wrote an interesting if modest article for the *Church Times* in which he called for Britain to be more 'evangelical' and 'confident' about its status as a Christian country. Crucially, he tempered that call by admitting, with impressive candour, that he himself was not that regular an attender at church services, and further that he was vague about 'some of the more difficult parts' of his faith. Indeed, he somehow managed to suggest that overmuch Christian fervour was not to be encouraged; he admitted that he wrote as a 'classic Anglican', meaning, I think, that he was restrained, not combative, in his Christianity and that he did not want to be too forceful in pushing his religious views down others' throats. His article seemed to me to be careful, cautious and almost verging on the timorous. As befitted an Anglican, it was far more Cranmer than Knox.

However, this apparently innocuous piece prompted a spectacular, if somewhat shrill, blast of indignation from angry secularists and militant atheists, who reacted with apparently genuine fury. The prime minister's article was described, variously, as sectarian, divisive and authoritarian. Mr Cameron was accused bitterly of 'forcing his faith on the people'. You could have kidded me: I thought that his remarks were notable for their mildness and vagueness. There was certainly nothing divisive or hostile to non-believers in them.

So, I waited for Cameron to be defended. Few seemed prepared to do so, though a prominent Jewish journalist forcefully insisted that it was ridiculous to claim that England (not the UK) was not a Christian country. He pointed out that the brouhaha was taking place over the Easter holiday – 'a Christian festival' – and that the Church of England was England's official established Church, and that the head of state, the Queen, was a strong and committed Christian who often professed her faith. Others pointed out that the first word of the UK national anthem was 'God', and that the UK calendar was dominated by Christian holidays and festivals.

The deputy prime minister, Nick Clegg, did follow up Mr Cameron's remarks, somewhat timidly and obscurely. He called for the disestablishment of the Church of England. As for the head of the Anglican Communion, the Archbishop of Canterbury, Justin Welby . . . well, it took him a good week to intervene. He eventually backed Cameron, but in fairly cautious terms, confessing to being 'baffled' by the contretemps. A much more controversial contribution came a week or so later when Welby's immediate predecessor, Lord Williams of Oystermouth, pronounced unequivocally that Britain – not England, note – was no longer a nation of believers. He claimed that Britain had become 'post-Christian'. At the same time, an ICM survey, undertaken across the UK, indicated that 56 per cent of the British public regarded the UK as Christian. But another poll suggested that only 29 per cent of British adults claimed to be 'religious'. (Yet, in the 2011 census, 59 per cent of Britons had indicated that they were indeed 'religious'.)

In yet another poll, two-thirds of those interviewed claimed that Christians had become afraid to express their faith. The same proportion felt that Christians were vulnerable to abuse or discrimination because of their faith, and that those of other religions were afforded greater protection. Only 14 per cent of those surveyed claimed to be practising Christians.

There ensued a further, lesser debate about what, if not Christianity, was Britain's religion – if indeed it had one. One suggestion was the National Health Service; but then it was pointed out that its main political architect, Aneurin Bevan, had described it as a Christian institution.

Meanwhile, the responses to David Cameron's original remarks dribbled on, in a disjointed and inconclusive way. Non-Christian spokesmen for the Sikh and Muslim communities expressed some support for Mr Cameron. The response from the Church of

Scotland suggested that the prime minister had been playing politics with religion and that he was guilty of posturing.

This was too much for Murdo Fraser MSP, a leading Scottish Tory politician who maintains a keen interest in Kirk affairs. 'It beggars belief that the first response from a representative of the Kirk was to question Mr Cameron's good faith'.

And so the row rumbled on and on, right across the UK. A further poll indicated that one in three of the UK population thought that the prime minister had succeeded only in 'undermining' Christianity, partly because of his support for gay marriage, and partly because of his suggestion that Britain should be more evangelical in its Christianity.

All this presented a confused and very unedifying picture. The champions of Christianity seemed uneasy and cautious and just occasionally truculent; they were not particularly confident or clear in asserting their faith. On the other hand, the anti-Christians seemed forceful and angry, and sometimes surprisingly ad hominem.

Further, it was evident that many people could not distinguish between Britain and England. There was a protracted, messy and at times virulent period of disputation. It was not an enlightening episode, and certainly not an encouraging one for a Scottish Christian.

My view is that Douglas Alexander had originally intervened with considerable authority, as a committed Christian himself. The follow-ups were far less impressive.

Douglas Alexander's father, the Revd Douglas Alexander, served for many years as the (much-loved) minister of Erskine Parish Church. He was never a minister to seek the national limelight, although in 2000 he presided over the very moving funeral service for Donald Dewar, the 'Father of the Nation' – the man who, more than any other politician, had ensured that Scotland should receive its own Parliament at Holyrood. This was an extraordinary occasion, possibly the most inclusive major Christian service I have ever attended in Scotland. Glasgow Cathedral was packed to overflowing. Inside were many figures from the ranks of the great and good, including English as well as Scottish politicians and statesmen; outside, there was a huge throng of ordinary Glasgow folk. I recall wondering at the time why and how the old Scottish links between socialism and Christianity had somehow become so severed.

Douglas Alexander had spoken with authentic authority because he himself had brought an undoubted Christian edge to his work, especially during the premiership of Gordon Brown, when he was UK Secretary of State for International Development. So, his remarks carried weight; they were not an idle or shallow grasp for a few headlines.

※

Meanwhile, within Scottish national politics there is now little sign of overt Christian influence. Alex Salmond, the nationalist leader who dominated Scotland's domestic politics, and the push for independence, for over a generation, was brought up, like so many Scots in the 1950s, in a home where Christianity was a central part of everyday life. When he was christened, his two middle names came from the minister who presided over the ceremony at St Ninian's Parish Church in Linlithgow.

Salmond's grandfather and father were both kirk elders. He was a regular churchgoer as a boy and a youth; then, when he was a student at St Andrews University, his Christian commitment apparently became more tenuous. This followed a very common pattern in Scotland in the postwar years: children were often brought up in strong churchgoing families, but somehow, generally around late adolescence or in their early twenties, the Christian commitment seemed to evaporate.

Frank McElhone

There were, of course, exceptions. Frank McElhone, a couthy, shrewd and altogether delightful Labour MP of the old school, was a fast-talking Glaswegian who represented the Glasgow Gorbals constituency (renamed Queen's Park) in the 1970s. He had formerly run a greengrocer's shop in the constituency; this he had developed into the so-called Frank's Bank, a place where poor people could come for credit and for friendly and useful advice if they were having problems with the social services or even with their own family. But even 'Frank's Bank' could not deal with all the problems of his constituents; and his separate constituency surgeries were among the most popular in Scotland, often attended by around 100 people. When he was (surprisingly) appointed Under-Secretary for Education and Sport at the Scottish Office by prime minister Jim Callaghan in 1976, he found the conduct of these surgeries increasingly onerous, coming as they did on top of his many ministerial duties. He used to hold them every fortnight, when he was often tired and weary.

One night, a wild-looking man came into the constituency rooms brandishing an axe. The many waiting constituents all got up and left at once. A fortnight later, the same desperate fellow reappeared, but this time without the axe. Quick as a flash, Frank said to him: 'For God's sake, man, where the hell's your axe?'

I suggested that Frank's appointment as a minister of the Crown was surprising. The element of surprise was twofold. He had been rather patronised as a good and decent constituency MP, but had not been regarded as ministerial material. Second, and this had a more sinister tinge, his Catholicism – which was strong and proud – was regarded as a potential issue, particularly as he would be dealing with Scotland's state schools. There had already been one or two Scottish Office ministers who were Catholics, but they had been rarities.

At the conference in Edinburgh when he 'met the press' to introduce himself immediately after his appointment, there was a lot of talk about his Catholicism. Typically, he dealt with pointed questions with a disarming candour and a quick Glaswegian wit. He said with a smile that he 'confessed' to being a 'devout Catholic' – and then he asked the gathered hacks why Catholics were generally described as 'devout' while Protestants were 'staunch'. This conundrum defused the issue, but it lingered. Later, I was told that his denomination had indeed been a matter of concern to some senior civil servants at the Scottish Education Department. Such sensitivities, however, were of little concern to Frank; he did not always take his senior advisers too seriously, and was quite happy to go against them when his instincts told him he was in the right.

Frank McElhone was indeed a committed Catholic, and his faith meant much to him. He was a reforming and effective junior minister, and in all he did he brought a strong and direct Christian commitment to bear. In this, he was politically unusual. He was a useful Christian of the very best kind. He certainly saw it as his duty, in his work at the Scottish Office, to deal with such issues as the abuse of alcohol and related thuggery by Scottish football supporters, and the appalling conditions at List D schools, to take just two examples. Other ministers, who preferred an easier political life, might well have avoided such difficult and contentious policy areas.

Frank McElhone died, far too young, in 1982. His funeral mass in the Gorbals was a smaller and more intimate service than Donald Dewar's funeral, but it was just as, if not more, moving. It took place on a very wet and wild autumn day – yet his constituents, many of them looking ragged and careworn, turned up in their hundreds.

I think that very few Scottish MPs in the modern era have had such a close and authentic affinity with their people. Frank believed in trying to combine his Christian faith and his political vocation; his main mission was to try to help people who could not work 'the system', people who were poor or in trouble or even outcast.

The press

If Scotland's politicians have been generally reluctant to 'do God', the same might be said about Scotland's journalists. When I started work on the *Scotsman* in 1969, I soon became aware that several of the paper's senior journalists were elders in the Kirk, including its distinguished lead critic and arts editor, Allen Wright. Its pages took the affairs of the national Church seriously – the Catholic Church received far less attention, but there were very few Catholics on the staff – and the General Assembly, each May, was regarded as a major news event. A team of three reporters was allocated to cover the proceedings; a full page was allocated for their reports. Sometimes a fourth, more junior, reporter was sent up to the Assembly Hall in the evening; ironically, this was often the time when the best stories tended to develop.

There was then still an authentic respect for the Assembly in the wider Scotland; it was felt that it was the nearest thing Scotland had to a serious national forum. Whether many actually regarded it as a kind of substitute for a Scottish Parliament is another matter.

Allen Wright was very friendly with the minister at his West End church, the Revd Bill Cattanach, and often invited him to pop into the *Scotsman* editorial offices. Cattanach had been the minister of Beechgrove, Aberdeen, in the late 1950s – and my parents knew him well. I sometimes had a coffee with Bill in the *Scotsman* staff canteen and found that he was rather perplexed as to what exactly his function, vis-à-vis the paper, was supposed to be. At one time, I think he thought he was going to be an informal chaplain or almoner for the editorial staff; at other times, he believed it was his job to offer religious commentaries for the paper. These were not actually rejected but were held for weeks or even months by the then features editor, Bill Watson, before they were eventually printed.

Bill Cattanach was a very genial and open man, not given to repining or reproaching; but, in retrospect, the sight of him wandering amiably round the *Scotsman*'s venerable corridors, uncertain of his role, could serve as a kind of metaphor for the diminishing status of the Church of Scotland ministry, and by extension a loss of confidence in the role of the ministry, whatever that should have been. Newspapers, in the same way as the Church of Scotland, have declined considerably since that time over 40 years ago. But, even then, it was slowly becoming clear that the media in Scotland were not as interested in sermonettes from clerics as in insights (well-informed and, ideally, controversial insights) into internal church politics. Journalists were increasingly interested not in the story the Kirk had to tell, but in the stories within the Kirk itself.

At that time, Scotland's other august heavyweight daily paper, the *Glasgow Herald*, also took the Assembly seriously; but the rest of the Scottish press, including the *Scottish Daily Express*, while generally respectful, took less interest. The *Scottish Daily Express* was given, occasionally but spectacularly, to posing bombastically as the champion and defender of Protestant Scotland. It became ridiculously enraged in the late 1950s when the Kirk was embroiled in a spectacular, if spurious, controversy following a somewhat preposterous proposal, emanating from the Kirk's Inter-church Relations Committee, that the national Church should allow its Presbyteries to elect bishops. The megalomaniac proprietor of the Express Group, Lord Beaverbrook, was apoplectic (he came from a Presbyterian Canadian background) – and, via his editor, Ian McColl, he ordered some of his Scottish staff (many of whom were atheists, though McColl himself was a deeply Christian man) to wage a vigorous campaign against the proposal.

To the confusion and amazement of the bulk of the *Scottish Daily Express* readers (there were then over 750,000 of them) and many of the paper's editorial staff, including, for example, the fine journalist who ran the paper's Aberdeen bureau, Adam Borthwick, the group of journalists carefully picked by McColl did as they were told. They were egged on by various outspoken figures in the Kirk, who regarded the proposal about bishops as something that had literally come from hell. A professor at Glasgow University achieved brief notoriety for announcing that God didn't think like 'these Anglicans' because God 'wasn't a bloody fool'.

The much-loved minister of the High Kirk of St Giles in Edinburgh, Dr Harry Whitley – a fine man who was anything but a Presbyterian bigot, although his judgement was not always of the best – threw himself eagerly into the row. He lambasted those associated with the so-called 'bid for bishops' – and they included venerable figures such as George MacLeod – as people who were willing to sell their birthright for 'an unsavoury mix of Anglican arrogance, ignorance and impudence'.

The General Assembly rejected the proposal, and the controversy quickly fizzled out, leaving many onlookers to wonder why so much energy had been spent on something so spurious when the national Church would not address the real causes of its decline. But then the full, disastrous extent of that decline was not yet fully apparent.

Meanwhile, Ian McColl, who was editor of the *Scottish Daily Express* from 1961 to 1971, and editor of the *Daily Express* in London from 1971 to 1974, was a rare Scottish newspaper executive in that he was always eager to take the Kirk and its standing in Scottish life very seriously indeed. The trouble was that his proprietor, Beaverbrook, was more interested in controversy and trouble-making than in considered reporting.

McColl served for more than 20 years as session clerk of the Sandyford Memorial Kirk in Glasgow's West End, and he personally regarded what might be called the politics of Presbyterianism as every bit as important as the politics of Westminster. But he was a canny editor, and, while he honoured the Kirk and cherished its place in Scottish life, he also understood that too many Kirk stories in his pages might eventually prove counter-productive. The bishops story was the only time his judgement on religious matters could be seriously questioned; and he was at that point undoubtedly under extreme pressure from his proprietor.

The only other time I can remember the Kirk prompting similar excitement in the Scottish media was when the religious commentator Stewart Lamont (a writer and BBC producer who had a parallel career as a parish minister, and was a man blessed with many informants and superb sources) revealed in the *Glasgow Herald* in 1983 that a new kirk minister was a convicted murderer. The story had been scrupulously checked over several days and was accurate in every respect – but many of the *Herald*'s readers simply refused to believe it. I know that, because they told me and my colleagues; I was the deputy editor at the time.

Stewart Lamont, a minister of enormous energy and zest who wrote many books on a wide variety of subjects (and in a variety of different styles), seemed to me to be typical of many of the more able parish ministers: he found the job slightly constricting, though he was diligent in carrying out his duties. He needed a broader context for his considerable creativity. This has been, I reckon, a growing problem for the Kirk: at times it has seemed all too keen to constrict rather than encourage its more able and energetic spirits.

As for the Roman Catholic Church in Scotland, it had to handle a serious scandal in 1996 when the Bishop of Argyll, Roddy Wright, eloped with his housekeeper (they had met on a pilgrimage to Lourdes). He had already, it soon transpired, fathered a child by another woman. The treatment of the story, which was manna for the tabloids, bordered on the frivolous. Meanwhile, various very serious scandals involving the abuse of children and youths by Catholic priests were, for one reason or another, not investigated in depth by the Scottish media. The darkest of them all concerned the persistent abuse of young people by Benedictines at the abbey boarding school in Fort Augustus, Inverness-shire; but there were others.

Scottish broadcasting

As television became the predominant medium in the 1960s and 1970s, religious broadcasting changed. With the notable and magnificent exception of William Barclay, there seemed a wariness about attempting anything that was explicitly evangelical or even anything that was explicitly Christian. So, a lot of religious broadcasting began to take the form of rather vapid, if articulate, discussion about ethical, moral and social issues; there was not always an obvious Christian perspective. Although I was not a church member at this time, I remember thinking that there was something slightly apologetic about much supposedly religious broadcasting, as if Scottish Christians were becoming demoralised and did not have the confidence to communicate directly.

In retrospect, I think the so-called religious broadcasters were often concerned not to cause offence; and I suspect that some of them thought that offence would be given if Christianity was propagated directly. There was a vague obligation for broadcasters to put out religious programmes, but often what actually materialised were quasi-religious documentaries on various topical controversies.

Dr Nelson Gray, a congregational minister in Glasgow, became head of religious programmes at Scottish Television (the main commercial station) in 1967 – and he excelled at organising this type of broadcasting. But the overtly Christian content was sometimes hard to find. Ironically, this was the very time when William Barclay, who is discussed later in this chapter, was emerging as a Christian communicator of genius – a man who had a glorious, natural gift for televisual exposition.

Barclay never strayed far from the Bible. His entire communication strategy was explicitly based on understanding and explaining the Bible. He had a sincere, strong belief that basic Christian communication should be utterly rooted in Scripture. But his approach, while clearly effective, was shunned by many producers and executives in the media.

Meanwhile, Arnold Kemp, then deputy editor of the *Scotsman*, was often invited to take part in televised discussions organised by Nelson Gray for STV. Arnold was not a religious man, and he did not speak publicly from a Christian perspective. He was happy to appear on the programmes, and thought they were professionally produced and of high quality; but, even so, he told me more than once that he wondered why they were not more slanted to direct Christian communication.

At this time, other religious broadcasters, with the notable exception of Barclay, and to a lesser extent the Revd Campbell Maclean of Cramond Kirk, were becoming more and more concerned with internal Church politics, and sometimes Church controversies and even scandals. There was very little, if any, direct evangelisation. Even indirect evangelisation, though Campbell Maclean was a master of this, was becoming unfashionable. All this indicated that most Christian communicators had lost confidence. Certainly, I can recall people asking pointedly, in the 1970s, why these supposedly 'religious' programmes were not much more religious.

STV's overtly Christian slot was a very brief late-night reflection called *Late Call*, the subject of much mockery. One kirk minister, after recording a week's worth of *Late Call*s, received a phone call regarding his payment. The story goes that the innocent replied: 'Oh, of course: how much do I have to pay you?' Nelson Gray had a very wide range of contacts; and some of the brief meditations on the *Late Call* slot were impressive, reflecting a pertinent Christianity. But sometimes they were banal and drab. The mockery of the slot intensified when STV's rival, the BBC, had the inspired idea of a series of *Late Call* pastiches called *Last Call*, in which the comedian Rikki Fulton played a lugubrious minister called I. M. Jolly.

The Kirk's publications

The Kirk itself was generally out of puff when it came to blowing its own trumpet. It had its own monthly magazine, *Life and Work*, founded in 1879 by the Revd Archibald Charteris, who held the chair of Biblical Criticism at Edinburgh University (and who also founded the Kirk's Women's Guild). A brilliant but very disputatious scholar, he was involved in a notable late-Victorian spat about the section on the Bible in the *Encyclopædia Britannica*.

In the 1950s and 1960s, *Life and Work* sometimes contained superb material but could also be dreary. Some of the subscribers found by far the most interesting section tucked away in the back pages. Here they could find details of all the various bequests and legacies donated to the Kirk and its agencies. In those days, a vast amount of money was handed over in this way. Many people were not at all certain what was done with it all, but they were fascinated by the magazine's monthly recording of very generous giving.

In the 1970s, the magazine was edited by a prominent Scottish intellectual, Bob Kernohan, who had been a formidable journalist with the *Glasgow Herald* and also a Conservative parliamentary candidate.

He was an elder at Cramond Kirk and was exceptionally well informed about internal Kirk matters. In the 1970s, along with the English broadcaster Vernon Sproxton, he provided a nightly radio commentary on the proceedings of each General Assembly; these programmes were notably intelligent and perceptive.

When he was the editor, *Life and Work* magazine set formidable standards and was taken seriously by many newspaper journalists as well as Kirk members, but it was sometimes criticised for its apparent suspicion of ecumenism.

After Bob Kernohan's long editorship, with falling numbers in congregations, *Life and Work* slowly declined, though even now it still contains a lot of interesting and worthy material. There has been a long succession of here today, gone tomorrow editors (including, very briefly, myself, although I only undertook the job on a short-term basis to assist the Kirk to fill a gap between permanent editorships). The journalists Muriel Armstrong and

Rosemary Goring both made very considerable contributions, the former in various roles over a very long period. Goring was one of the more distinguished of Kernohan's various successors – but she became understandably disaffected when she was ordered by the hierarchy at the Kirk's headquarters in George Street, Edinburgh, to pulp an entire edition – around 50,000 copies – that contained an anything-but-controversial piece about Prince Charles.

The twenty-first-century Kirk is unlike the Kirk of the glorious past; it dislikes offending the great and the good, if at all possible. The current *Life and Work* editor, Lynne McNeil, has lasted longer than anyone since Bob Kernohan and is doing a solid job in a very difficult context.

In terms of media relations, the Kirk has for some time been rather tentative, though, as I write, this is at last changing: there are very encouraging signs of much more proactive, rather than reactive, style. Two highly regarded journalists from the BBC, first Seonag Mackinnon and now also Rob Flett, have been recruited to develop this fresh approach, and they are already making a positive impression.

Across in Glasgow, the Catholic Church has its own impressive media office, presided over by one of the leading figures in contemporary Scottish Christianity, Peter Kearney. He is a personal friend, so I shall not embarrass him or invite charges of special pleading; but I am certain that his indefatigable media work on behalf of the Catholic Church in Scotland has been greatly appreciated by many Christians of a number of denominations. It has also annoyed some members of the Kirk, who admire his professionalism but, even so, cannot understand why the Catholic Church seems to gain so much more publicity (admittedly, not all of it benign) than the supposed national Church.

Relatively few print journalists – or their editors – have been keen to tackle the vexed issue of sectarianism in modern Scotland. A notable exception is Kevin McKenna, who has worked on various papers and is very well informed. He writes from a Catholic perspective – but, importantly, he is no stooge of the Catholic hierarchy in Scotland. Quite the opposite, in fact.

The BBC

The BBC has had a curious relationship with Scottish Christianity. It produced, as we've just noted, a superbly mischievous send-up of the late-night religious slot on commercial television. This was gently, but effectively, subversive.

Influential BBC figures such as the kirk ministers Melville Dinwiddie and Ronnie Falconer, who both had long careers as senior executives with BBC Scotland, were hardly ecumenical in their approach. Possibly because of this, they were very highly regarded in Church of Scotland circles; less so in media circles. In more recent times, the BBC has covered religious affairs with much more consistency and informed interest than the press; on the other hand, the press, while erratic, has at times shown far more flair in covering major religious stories.

Although John Reith was of course a stern Scottish Christian, he soon came to believe that the organised Christian churches, in both England and Scotland, did not respond to the considerable opportunities that, thanks in no small measure to him, the BBC's religious broadcasting had given them. His specific influence on Scottish religious broadcasting was not particularly noticeable, apart from perhaps during the years (on either side of the Second World War) when Melville Dinwiddie was its chief executive.

A genuine First World War hero, Dinwiddie had become minister of St Machar's Cathedral in Aberdeen in the 1920s; and then, at the BBC in Glasgow, he tried to implement the high-minded Reithian style in Scotland, but with only limited success. He once claimed that his great aim was to make Scotland a more Christian country; and he certainly failed in that task.

After the Second World War, Dinwiddie placed the Revd Ronnie Falconer, formerly a parish minister in Coatbridge, as the supremo of religious broadcasting. Falconer quickly excelled at broadcasting live church services, although he had to fight with Scotland's alternative religion (football) for outside broadcasting crews and equipment.

The Church of Scotland had plenty of inspirational preachers in the 1950s and 1960s, but for some reason relatively few of them were used regularly by Ronnie Falconer. I don't think that had anything to do with personal jealousy; by all accounts, Falconer was a gracious and open-minded man. And a good pulpit preacher was not necessarily an effective communicator on television. But to suggest that the pulpit style did not suit live broadcasting, and to leave it at that, is hardly good enough. Anyway, Falconer's preferred method of evangelising was to transmit live services, often from rural or suburban churches, in which the sermon tended to be short or even cut altogether. There was often an emphasis on music, which anticipated future trends in popular religious broadcasting.

The greatest Scottish preacher of them all, the Dundonian James S. Stewart, hardly ever appeared on television. Looking back, this seems utterly extraordinary. Stewart was minister at Beechgrove, Aberdeen, a fine 'preaching station', in the 1930s. Two decades later, a few members of the congregation could still recall his sermons with something akin to awe; indeed, it seemed to me, as a child, that they could recall some of them almost in their entirety. Later, Stewart was a distinguished professor at New College, Edinburgh. He was Moderator of the General Assembly in 1963.

In persona he was apparently a quiet, even reticent, man, but I am told that he caught fire in the pulpit, paradoxically preaching self-abandonment with fervour and eloquence but also careful Biblical sensitivity. (I am also informed that he was never a man to push himself forward. Possibly his fastidious nature made him regard television as a somewhat vulgar medium. But that is sheer speculation.)

Later, the religious programming at BBC Scotland was run by the Revd Ian Mackenzie, a thoughtful and gentle man whose style was always considered and reflective. Perhaps he was a little too cautious; in 2004, I debated with him at an event in The Ceilidh Place in Ullapool, and I thought he was the most reasonable man I've ever argued – or tried to argue – with. With us that evening was Mike Russell MSP, the former chief executive of the SNP (and, later, Scotland's Education Minister), who told me later at the bar that he thought everything had been much too conciliatory and careful. We'd never make politicians, he said – and I think he almost meant that as a compliment.

William Barclay

During Ronnie Falconer's time at the BBC, one genuinely great, and utterly natural, television communicator had emerged. This was the perhaps unlikely figure of Professor William Barclay of Glasgow University, a brilliant Biblical scholar possessed of a pleasant, if rather hoarse – and very Scottish – voice, a broadcasting manner that some-how managed to combine gruffness and charm, and the supreme gift of interpreting the teachings of Jesus – and in particular his parables – in a way that was lucid, intelligent and couthy all at once.

Barclay was an authentic and very clever scholar, but he was never an aloof academic. Indeed, I heard that he was occasionally patronised by some of his university colleagues who disapproved of his enormous popularity as a television broadcaster, finding this vulgar. But Barclay did not worry about such petty jealousies. I'm pretty certain that impressing his academic colleagues and peers was low in his priorities.

But most Scottish churchmen and most members of the various divinity faculties could put envy aside and appreciate Barclay for what he was: a master of direct, straightforward communication. Looking back, I'm really surprised that the Kirk and indeed organised Christianity right across Britain did not use him much more. He had his folksy side, but he always talked and wrote with supreme clarity and conviction. Here is a very brief example of Barclay at his best (and he was usually at his best):

The risen Lord was no phantom or hallucination. He was real. The Jesus who died was, in truth, the Christ who rose again. Christianity is not founded on the dreams of disordered minds, or the visions of fevered eyes, but on one who in actual historical fact faced and fought and conquered death, and rose again.

Just before the era of 'celebrities', Barclay became a genuine celebrity. People of all ages and backgrounds listened to him and enjoyed what he had to say. But he offered much more than mere enjoyment. He led many to Christ.

While he held the chair of Biblical Criticism at Glasgow University for 11 years, his avowed aim was simple and down to earth. It was to convey the results of scholarship to ordinary folk: the ordinary listener and the ordinary reader. He based most of his lecturing and teaching on the first three Gospels; he made less use of the more mystical and philosophical Gospel of John. He was convinced that the Gospels of Matthew, Mark and Luke presented a reliable account of the ministry of Jesus Christ. He was confident that they provided authentic accounts of the key events in his life and the essence of his teaching, and that they allowed those who studied them carefully to enter Christ's mind. At the heart of everything he wrote and said was one crucial constant: he was convinced that Christ was his Saviour.

As with many brilliant communicators, it is almost impossible to anatomise what made him so special. There was, first of all, his simple and strong faith. As a communicator, he was blessed with a lucid, uncomplicated style. He understood words and their power. He read very widely. His Bible studies are punctuated by many quotes from poets. As his son Ronnie noted, he had a huge love of literature and could have been a Professor of English Literature as well as a Professor of Divinity.

He greatly enjoyed the company of his own students, and of other students too. He was a very social man; he liked his whisky. I recall meeting him when he was holding court in the lounge bar of the Randolph Hotel in Oxford in the late 1960s. By coincidence, the most celebrated Oxford figure of the day, Professor Sir Isaiah Berlin (who was exactly the same age as Barclay), was also in the bar at the time, and also holding court; but Barclay attracted the larger audience.

William Barclay knew Scotland well. Born in Wick in the far north, in 1907, he was then brought up in industrial Lanarkshire. As a relatively young man, he knew the needs and demands of the parish ministry, for he was the successful minister of Trinity, Renfrew, for 15 years. He understood the realities of working-class life in some of the toughest parts of Clydeside. He was acutely aware of social problems and political issues, and he could always place them neatly in an appropriate Biblical context.

There are few people around now who have personal memories of his ministry in Renfrew, which ended in 1948, when he joined Glasgow University as a lecturer in New Testament studies. But I remember asking one of his former Renfrew parishioners, quite some time ago, what he had been like in the pulpit each Sunday. I cannot remember the precise reply, but surprisingly it was on the lines of 'nothing special'. Indeed, I was told that Barclay was more fondly remembered in Renfrew for his pastoral work. He was, in his time at Glasgow University, a genuinely ecumenical figure. He served as the Glasgow University Catholic Society's honorary president.

His *Daily Study Bible* series has been a remarkable, sustained success for Saint Andrew Press. First published in 1953, and updated and revised in a new edition in 1975, these superb, deceptively simple books were translated into many languages and reached a genuinely global audience of at least 8 million readers – probably many more. A third edition, again fully revised and updated, was supervised by Ann Crawford and launched at a majestic ceremony in Glasgow's Royal Concert Hall in 2001.

In that difficult decade for Christianity, the 1960s, Barclay was the supreme Christian communicator in Britain. As he moved around Scotland, and England too, he was frequently recognised by strangers. It was generally his very distinctive and much-loved voice, rather than his appearance, that first caught people's attention. It is fascinating to note how, two or three generations on, Barclay is much more affectionately and keenly remembered than his contemporary James Stewart, though Stewart was undoubtedly the finer preacher. But Barclay was the better communicator – and the distinction is important.

To reiterate: I have often wondered if the Kirk could not have made much more of William Barclay. This is one of the real mysteries of modern Scotland. The BBC and Saint Andrew Press both played their parts, and gave him the opportunity to reach out to very large audiences; but surely others, in the Kirk and beyond it, could have put far more effort into using this much-loved man's genius as a communicator when Christianity was in acute decline?

☒

Later, the Revd Johnston McKay was a minister who well understood how the media worked. He frequently broadcast for the BBC, and for a time he worked for the corporation in an executive role. He was always prepared to make waves; indeed, he relished religious controversies. He had a profound knowledge of the Kirk's history and was very well informed, with many contacts right across Scotland. But, as he was simultaneously pursuing the life of a parish minister for much of his career – he was at one time minister of Paisley Abbey – he could not always concentrate exclusively on journalism.

Sally Magnusson, a former colleague of mine on both the *Scotsman* and the late lamented *Sunday Standard*, became a very popular and effective religious broadcaster, but there were few others.

Richard Holloway

Scotland's most naturally accomplished religious communicator in the last years of the twentieth century, and into the new millennium, was Bishop Richard Holloway. But – and this in a way sums up the trends of recent Scottish religious history – he lost his faith, although his beautifully written autobiography, *Leaving Alexandria*, ends with what almost amounts to a tease: just a hint that he wonders if his faith has indeed completely disappeared.

Richard Holloway is a cerebral man, and he enjoys grappling with recondite ideas and notions. In person, he is delightful and charming. Brought up in a happy working-class home in Alexandria in the Vale of Leven, he was packed off as an adolescent to study for the Anglican clergy at a college in the English Midlands. He duly became a minister in the Scottish Episcopal Church, and eventually Bishop of Edinburgh. He has often talked of the ambivalence he felt as a 'Piskie'. He would insist that his church was a genuine Scottish denomination (which of course it was) and that it had played an honourable and patriotic part in Scotland's history (which was a more debatable assertion). He gently resented the common notions that his denomination was all too often regarded as the toffs' church or, worse, the 'English' Church of Scotland.

In the years 2009 and 2010, I took part in several public debates with Richard on the legacy of the Scottish Reformation. At this time, I became aware, at first hand, of what many Scots already knew: here was a man with the confidence to discuss complex historical and theological issues graciously in front of sceptical, secular folk. He had an equally impressive ability to achieve, very swiftly, a genuine rapport with his audience, whatever its size and nature. Altogether, he was, and is, a man of exceptional gifts, and one who should have been precious for Scottish Christianity. But his doubts must of course be respected.

I have found some of Richard Holloway's books quite difficult. This is certainly not the case with *Looking in the Distance*, published in 2004, which is among other things a very elegant rejection of God. As I was reading it, the no doubt banal thought occurred: if God exists (and I believe he does), how can he allow someone to write such a gracious and beguiling rejection of his existence?

Holloway starts this short and brilliant book with the assertion that, for many people today, religion is no longer a possible way of life. I'm sure this is true in Western Europe, though I'm not certain that it applies elsewhere. Anyway, starting from this premise, he moves on until he comes to the last great crisis in most lives: death. But his view is that it is Christianity that has turned death into a crisis 'with its diseased and ugly notion of Hell'. He claims that we need not worry about Hell, because there is no afterlife. Just – nothing. 'A blessed oblivion', in his phrase.

Many Christians would regard this as insidious, because it is providing exactly the wrong kind of assurance. I'm not so sure. Indeed, I think Richard is quite right in the sense that if you are certain there is no hereafter, then that makes everything a lot easier – whereas if you believe in some kind of life after death, far from always making things easier, it can render them more difficult. You must, unless your faith is incredibly strong, be subject on occasion to some doubts and fears.

But, in the overall context of Scottish Christianity, Richard Holloway's long and distinguished career eventually becomes a sad loss, though all too typical of our times. Yet again, we have a good and potentially prophetic life marked by the loss of Christianity. This is a constant theme of these pages: exceptional twentieth-century Scots who were Christians in their childhood, youth and early adulthood but who somehow lost their religion along the way.

Papal visits and the All-Scotland crusade

In recent years, there have been two enormously successful papal visits to Scotland. Both passed off peacefully, with most observers and commentators agreeing that there had been very little obvious dissent or unpleasantness. The first visit, by the most charismatic Pope of modern times, the Pole John Paul II, in the early summer of 1982, was however surrounded by controversy that had been totally unseen three or four months earlier. This was because of the Falklands war, which suddenly flared up in April. The efforts of Archbishop Tom Winning, more than any other individual, ensured that the visit went ahead, despite undoubted diplomatic and political strains.

The highlight of the visit was a great mass in Bellahouston Park, Glasgow, attended by around 250,000 people. This was the biggest gathering ever recorded in Glasgow, Scotland's largest city. Other highlights were a youth rally in Murrayfield Stadium, Edinburgh, and the moment when the Pope met the Kirk's Moderator right under the statue of John Knox at New College, Edinburgh.

One of the notable things that attended this papal visit was that it inspired an enormous amount of good writing. Indeed, as a journalist who has worked on various papers and at various levels in Scotland for the past 44 years, I can think of no other single event or episode that has inspired so much fine reporting and commentary. Here are just two brief examples, both from the *Glasgow Herald*. (I was actually working on another paper – the *Sunday Standard* – at the time; this is not a case of biased selection.)

First, by Colm Brogan:

The servant of the servants of God was himself well served in Glasgow. Bellahouston was not a park. It was one vast open-air cathedral, made not of stone but of people. The numbers did not matter, immense though they were. It was the effects of this enormous congregation slowly building up from early morning, tangibly taking on a character of its own, that transformed a simple piece of open ground into something entirely sacred – and at the same time entirely human . . . How the 7,000 stewards, some of them veterans of Lourdes and showing the experience, manipulated that vast congregation into a human cathedral, God really does alone know . . . During Mass, concelebrated with almost 100 priests, where communion was distributed to the crowd by 1,000 ministers of the Eucharist, the crowd heard the Pope amend Glasgow's motto slightly: Lord, let *Scotland* flourish, through the preaching of the word and the praising of thy name.

So the city could afford to be generous and give of its own to the whole of Scotland.

And second, by Anne Simpson:

There is little doubt about the durability of the greetings exchanged between the Moderator (of the General Assembly of the Church of Scotland) and the Pope. They will survive through time as a dignified and moving testament to two holy men's mutual goodwill . . . In Edinburgh, and in the shadow of John Knox, such welcome, pleasure and gratitude, expressed without triumphal trapping, was wholly appropriate, quietly momentous – and illustrated how poorer Christianity would have been if Pope John Paul had cancelled his visit.

Anne Simpson also wrote:

In the long run, what the Pope will be seen to have given Scotland specifically will be a *special identity*. He chose his words about the nation brilliantly, acknowledging the sense of isolation Scotland has often felt situated on the remote edge of Europe. Thus he recognised its loneliness and the heroism of its early Christians. And if there has been a sense of inferiority, John Paul may have relieved that in some large measure by restoring pride to Scottish Catholics, by telling them he loved them and putting Scotland in blissful mood on the world's television screens.

Both these writers were, as it happens, Catholics; but there was plenty of other sympathetic and well-turned writing by Protestants and, possibly more surprisingly, by avowed atheists. As for the hope expressed by Anne Simpson – a sentiment echoed by other commentators at the time – that the symbolism of the Pope meeting the Moderator more or less under the great statue of Knox in the New College quadrangle would be durable, would survive through time – well, I do wonder. Also, Anne Simpson made the large claims that the Pope had given Scotland a special identity, and that Christianity (note: not Catholicism) would have been poorer had the Pope not come. She was right, of course – but that these words were written in a Scottish national newspaper indicated that Scotland had travelled quite a distance in religious terms. Having written that, it must sadly be acknowledged that sectarianism and bigotry still fester in Scotland, more than 30 years on.

The visit did in a way enfranchise Scottish Catholics, making them feel that at last they had a proper place in the nation's life. One specific and positive after-effect of the visit was that it helped to give Tom Winning the confidence to push for Catholics to have a more prominent role, and more influence, in Scottish public life.

On the other hand, this was a one-off. Some grumpy Protestants I know emphasised that: fair enough, a genuine world figure had inspired a very special moment in the nation's teeming religious history, but the very point was that he could do so because he was a global, not a local, figure. Being a global figure, he was here today, gone tomorrow. That sums up some of the genteel Presbyterian dissent, if that is the right phrase, that I heard at the time.

Meanwhile, there were many who simply could not understand what all the fuss was about. I know two intelligent, professional

Scottish women who were on a brief break in the far north-west of
Scotland at the time of the visit. This trip north was arranged coin-
cidentally; it was not an effort to escape from the Pope-fest, as some
called it. Neither of them is a believer, but I stress that neither of
them harboured any anti-Catholic sentiment. Both, on their return
to the central belt, were quite unable to understand the euphoria the
visit stimulated – one of them described it as baffling and bizarre.
She said she was very surprised, in particular, that so many young
Scots appeared to regard Pope John Paul as some kind of authentic
superstar. (This is admittedly anecdotal – but I checked, 21 years
on, with the lady in question, and she confirmed that this was very
much what she thought at the time, and her view had not changed.)

There was also the Falklands factor. The problematic on/off
build-up to the visit meant that it was all the more eagerly anticipated. Before the Pope actually arrived, there was a fervent longing
in many Scottish hearts that, please God, he would indeed come. A
further special factor was the charismatic nature of this particular
Pope. That has been much discussed, and need not be rehearsed
here.

What is indisputable is that when his successor Pope Benedict
XVI visited Scotland later, the whole occasion was rather more
subdued, more matter-of-fact. Benedict also celebrated mass at
Bellahouston Park, but this time there were only about 65,000 people present – a drop of 185,000. This suggested that there might
have been no lasting benefit from the earlier papal visit. I heard one
cynic suggesting that, at this rate, the next papal visit would have
an attendance of minus 120,000.

Pope Benedict XVI also met the Queen, in a carefully stage-managed
event full of protocol but lacking spontaneity, at Holyroodhouse in
Edinburgh. (The then Moderator of the General Assembly was not
in the line-up of dignitaries who were presented to the Pope – and of
course this was manna for conspiracy-seekers. It transpired that he
had taken a 'wrong turning', and a presentation was hastily fixed up
later on; there was no question of a deliberate snub.)

As the Queen had invited the Pope to Scotland, it was officially
a state visit, and he was in Scotland not just as the head of the
Catholic Church but as a head of state: the tiny state of Vatican

City. This technicality was emphasised by some Protestants in a neatly nuanced put-down. One friend of mine seemed very keen to stress that a head of state had met the Queen rather than the head of a church.

I sensed that altogether it was a less joyous and altogether much less remarkable visit than that of Pope John Paul II some 28 years earlier. The German Pope, unlike his Polish predecessor, was not a natural crowd-pleaser. But he was well and warmly received, and overall the visit was a success. For me, the only slightly peculiar note was when Benedict praised Britain's fight against Hitler's atheism. Maybe he felt that, as a German, he had to say something about the Second World War. But surely Britain was fighting to defend itself, and the fact that Hitler was an atheist was neither here nor there. If Benedict was trying to present the Second World War as some kind of holy war, I think hardly anybody in Britain would endorse that interpretation.

⊠

Overall, the two visits undoubtedly made an impact – the first spectacularly so. The visit of Pope John Paul II was the most significant and successful large public event that Scotland has hosted for many generations. The key, residual, ecumenical memory is that Christianity in Scotland had been seen *en fête*. Whether the spiritual life of the nation had received any lasting boost is another matter.

For many Scottish Protestants, the visits were dramatic reminders that Roman Catholicism is a worldwide phenomenon. The Pope is a great global figure. Their own Presbyterian version of Christianity could never ever put on a show like this. (Perhaps, some might add, they would not want it to. But I think that would be grudging.) And yet Scottish Protestantism had managed, in the 1950s, to produce a great Christian show, or series of shows, that engendered something akin to the enthusiasm and excitement that attended the first papal visit.

The US Baptist Dr Billy Graham was, in the 15 years or so after the Second World War, a powerful and charismatic, if somewhat simplistic, evangelist. He was extraordinarily popular, and in private he was a man of considerable grace and charm. When in front of a mass audience – and he often was – he could apparently take on a slightly different quality: for some, he became an evangelist who was all too easily intoxicated by his own power to move people and redirect lives. His very powerful approach offended fastidious Christians in Scotland and elsewhere.

Billy Graham visited Scotland in 1955 at the invitation of the Revd Tom Allan, a kirk minister who was himself no mean evangelist, although on a much smaller scale than the cosmopolitan Baptist showman. There is an interesting back story here.

Allan was an Ayrshire man, but he made his name in Glasgow, where he became a very popular figure. He was parish minister of North Kelvinside and was, for the Kirk, an unusually effective communicator and broadcaster. He had rather less impact in the rest of Scotland. Anyway, the Kirk, abetted by the BBC in Glasgow, decided to use his talents to embark on a new national mission, called Tell Scotland. Other churches were invited to take part, although the Roman Catholic Church stayed aloof.

As for Billy Graham, in 1955 he sparked something akin to mass hysteria. Around a million people attended his various rallies, held in venues such as the Kelvin Hall in Glasgow. Of this very impressive accumulated audience, around 25,000 'came forward' to make a serious long-term commitment to change their lives and serve Jesus. Of these thousands, several went on to become Church of Scotland ministers. (As Graham was reaching out to non-Christians, or to lapsed or inactive Christians, there was no reason why Catholics should not have attended his rallies. But I have not heard of any Catholics who were in any way influenced by him.)

Even if Graham's somewhat simplistic and crude evangelism prompted much distaste, there can be no denying that it produced results. The residue of his great 'All Scotland Crusade', to give it the preferred, official title, was on the whole benign, if not long-lasting. Indeed, the late 1950s was the last period in the modern era when Scottish Christianity was solid and confident – if at times distinctly complacent and rather non-ecumenical in spirit.

There was one very unfortunate side effect of Graham's spectacular evangelisation. It prompted a falling-out between the Church of

Scotland's two most charismatic figures of the day – Tom Allan and George MacLeod. Tom Allan's own evangelical movement, Tell Scotland, had been a sustained attempt to reach out to Scotland's many thousands of 'unchurched' souls. Allan proved that there was real potential for energetic popular evangelism in Scotland, so in a way he paved the way for Graham's rallies in 1955, although unfortunately Allan allowed his own movement to be subsumed into the American's more theatrical, and more transitory, campaign.

George MacLeod enjoyed good relations with Billy Graham at a personal level, but he disapproved of the Baptist's over-the-top style. MacLeod himself could of course get carried away with his own prophetic rhetoric, but he was less populist and more subtle than some have since imagined. He could rouse large crowds of ordinary people, as he did in Govan in the 1940s, but there was also a fastidious side to this very complex man. His Christianity was mystical and prophetic, but he also wanted it to be directly engaged in specific social and political issues, though never at the cost of spiritual integrity.

Tom Allan, while every bit as left-wing as MacLeod, did not think that social and political involvement mattered quite so much, although in the last years of his ministry he was exemplary in his practical outreach. As for Billy Graham, his approach was, in retrospect, rather too crude and emotional. Church attendances in the Glasgow area increased after his rallies but soon declined again.

You sense that Tom Allan was trapped, and neutralised, somewhere in the middle. His endorsement and encouragement of Graham displeased MacLeod. And more's the pity; he was a man who had much to offer Scotland. He understood the need for effective popular communication, but somehow his own plans were usurped. Tell Scotland was totally overshadowed by Billy Graham's spectacular mass evangelisation.

Allan went on to serve for a decade as the minister of St George's Tron in the centre of Glasgow. Here he practised social outreach with considerable success, and his ministry made an impact on both the city's business community and its outcasts. He was awarded the St Mungo Prize in 1965, the year he died.

Aberdeen

Growing up in Aberdeen in the 1950s and 1960s, I soon realised that I wanted to be a journalist. From an early age, I was an avid reader of newspapers. From today's perspective, the Scottish press in the late 1950s and through the 1960s was remarkably full of reports and commentary on religious matters.

In the north-east of Scotland there was still a very strong tradition of local literary and historical journalism, which flourished in particular in the Aberdeen morning paper, the *Press and Journal*. On the front page of its Saturday supplement, the *Press and Journal* always carried two fine articles by excellent local journalists, Dr Cuthbert Graham and John R. Allan. Graham wrote mainly about buildings and hamlets and villages in the vast countryside around Aberdeen; he often enthused about relatively obscure country churches.

Allan wrote about anything and everything. He was a notably contrary writer, sentimental yet hard-headed, and always full of subtle mischief. He farmed at Methlick, about 18 miles north-west of Aberdeen, but I think he wrote with even more zest about the fishing folk on the coast than about the farming communities. One of his themes was that these fishing communities were zealously and sometimes comically religious. He observed with detached fascination all the obscure Christian sects that flourished along the long coast of Aberdeenshire. He noted that the fishermen adored fiery political speeches, especially if they contained Biblical references. That was 'as good as an orgy to them'. He also turned his mordant eye on the regular, short-lived evangelical revivals in the many fishing communities.

An even more high-profile author-farmer was Dr Sandy Keith, a man of very many parts, and a great admirer of north-east clerics. His farm was near Balmedie, a few miles north of Aberdeen. He was a celebrated breeder of Aberdeen Angus cattle, and founder-secretary of the Aberdeen Angus Society. Once, my brother and I were fooling around with a football as we walked along one of the paths that led to the famous dunes at Balmedie beach. The ball bounced into a field where a very large Aberdeen Angus bull stared malevolently at us. We were wondering what to do when who should appear but the farmer, Dr Keith. With a kind of showy bravado, he walked almost under the bull's nose and kicked the ball back to us.

He seemed ubiquitous in Aberdeen itself. He was always writing articles, giving talks, taking up campaigns. He collected local songs and ballads. He was a fine if very opinionated historian, a biographer and a broadcaster. One of his most persistent themes was that kirk ministers in north-east Scotland had made a colossal contribution to local life in areas well beyond the ecclesiastical. Indeed, in his view, their actual ministry was often far less significant than their other activities. He insisted that they had excelled in commercial, cultural and even industrial work.

One of his particular heroes was the eighteenth-century cleric Dr John Chalmers, who combined successful farming at Kinellar with a distinguished career as an academic at Aberdeen University. Another was the Revd George Keith of Montgeggie, who organised the first major agricultural survey of Aberdeenshire. At the back of his manse, this splendid cleric kept a barrel of ale; no minister, observed Sandy Keith, was ever more popular. Yet another minister hero was the Revd Alex Forsyth of Belhelvie, who invented the percussion lock which was the key development in the evolution of the modern military rifle.

The hero of heroes was James Robertson, the minister of Ellon, a small town north of Aberdeen. Robertson was a scientist and a progressive farmer as well as a man of the cloth. And an educationist too – he was for a time headmaster of the famous Aberdeen school Robert Gordon's College. For Sandy Keith, his greatest claim to fame was that he was a pioneer of chemical fertilisers.

Such men, Sandy Keith well understood, would not necessarily insist on strict Sunday observance. They knew that successful farming often entailed hard labour on the Sabbath day. As for Robertson, he was perhaps the most distinguished of the ministers who remained in the old Kirk at the time of the Disruption. His response to the new Free Church and its enthusiastic building of new churches, manses and halls was to set up a committee that presided over the building of nearly

100 new churches for the old Church. It was almost as if a grotesque rivalry in church-building had broken out.

My view is that this extravagant and unnecessary church-building, of which Robertson was a leading exponent, was a colossal waste of money and energy when the Church had much better things to be getting on with – but there can be no denying Robertson's extraordinary energy, or indeed Sandy Keith's huge enthusiasm for him and his like. I do not know what Sandy Keith thought of the clergy in Aberdeen in his own time, but I'm pretty certain he regarded most of them as lesser, greyer men.

✕

My mother and father were married in Glasgow at the end of 1938. My father was in the army from 1940 until early 1946, when he was demobbed at a camp in Norfolk. He had served in North Africa, Italy, France and Belgium. For five years, he did not see his new wife. Like many couples who had their lives appallingly disrupted by Hitler, they were, I think, uncertain of themselves in the supposed brave new world of the late 1940s and early 1950s. The Church was a source of strength for them – social as well as spiritual.

I was born in 1947. My parents were then living just south of Glasgow's city boundary. They were members of Netherlee Kirk, where I was christened. Looking back, I sense that, through my childhood, the Church of Scotland was very important indeed to my parents, not so much in a directly religious sense but because it provided a social solidity, a binding sense of assurance after the very difficult war years.

In the 1950s, the Church of Scotland was able to provide an antidote to all the disruption and danger of the war (in which well over half a million Scots served in the armed forces). When my father got a new job and we moved to Aberdeen (when I was 5), one of their most urgent priorities was to find a church, to join a new congregation. I recall this very clearly. It was, more than anything else, how they chose to become part of their new community, how they achieved a sense of settlement and context.

The two churches that were nearest to our new home both loomed over the gracious junction of Queen's Cross, where no fewer than five West End avenues meet. Here, there were, and still are, two fine church buildings, strong physical testament to the competitive church-building that followed the Disruption. Rubislaw Church, built for the old Church in the 1870s, was fairly modest in size, even with its fine Gothic tower, which was added later. On the other side of Queen's Cross is the church that bears its name, built as a spectacular statement by the Free Church in 1880–1, and the masterpiece of a brilliant architect, J. B. Pirie. (This particular church was to receive considerable media attention much later when its minister was the openly gay Revd Scott Rennie.) Also situated at Queen's Cross – for some reason never designated Holy Cross – was a large Roman Catholic convent with an attached school.

My parents rejected the two churches at Queen's Cross and chose the congregation of Beechgrove Church, about half a mile farther away to the north-east. The main reason they chose Beechgrove was the minister, the Revd Stuart McWilliam. They liked the fact that he came from the industrial west of Scotland; it also helped that he was a superb preacher. They also realised that it was a very active congregation: during the week, the church hosted many social events.

The church was attended by between 600 and 700 every Sunday morning; there was a smaller, though still healthy, attendance at the evening service. The organist and choirmaster, an Englishman called Donald Hawksworth, was a distinguished musician, and the church music was always of an exceptional standard.

It is important to note that Beechgrove was not unusual; it was typical of very many churches in Scotland in the 1950s. If it was in any way exceptional, it was because it was regarded as a 'preaching station'. Stuart McWilliam was an exceptional preacher, and some distinguished guest preachers came, among them George MacLeod and Murdo Ewen Macdonald.

I describe the later decline of Beechgrove elsewhere. What I'm trying to suggest here is that this particular kirk was – and no doubt many others in Scotland in the 1950s were – very much a focus of social as well as spiritual activity. It provided warm assurance and a promise of protection against sudden change and upheaval.

The 'nearly men'

Thomas Chalmers, John White and John Reith

Thomas Chalmers

Thomas Chalmers was the great 'nearly man' of nineteenth-century Scotland. If Scotland was to be taken seriously as a Christian country, it needed to find somebody with vision, tenacity and evangelical energy, with political skill and, above all, determined and focused Christian compassion to lead the Church's response to the horrors – the word is used advisedly – of mass industrialisation.

It is all very well to note smugly that the Battle of Culloden in 1746 was the last major military confrontation on Scottish (and British) soil, and that Scotland was never again to be invaded by rebel forces. But so what, if so much damage was to be visited on the country from within? The persistent misery and suffering that were endured by so many men, women and – worst of all – children in Victorian Scotland is a serious and continuing stain on Scottish collective consciousness, a perpetual challenge to our ideal of ourselves as a decent and civilised people. The lack of an organised Christian response for generations was particularly deplorable, given the enormous effort and energy that Scotland's Christians put into other comparatively frivolous activities such as competitive church-building.

Chalmers, a man of fine intellect and real evangelical power, was the man who could and should have taken the lead. That he did not is both a personal and a national tragedy. He was without doubt a good and decent man, blessed with charisma and considerable leadership potential. He did genuinely care about the poor; he was ecumenical and liberal in his dealings with Catholics; and, far from being a firebrand, he preached tolerance and reconciliation. So, what went wrong?

I suspect the key is to be found in his years as minister of St John's parish in central Glasgow. Here, there were many folk in extreme poverty, living – just about – in the most wretched of conditions. Chalmers was well aware of this, and he was tireless in visiting the poor, often with volunteers from his church. He thought this was the right approach; he was resolutely opposed to any organised system of state welfare. At a time when various experts, particularly in the medical profession, were beginning to agitate for – at the very least – radical reform of the Poor Law, and preferably organised state support for the poor, including the unemployed, on an ambitious scale, Chalmers remained adamant in his opposition to such progressive thought, fearing the consequences of overzealous intervention by the state. There is also a slight sense that Chalmers was propelled slightly against his will as he moved to lead the evangelical wing in the Church of Scotland.

He was a Fifer, born (in 1780) and brought up and educated in the East Neuk, before he went to St Andrews University at the tender age of 11. After graduating, he served for a dozen years as minister of Kilmany, and then moved to Glasgow Tron. In 1823, he returned to St Andrews as Professor of Moral Philosophy, and five years later he was appointed Professor of Divinity at Edinburgh. This smooth progression marked him as very much the coming man in the Kirk, although for some he was beginning to evince what the Kirk establishment saw as dangerous evangelical tendencies.

He was, of course, the man who eventually led the evangelicals out of the Kirk at the time of the Disruption. In that sense, he became a leader, and a brave one; but already there had been doubts about his focus. At Kilmany, he spent a lot of time dabbling in intellectual pursuits – mainly mathematics and economics – when he should have been devoting more attention to pastoral matters.

Thomas Chalmers was a kind and charitable man, yet he never really understood how desperate, and how tenaciously exploited, the new urban poor were. When Andrew Marshall, a genuinely radical and prophetic minister, if deeply flawed, started to advocate nothing less than the break-up of the organised Church, Chalmers refused to endorse his views or even to take them seriously.

Marshall was a maverick who believed, in the face of incipient social breakdown, that the Kirk should in effect start all over again.

This was a melodramatic yet also realistic response to the inertia of the early nineteenth-century Scottish Church, and it was one that Chalmers wholly rejected. How ironic it was that, just a few years later, he was to be responsible for the most serious split in the entire fissile history of the Church of Scotland.

To be completely fair to Chalmers, it is true that, when he was in Glasgow, he quite understandably reacted against the smug bureaucracy with which the city fathers, the merchant class and the many ministers of the city meddled with the growing problem of welfare. He was, for example, very angry after he endured a long discussion on whether pork broth or oxhead soup should be served in city hospitals. But anger was not enough. He needed to come up with some plan of action that was both visionary and viable.

Convinced that kirk elders and deacons could attend adequately to their social responsibilities via the parish system, he did not see the need for the Kirk and the agencies of the state – such as they were – to co-operate more closely.

After his early and rather idle ministry in Fife, his career had progressed serenely. Eventually, he was off to the capital, to the chair of Divinity at Edinburgh University. From then on, his main concern was church extension, a necessary cause; and he saw to it that the Church of Scotland built many new churches, even if they were not always built where they were most needed. But he could not sort out the perennial problem of patronage. He passionately believed in the Scottish Reformation principle of the parishioners, not some aloof and grandiose patron, appointing the parish minister. It was, of course, this very long-running and debilitating row that eventually led to the great Disruption of 1843, which was a calamity for the national Church.

Chalmers had, as we saw, been genuinely concerned about the condition of the poor; but, partly because of his growing concern about patronage, he was suspicious of any suggestions that the Kirk should work closely with other agencies to ameliorate distress and squalor. In fact, he had become obsessed with the need to protect the established Kirk, although expanding its role.

After the great breach in 1843, it finally became clear that it was the British state (flawed as it was), not the Scottish Kirk, that would have to undertake the main work of ameliorating the hellish conditions in which the new, rapidly growing proletariat worked and lived. Many no doubt think that was as it should have been; but it took generations for the state to get its act properly together. At this very time, indeed, the great administration of Chalmers's friend Robert Peel – a supposedly right-wing prime minister, let it always be remembered – was at last embarking on much-needed legislation to improve the conditions in the mines and factories.

Chalmers had undoubtedly nurtured a vision of practical Christian communities, doing their best amid the ever-growing tide of disease, extreme poverty, malnutrition and grievous exploitation. But this was nothing like enough; and the Disruption of 1843, which he helped to lead, finally meant that the Church of Scotland simply could not cope with the responsibilities of parochial poor relief, as it had tried to do since the Reformation.

Chalmers was a fine, popular preacher, and was much admired by his contemporaries. After the Disruption, he was, for the four years until his death in 1847, the charismatic and impressive leader of the new Free Church. He, more than anyone else, gave it the foundations that allowed it to flourish, as it did for several generations: he was a good organiser, and he presided, as he had already done for the old Church, over an extraordinary building programme – of churches, schools and manses. But, in a sense, all this energy, effort and expense was wasted; they could have been much better spent in other directions.

John White

If Chalmers was the charismatic and very distinguished 'nearly man' of Scottish Protestantism in the early nineteenth century, his equivalent in the early twentieth century was the Revd John White. In an earlier book for Saint Andrew Press (*Outside Verdict*, 2002), I devoted much of a chapter to a discussion of White, and the chapter was entitled 'The Kirk's Bad Man'. I know that this offended some people; and it was perhaps a misjudgement.

In many – probably most – ways, White was a distinguished man, a great Christian leader. He presided over the great reunion in 1929, when the Church of Scotland and the majority of the Free Church, after 86 years of essentially unnecessary competition and feuding, became one Church again. This was the apogee of his career. But, before and after that great moment, he had been running a racist – his own word – campaign against Irish immigrants to Scotland. This was bad in itself, but it was worse because it tainted the reunited Church just when it was starting; and it encouraged lesser men than White to engage in bigoted and sectarian hatred, which sometimes spilled into violence. Indeed, the decade from 1925 to 1935 was a dark one for Scotland because these years were marked by especially intensive sectarianism. I believe that White was disingenuous when he claimed to be concerned with race, not religion. He was without doubt an anti-Catholic zealot.

In 1930, when he had just presided over the official reunification of the Kirk and was still Moderator of the General Assembly, he announced that 'Rome now menaces Scotland as at no time since the Reformation'. The timing was utterly extraordinary, if for no other reason than that the Presbyterian Church was suddenly far stronger, thanks to his efforts as much as anyone's, than it had been for generations. But White, possibly fired up by the supposed power of the new reunited Kirk, devoted his considerable oratory to the cause of deporting Irish Catholics.

When I was researching *Outside Verdict*, I asked Professor Tom Devine, the distinguished Scottish historian, why a man of such obvious gifts and brainpower should have been mired in such a wretched, cowardly action. Tom told me that White was greatly concerned about the growing assimilation of Catholics into all parts of Scottish society. In essence, White, a very brave man, was afraid.

Tom Devine explained that White, a staunch Tory, was also worried about the rise of the Labour Party – and of course Irish immigrants tended to support that party. White hated socialism, and he had led the campaign to reunite Scotland's two main Protestant churches at a period of very bitter, sometimes violent, labour agitation in west industrial Scotland.

White was born in 1847, the son of a Kilwinning miller. He had a brilliant career at Glasgow University, where he studied theology and philosophy. He was much influenced by the Caird brothers, sons of a Greenock foundry-owner and both brilliant theologians and philosophers. Edward Caird was Professor of Moral Philosophy at Glasgow and later master of Balliol College, Oxford. His older brother John had been appointed Professor of Theology at Glasgow after serving as minister of Park Church in the city's West End.

John White had a brilliant, rigorous mind and could have become a fine academic theologian. But he preferred the ministry to academe, and when he was 26 he was called to the parish of Shettleston in east Glasgow. He moved on to South Leith, and then returned to Glasgow as minister of the prestigious Barony Church near Glasgow Cathedral, and, for some, a greater 'preaching station'. He served there for 23 years until he retired aged 67. There was, however, a significant break from the parish ministry during the First World War, when he served, with considerable distinction, as a chaplain on the Western Front.

He was virulently opposed to pacifism. He could deploy his right-wing arguments with both force and passion but also with intellectual finesse. He was an exceptionally powerful speaker and a rigorous – some said relentless – debater. It is not surprising that, by the mid-1920s, he had become the dominant force in the Church of Scotland.

In the 1930s, he saw the main tasks of the Kirk – even more important than resisting Irish immigration to Scotland – as being church extensions. He understood that too many churches were in the wrong places. Ironically, the Disruption in 1843 had led to a frenzy of competitive church-building. Now that those two churches were reunited, White once again wanted a programme of church-building; but this time the process was to be focused on the new housing schemes. He was not wholly successful, but under his leadership around 35 new churches were built.

From today's perspective, White's strong Toryism might seem strange; but, in the 1930s, many, possibly even most, working-class Presbyterians in Scotland tended to vote Tory. It was not his Toryism that made him errant but his suspicion and downright fear of the Irish who were being assimilated, despite his efforts, into Scottish society.

By twenty-first-century standards and values, White seems something of a maverick. He had many sterling qualities: he was physically brave, he was a brilliant orator and, in his own way, he was as Presbyterian as George MacLeod, a very different kind of leader, who respected him and wanted him to be one of the Iona Community. But something perverted the goodness that was undoubtedly in him; and so, like Chalmers in the previous century, he never managed to be the outstanding churchman he should and could have been.

White's legacy was twofold: the reunited Church of Scotland, and also a potent sociological, religious and political association that linked Protestantism, Toryism and Scottish patriotism within a Unionist context. The political manifestations of this were perhaps more obvious than the religious ones. In the 1930s, 1940s and 1950s, Scotland was very much a Tory nation. There was little overt Scottish nationalism; the Liberal Party was in decline; and the Labour Party – while significant – was still a long way from the dominance it slowly acquired through the 1960s, 1970s and 1980s. I would not claim that John White was the architect of this informal association; but he undoubtedly gave it both a powerful voice and a fusion of religious confidence and political respectability.

When I was working on the *Scotsman* in the 1970s, I became friendly with the Scottish psephologist David Denver, who was then working at Lancaster University. He contributed political analyses and commentaries to the *Scotsman*, and I always found conversing with him fascinating – particularly when he told me that the Conservatives' residual strength in Scotland had been largely predicated on the support of the Protestant working class. This surprised me, because I thought that the Tory Party in Scotland was essentially bourgeois. But not only did David insist that much of its strength within Scotland was with the workers, he also correctly predicted that if the Church of Scotland declined, and lost *its* working-class support, it would be bad news for Scottish Conservatism. Of course, he did not foresee the rise of Thatcherism and its toxic effect on the Conservatives in Scotland –

hardly anybody did in the early and mid-1970s – but, in every other respect, his predictions were right.

John Reith

John Reith was the creator of the BBC, but not the BBC as we know it today. He was a Scottish Calvinist of the old school, tormented in his excessive internal religiosity (despite the fact that he was not a naturally pious man); and he was really more of a nineteenth-century – or even a seventeenth-century – figure than a twentieth-century one. (He was born in 1889, and could trace a Covenanting lineage.)

If Reith could assess the BBC as it is today, I suspect that he would be immensely proud of its role as the pre-eminent newsgathering organisation in the entire world, and deeply disgusted with its parallel role as a purveyor of what used to be called 'light entertainment', much of which I'm sure he would regard as sleazy and disgusting. (He would have been even more appalled by the series of sex-abuse scandals involving BBC personalities on BBC premises.)

He was head of the BBC for its first 16 years, a period when he was feared by many, respected by many – and heartily loathed by more than a few. He was not really a journalist; but, insofar as he was, he was important in his insistence that broadcasting should be embedded as a public service – and, even more significantly, in his willingness to take on the powerful, the great and the good of his day if he felt it was necessary to preserve the BBC's integrity. His clashes with Winston Churchill were particularly virulent, as when, during the General Strike of 1926, he steadfastly refused to allow the BBC to be used against the strikers.

⚒

Reith's religion was deeply personal; he was brought up to attend church twice every Sunday, but in later life he was not a regular attender, sincerely believing that his spiritual state was actually worsened by church attendance. At the same time, he thought Sundays should be very special days, 'quiet islands on the tossing seas of life'. Again, he would have been appalled by some of the programmes the BBC broadcasts on Sundays today.

He was born in Stonehaven, the last of seven children of a minister of the Free Church, George Reith, and brought up in Glasgow. When he left Glasgow Royal Technical College, he was apprenticed at the works of the North British Locomotive Company. After distinguished service in the First World War, he returned to Scotland and worked as an engineering manager in Coatbridge. Increasingly frustrated, he sought a political career, which he thought might suit him better; he had a very high opinion of his own abilities, though this was tempered by bouts of Calvinist self-loathing.

He sounded out representatives of the Liberal and Labour Parties, but instead he worked for Sir William Bull, a Tory MP. This suggests a promiscuous approach to politics; and Reith was never politically partisan. Perhaps that was why he was to be such an effective pioneer of public broadcasting. In 1922, he saw an advertisement for the post of general manager of the new British Broadcasting Company (soon to be Corporation, rather than Company). He applied, and the rest is history.

A few years later, he was told by a senior Anglican cleric that he had more influence than any other man alive. Yet, given his power and his Sabbatarian instincts, he was modest in his Sunday scheduling. The early Sunday format consisted of a 75-minute service, followed by a period of silence, followed by some talks and music. Then there was a second service in the evening. Despite this restraint, Reith could sometimes play the Presbyterian bully. Once, interviewing an applicant for a post at the BBC, Reith demanded: 'Do you accept the fundamental teachings of Jesus Christ?'

Always a restless man, he became bored with his own creation. Deciding he needed a fresh challenge, in 1938 he left the BBC to become chairman of Imperial Airways. The rest of his life was a rancid anticlimax. He held several relatively important posts that did not fulfil him; he felt his life was wasted. He became embittered, though he was pleased when the prime minister of the day, Harold Wilson, asked him to serve as Lord High Commissioner of the General Assembly of the Church of Scotland in 1967 (when the Queen Mother had to call off) and in 1968. He appreciated the ceremonial that went with the somewhat meaningless office, but – in typically graceless style – he let it be known that he wanted few ancillary engagements, as these would be 'silly and boring'.

He died, disgruntled and peevish, in 1971 – a tormented, trapped Calvinist to the last. He had always felt himself essentially fore-doomed. He was not instinctively devout, yet in his darker moods he was deeply afraid of an avenging God. The downside of Calvinism can be seriously overplayed in analyses of Scottish people in the twentieth century; but, in John Reith, the stock notion was lived out to particularly unhappy effect.

Army chaplains

Being a minister is a most stressful job. If I were asked to name the branch of the Christian ministry in Scotland that is subject to most stress and strain, I'd unhesitatingly cite those who serve as chaplains to our armed forces. The Church of Scotland has a committee tasked with recruiting chaplains for both the regular and the auxiliary forces. The Service view is that 'chaplains take the Church where it's needed most'. Chaplains are not concerned with rank or religious background; they provide spiritual and pastoral support in war zones as well as in camps and barracks. They also support the families of serving personnel.

In November 2009, I was asked to address a conference of British Army chaplains at the UK Defence Academy, Amport House, near Andover. The chaplains proved to be pleasant and open-minded people, though some of them were clearly somewhat stressed. I think my talk went quite well; but what was more important for me was that I had been allowed to attend a 'fireside chat' after dinner the night before. This was both an enthralling and alarming experience. Some of these men were clearly operating under very considerable strain. It was enthralling because they were clearly so engaged in their many duties, and so committed to the troops they served with, some of whom had come from pretty problematic backgrounds.

I'm not suggesting these chaplains were 'on the edge'; but they clearly appreciated the opportunity to talk freely, among their peers, about the many challenges and difficulties of their exceptionally demanding ministry. They were dealing, for the most part, with young soldiers who were completely 'unchurched' – that is, they had no understanding of the basics of Christian life in Britain, let alone any elementary knowledge of the Bible or of Jesus Christ. There is a certain complacency in the ranks of many, possibly most, ordinary Christians in Scotland – and what I heard was alarming in the sense that it smashed right through any such complacency.

While there seemed to be general agreement that new recruits tended to struggle in their first few weeks, there was a threshold after which those who were going to make the grade suddenly became more self-confident. The chaplains also discussed the difficulties in helping and supporting those involved in combat; but I must not write anything beyond these generalised observations, because I was an outside guest at what was essentially a very private, and very candid, session. It was a privilege to be present. I'd sum up by saying that I heard far more that was positive than negative.

In that spirit, let me fast-forward to the spring of 2014. Here are a few pertinent and moving thoughts from an excellent Church of Scotland padre, the Revd Dr Scott Shackleton. As his words imply, Scott has seen a great deal in various, very different, theatres of war. When he wrote these words for me, he was serving as chaplain to the Royal Marines Corps, based at Plymouth.

Earlier, Scott had served as a parish minister in Dundee (where he organised a notable conference called 'Dundee: Geneva of the North?'); and, before that, he had done an earlier stint as an army chaplain. Scott is the son of a well-loved Glasgow minister, the Revd Bill Shackleton, and is a man who is naturally strong in spirit and cheery in disposition. But he also has his reflective side. Here is his testament:

In a country far, far away, I once uncovered the truth – or maybe it found me. The truth was on the verge of what some might describe as heresy, if one believes in such a thing. Our Bible, it would seem, is not always 'the thing itself' any more than anything else might be so. A Bible versus Pope or Patriarch argument was superfluous – Christianity versus Islam or atheism, irrelevant.

One discovers such things when one is given eyes to see the LIGHT, because the darkness is so dark. The light that shines thus cannot be diminished, just as the stars shine more brightly to our eyes when we are in the high mountains of Afghanistan, and there is no ambient lighting. For a fleeting moment, one gets it.

'Woodbine Willie' (Studdert Kennedy), the World War One padre, wrote that the priests of France and the Great War were a new race of clergy – if they were honest, or not corrected/recalibrated by the civilian, orthodox church when back home. He said that never again could they be satisfied with the domestic church which seemed to dim the light of truth.

Somehow the truth shines its light into corners of the church we do not want to be exposed. Most noticeably, prejudice and intolerance to children of God for whose sake his Son died, and in his resurrection remains tied to their cause, situation and person.

God with us.

'Woodbine Willie' said: 'that's all'. He is right. Operational tours with the Royal Marines Commandos have taught me over the last 21 years that whether it be Northern Ireland, the Balkans, Iraq or Afghanistan, or indeed on humanitarian operations, that's all . . .

Tony Bryer

Comparisons are odious, as John Fortescue opined all these years ago. Yet I've heard more than one Church of Scotland cleric complaining that Church of England clergy have it much easier than their Kirk counterparts. Such people might well listen to the Revd Tony Bryer.

Tony is an Anglican clergyman who was director of outreach for a city-centre Church of Scotland parish for several years before he returned to England to be parish minister of Towcester, a South Midlands town near the Silverstone motor-racing track. As well as Towcester itself, Tony had to serve various rural villages and smaller communities. Altogether, his ministry covered four parishes and five actual churches (four of them venerable Grade I listed twelfth- or thirteenth-century buildings that were expensive to maintain and difficult to adapt to flexible use).

His workload included about 30 weddings, 40 baptisms and 50 funerals a year; at least the weddings and baptisms could be planned well in advance. Four of the five churches had parishioners who were very traditional in outlook. A conservative approach to worship and liturgy, and a general resistance to change, made the flexibility and adaptability that Tony simply had to practise all the more difficult.

Yet, to do his job properly, Tony had to introduce much change. He was supported by three different 'passing through' curates over the seven years, plus one permanent female curate, and a lay ministry including a reader, two licensed 'pastoral ministers' and a specialist in evangelism. On an average Sunday, attendance at the five churches totalled around 130, including about 70 at the parish church in Towcester. It was simply impossible to perform as a traditional parish minister in these circumstances. Tony worked at least 60 hours a week, but he readily admits that he became proficient at what he calls 'planned neglect' – that is, prioritising the urgent and essential tasks and duties, and leaving all the others to be 'fitted in'.

It did not help that people were less and less willing to volunteer for the traditional 'officer' roles such as church warden and parish treasurer. Needless to say, there were many meetings to attend around the various parishes, and Tony reckons he could easily have spent all his time in the town of Towcester itself, there was so much to do there. After seven years, Tony decided to return to Edinburgh, to take up a senior ecumenical post in the city centre.

I asked him, now that he has been back in Scotland for several years, to reflect on the differences between the two national churches, especially in their relations with their host nations. I found his response fascinating. 'For all its faults, the Church of England still manages to think nationally,' said Tony, 'whereas the Church of Scotland finds it difficult to think or act nationally. I feel that the annual General Assembly can be too dependent on what is produced and prepared for it in advance by the various councils and centralised departments.'

He reflected that the Anglican Church's structure, with a more permanent hierarchy, helped it nationally. 'Most people notice the Archbishop of Canterbury, whether they are religious or not. Attention is paid, even here in Scotland, when a new Archbishop of Canterbury is chosen. Also, in each diocese, the bishop provides focused leadership. In Scotland, the coming of the Holyrood Parliament may have contributed to the national Church losing at least part of its national role.'

Tony Bryer, a wiry, charismatic and very energetic man, arrived for his first 'tour of duty' in Scotland in 1996; before that, he had worked for the Church of England in Bristol and the East End of London. When he came to Scotland for the second time, he definitely sensed that the country had become considerably more secular.

Tony's reflections on these matters – and these comparisons – seem to me to be apposite because the Church of Scotland is facing a desperate crisis in pulpit supply – that is, the provision of new ministers. The growing shortfall presents an acute crisis. Some figures in the Kirk reckon that ministers may soon have to serve eight or even ten parishes.

In that context, Tony's experience is most relevant. Without being officious, I reckon it might be useful if the national Kirk were to appoint him as an informal adviser on managing the challenge of leading and looking after several parishes.

Christianity and the
Scottish Parliament

Murdo Fraser

The very first debate held in the new Scottish Parliament, on 18 May 1999, was on a motion put forward by the Conservative MSP Alex Fergusson (later to be the Parliament's Presiding Officer), calling for consideration to be given to prayers to be said, in one form or another, at every meeting of the Parliament at its then home, the Assembly Hall of the Church of Scotland.

Scotland's inaugural First Minister, the late Donald Dewar, was opposed to the whole notion of having prayers. Having come direct from Westminster, he wanted Holyrood to be different, in this instance rather unfortunately equating modernism with secularism. But his wishes were overruled: the Parliament backed the motion by a majority of 2 to 1, and as a consequence a weekly 'Time for Reflection' was introduced, which even today continues to have a predominantly Christian ethos.

It was an early victory for those who wanted to see recognition of Scotland's Christian heritage, and contemporary Christian life, within the nation's devolved Parliament. Scotland's churches were enthusiastic about engaging the new institution, establishing the Scottish Churches' Parliamentary Office. This has helped provide regular Christian input to the work of the Parliament, particularly focused on lobbying on legislation impacting on areas of interest to Christians.

This active engagement does not necessarily mean that the views of churches have been listened to. Indeed, there is little evidence that outcomes from Holyrood have been any more beneficial to the Christian viewpoint than those from Westminster. To give an example, amendments to the Bill to legalise same-sex marriage to enhance protections for churches and other faith groups were heavily defeated, despite strong external lobbies in their favour.

It is not just the churches who have sought to use Holyrood to extend their influence. The small, but militant and aggressive, Scottish Secular Society has been active in trying to use the Parliament to pursue its own agenda. Making good use of the public petitions system, the Scottish Secular Society has attacked religious observance in schools, public funding of chaplaincy services in the public sector, and the predominantly Christian nature of 'Time for Reflection'. It might appear to many observers that the churches are fighting a rearguard action.

MSPs – with a few notable exceptions – seem reluctant to champion Christian causes, even when these appear to be relatively uncontroversial. In the run-up to the 450th anniversary of the Scottish Reformation, the Scottish government was most reluctant to get involved in any official celebration of this important date, apparently for fear of upsetting the Catholic community. In the end, a parliamentary debate on the subject was held, followed by a formal reception at Edinburgh Castle hosted by the First Minister; but, without pressure from across the political spectrum, it is debatable whether even these gestures would have been made.

There has always been an active Christian presence at Holyrood, not least in the form of Parliamentary Prayer Scotland, who meet weekly to support the Parliament, its members and staff, in prayer, and have a visible presence (in bright red jackets) every week in the public gallery during 'Time for Reflection'. Christian organisations and lobby groups use parliamentary facilities for receptions and promotional events, and are always warmly welcomed. But, with the exception of 'Time for Reflection' itself, there seems to be an institutional disconnect between Scotland's churches and its Parliament.

The irony is that the churches have a lot to offer in advancing the public debate. While it was broadly accepted that there was no singular Christian view on the question of independence, during the referendum campaign churches up and down the country were happy to host debates, giving each side the opportunity to present their views. In my experience, these were better informed, more thoughtful and more graciously conducted than similar debates in more secular settings. The Kirk even made time at its General Assembly for a debate, with fine contributions from Doug Gay and Douglas Alexander MSP, and from the floor, but (typically) bottled out of allowing the Commissioners a vote.

There are those within Scottish politics who are instinctively hostile to any influence from the Church either in the institution of Parliament or in the broader public debate. There are others who, while not actively hostile, are nevertheless wary of being seen to be too much under the sway of what is now undoubtedly a minority interest. Even the limited influence of Christian thinking on law-making that exists today appears to be constantly under attack.

And yet the churches, as was demonstrated during the independence debate, have a huge amount to contribute. Perhaps they need first to regain their own sense of confidence in the gospel message before they can expect parliamentarians to take them more seriously.

PART 3

History

Highlands and Islands

The most remote part of Scotland is St Kilda, a group of islands around 112 miles north-west of the Scottish mainland – in other words, well out into the Atlantic Ocean. The islands are not just remote; the weather is sometimes ferocious, and the storms can reach a pitch of fury that is well-nigh unimaginable to people living in gentler parts of Scotland.

The main island is Hirta, and it is quite big, covering around 1,600 acres. There are three lesser islands. This is by far the most significant breeding ground for seabirds in the entire British Isles. Hirta is also, for some of the year, a very agreeable place for human beings, though needless to say, as it is part of Scotland, its religious history has not been altogether smooth.

For many centuries, St Kilda was virtually ignored by the rest of Scotland. The small number of inhabitants, mainly descended from early Christian missionaries and Vikings, got on with their lives in comparative peace – if it was possible to be consistently peaceful when the winters were always wild and turbulent. But the St Kildan summers were generally notable for their serenity.

At the beginning of the eighteenth century, the population consisted of 180 people. They lived on birds rather than fish. Indeed, fishing was unpopular, partly because it was very dangerous. There were also plenty of cattle and sheep.

The islanders built a kind of democracy. There was an assembly which met every day except Sunday; and a kind of almost utopian co-operative socialism was practised. The people sustained a basic but adequate economy. For centuries, the islands were technically owned by the MacLeods of Dunvegan in Skye, who generally ignored them. The islands were not inaccessible, but landings were often difficult, and the big seas around them could be terrifying.

The spectacular sea cliffs are the highest in Europe, rising to over 1,400 feet.

It seems safe to assert that the people were on the whole content until the nineteenth century, when religion intervened. In 1822, the islanders were subjected to a blast of hardline Scottish Christianity by the self-styled Apostle of the North, an impressive preacher called John MacDonald, who in one month in 1822 sermonised to the islanders no fewer than 13 times. Up until his arrival, a kind of basic Druidism had been the informal religion. MacDonald should not necessarily be blamed; but what followed had an unfortunate effect on lives that had been, if not idyllic, then certainly peaceful and co-operative.

Indeed, the Catholic writer Father Francis Marsden believes that later missionaries from the Church of Scotland had a most deleterious effect on the lives of St Kildans. The worst was John Mackay, in the later nineteenth century. Mackay organised three Sunday services, each of them lasting for more than two hours. In addition, there were further services, complete with rigorous religious instruction, on four of the other six evenings. Attendance was obligatory for those who wanted to escape eternal hellfire. No cows or ewes could be milked on the Sabbath day, and no non-religious conversation was allowed from Saturday evening until Monday morning.

Father Marsden has suggested that Mackay was a zealot who turned a potentially paradisiacal place into a pit of gloom and misery. Mackay discouraged spontaneity and any expressions of happiness. The children had to carry their Bibles at all times; and all fun and games were forbidden.

Something of Mackay's sternness has lingered to this day in various parts of the Hebrides. You could argue that, in much of contemporary Scotland, an overtly Christian counter-culture would be a justified antidote to wasteful, indulgent and selfish ways of living. Whatever; in modern Scotland, there is still much mockery of Christianity. Those who wish to traduce organised Christianity generally head for the Highlands and in particular the Western

Isles. There, the celebrated 'long island' of Harris and Lewis (two names, one island) has been the subject of much controversy.

The long-serving and distinguished Highland correspondent of the pan-Scotland *Herald* newspaper, David Ross, covers a huge area the size of Belgium, but with a population of only circa 450,000. He reckons that the Highlands and Islands can still be the stuff of caricature, even in the twenty-first century. He insists that parts of the media still have a tendency to ridicule Highland Presbyterianism – a treatment, he wryly notes, that journalists would hesitate to accord to Roman Catholicism and would never contemplate for Islam.

Another distinguished Scottish journalist, John Macleod (himself the son of a much-respected Free Church theologian, Professor Donald Macleod), has written with impressive pungency about the almost routine sneering and mockery that the Presbyterians of the 'long island' have to thole. For many of these church folk, protecting the Sabbath remains a key Christian duty. It may be a losing battle, but they have fought hard to prevent Sunday ferry services, or supermarkets opening on Sundays.

When it comes to incomers who have little interest in, or sympathy for, the traditions of island Presbyterianism, Macleod can be scathing. He reckons that an 'alarming' number of the new 'settlers' have simply shown contempt for the folk who have tried to protect the Sabbath from secular attack. He is scathing of those who have truculently demanded their supposed rights when it comes to Sunday sport, Sunday drinking, Sunday shopping and so on. He characterises such attitudes as 'unfathomable colonial arrogance'.

Macleod lives for much of the year on Harris and has a keen understanding of the culture, history and theology of these parts. His indignation is, I believe, completely justified, although unfortunately the occasional excesses of overzealous Highland clerics do not help his cause.

⬕

After the Scottish Reformation in the sixteenth century, the Highlands and Islands were among the last parts of Scotland to embrace the new forms of Christianity enthusiastically. But it is difficult to generalise, for there was much confusion.

This confusion was embodied in the somewhat slippery and self-serving personage of John Carswell, an ambitious and greasy clerical grandee who was educated at St Andrews, became treasurer to the little cathedral on the isle of Lismore, and then chaplain to the Earl of Argyll. Influenced by the reforming sympathies of the earl, he converted to Protestantism; and, soon after the Reformation was secured in 1560, he was appointed 'Superintendent' for the vast area of Argyll and the Isles. (Some thought that 'superintendents' were just bishops by another name – and, as if to confirm this, Carswell actually accepted the offer of a bishopric from Queen Mary a few years later. He was generally regarded as a man on the make.)

Carswell was without doubt a notable Gaelic scholar, and he translated at least one of the works of John Knox into Gaelic, although he was also to condemn the 'ignorance and perversity' of those who taught and preached in Gaelic.

There was less ambivalence in his building of the splendid Carnasserie Castle, which has a fine hillside site a mile or so north of Kilmartin. Essentially a very large fortified house (it has been compared to a Renaissance palazzo) that is now in a partly ruined but very picturesque condition, it commands the narrow Kilmartin valley. There is a large parking area beside the busy A816. From here, you can walk up the steep hill and then clamber over the well-preserved shell of the building; and indeed you can still climb right to the top of it. Carswell had it built when his career was blossoming after the Reformation; he employed masons and builders from far afield.

In the years after the Reformation, Gaelic-speaking Irish Franciscans made a concerted effort to evangelise across the Scottish islands, for they were regarded as one of many mission territories across Europe, areas ripe for reconversion; and this work was formalised by Pope Gregory XV in 1622. The Scottish Reformation had been predicated on the parish system. But, in the Highlands and Islands – about half of the total Scottish land mass – there were not enough ministers to work in the vast and scattered parishes. Itinerant missionary-ministers tended to be used rather than settled parish ministers. For centuries, the far north and west of Scotland proved problematic territory for the creation of a coherent parish ministry. Clan chiefs were sometimes disposed to help by providing patronage; but then that raised other problems.

After the Disruption of 1843, there was, inevitably, more confusion. Most of the Highland congregations joined the new Free Church, but far fewer ministers did. Partly because of these difficulties, the Roman Catholic Church recovered considerably. In 1878, the appointment of the first Bishop of Argyll and the Isles, Angus Macdonald, was a key development. A notable and very energetic man, within a dozen years he had presided over the building of several new churches and convents and the creation of new missions. He also introduced Scottish saints into the liturgical calendar and organised pilgrimages to Rome and Lourdes.

Meanwhile, the various Presbyterian churches split, and split again. The great reunification of 1929 only partially resolved this tendency.

The churches had not always reacted well to the tumults in Highland life, not least the Clearances. Twentieth-century writers such as Iain Crichton Smith and Fionn MacColla wrote very angrily about this, while twentieth-century preachers like Murdo Ewen Macdonald were not slow to indict their predecessors for their pitiful complicity in a great evil. Scottish Christianity has occasionally had an unfortunate tendency to compromise with the secular powers that be; and this has sometimes produced, in turn, justifiably bitter responses.

The view of some historians has been that the Highlanders' Christianity sustained them, giving them strength in the face of organised oppression; at the same time, their faith rendered them supine, leading them to accept the horrors visited on them as some kind of punishment or even judgement. Some ministers managed to sympathise sincerely with the victims while defending the vicious actions of their patrons.

There were clerics, not least the Revd Lachlan Mackenzie, who were fearless in the pulpit and visceral in their condemnation of evictions. Yet, at the same time, Mackenzie believed in obedience; oppression was the result of sin. This ambivalence was linked to a theology of submission. The distinguished educationist and great poet Sorley MacLean claimed that not one in ten of the Highland clergy supported the crofters in any tangible way. One of the worst aspects of the Clearances was that some of the young and virile Highlanders left Scotland, often leaving behind the most vulnerable: women, children and the old.

Much of the Christian effort in the Highlands and Islands continued to be described, without any intention of being patronising, as missionary work. It was undertaken by itinerant Gaelic-speaking preachers who were often more than mere freelances: there was also a formidable elite, simply known as 'The Men', lay preachers who spoke with exceptional power and impressive Biblical knowledge. But, impressive as many of them may have been as individuals, they were just that – individuals, and they hardly helped to heal the religious divisions that so beset their wild and fierce territory.

Foreign visitors loved to visit the Highlands, and they were often mesmerised. A very observant Pole called Krystyn Lach Szyrma was a case in point. He arrived in Edinburgh in 1820 as the tutor of a Polish prince and princess who were already studying at Edinburgh University. Later, he became a Professor of Philosophy at Warsaw University, an active Polish patriot and political activist. On his travels across Scotland, he was more than a mere tourist; he was concerned and almost obsessively curious. Not all his conclusions were mature, but he was generally shrewd and sympathetic. His account of his tour of the Highlands is particularly vivid. He found the Highlanders a very warlike people, and contrasted them with the douce Lowlanders. He described how a Highland chief intent on vengeance for some slight, real or imagined, would set fire to a wooden cross which had been dipped in the blood of a newly slain animal. The fiery cross was a call to aggression and violence.

He reckoned that in no other place in Europe was Sunday so carefully observed as a day apart. He also found that the Scots were very eager for religious argument, and that they did not give ground easily. Indeed, he felt that religion had given the Scottish nation its essential character, had been the basis of its morality and had been the true source of the people's welfare and also their happiness.

✉

The main difficulty in developing and maintaining organised Christianity in the Highlands and Islands was physical. Folk often had to walk, and/or sail, very long distances to church – journeys of a dozen or so miles were commonplace, and sometimes there was a round journey of as many as 30 or even 40 miles. Parishes were far-flung, and the terrain was tough. So, simply getting to church could be an arduous business, requiring much time and effort. Was it worth it, to sit for a very long time in a dreich, cold building, sometimes little more than a shed, perhaps to hear a harsh message full of bleak force but devoid of any suggestion of softness or joy? Many thought that it was indeed worth it. Even so, the sheer physical effort involved in getting to worship must, in many instances, have militated against concentration. Worshippers must have struggled to stay awake and keep warm.

Of course, sometimes the ministers went to the people; some of the itinerant preachers whose missions were sketchily recorded were clearly effective, for their preaching changed lives. These men had to be resourceful and resolute. They were constantly on the move, travelling through high mountain passes and across vast bogs, and sailing over stormy and capricious waters.

Some parishes consisted of several small islands. One celebrated parish consisted of the southernmost part of the very large island of Skye, plus the much smaller isles of Canna, Eigg, Muck and Rum. In the 1970s, I spent two summer holidays on the tiny island of Muck, and on both occasions I attended the Sunday service. There were about a dozen folk present. What I remember most is not the two extraordinarily long and grim sermons, but seeing the little boat arrive at the harbour, with the preacher standing aloof in the bow, and the boatman sitting back at the stern, about 15 feet away, clutching the tiller. The preacher was holding a large black Bible, and he could not have looked more fierce and severe had he tried. Perhaps he was trying.

A little south of the Isle of Muck is the promontory of Ardnamurchan, a long, gnarled and magnificent finger of rugged land pointing into the Atlantic. It is the westernmost part of main-land Scotland, and at its eastern end is what for me is the finest mountain in all Scotland, Ben Resipol, which is not quite a Munro but from its top affords views north, south, east and west that are so extraordinarily beautiful that it would be insolent to try to describe them. If you regard the 'view' as the proper reward for peching up a Scottish mountain, then Resipol's reward is bounti-ful beyond belief. I holidayed in Ardnamurchan as a child and was privileged, much later, to see in the new millennium at the tiny community of Portuairk, near Sanna on the north-west corner of the peninsula.

Meanwhile, of the various eminent Scottish literary figures I have interviewed, perhaps the most impressive was the distinguished poet Alasdair Maclean, who was, until his death in 1994, among many other things the severe but clear-sighted laureate of Ardnamurchan. I wrote a feature on him in the early 1970s. The then editor of the *Scotsman* was delighted when he heard that I had secured an inter-view with Alasdair Maclean, but was then somewhat aggrieved when he discovered that I was to meet not Alistair MacLean, author of *The Guns of Navarone*, *Night Without End* and so on, but a – for him – obscure poet.

Maclean's poetry should be better known. It is similar to that of Seamus Heaney, and, for me, better. Maclean wrote with both rugged candour and beguiling tenderness of life on the peninsula. His family had a croft at Sanna, and he wrote a moving, elegiac account of life and work there. It is partly the story of his own struggles, partly a memoir of his father – he quotes copiously from his father's journal – and partly an introduction to the culture and history of that unforgiving promontory. This superb book is called *Night Falls on Ardnamurchan*.

Needless to say, there are passages that deal with religious life on Ardnamurchan. The Macleans had enjoyed – perhaps the wrong word – a kind of dual religious identity. Members of the Church of Scotland, they were regular attendees at the Free Church services that were held at Sanna.

Maclean's account of the funeral of his father at Kilchoan, a larger community a few miles to the south of Sanna, is most revealing. He tells of how the Free Church minister droned on and on and on, invoking the gloomier prophets, especially Jeremiah. This man appeared to think that Mr Maclean senior had crept off in mountainous guilt and shame at last to his terrible eternal fate. The Church of Scotland minister sat alongside the preacher, growing ever more impatient and annoyed. At last, he rose to his feet and announced that the mourners had had enough. The Free Kirk minister, black with fury, strode down the aisle and away, with his billowing clerical gown likened to a 'dark cloud'. As for Maclean, he was simply sorry for his father; he felt the interruption would have shocked him profoundly.

Alasdair Maclean delved into the religious history of Ardnamurchan. He found that, over several generations, the Church of Scotland was almost the sole source of charity and did what it could to alleviate hardship, of which there was plenty. The Kirk's income came partly from small legacies and smaller collections, but mainly from fines – for non-attendance at services, or for illicit sex. The latter punishment made Maclean, in retrospect, enormously indignant.

Nonetheless, the fines were collected and helped the Kirk to provide social service of a kind. Among many things, it paid for the funerals of the poorer members of the community. In the late eighteenth century, the main funeral expenses were three shillings for a wooden coffin – and a shilling for a bottle of whisky.

⊠

I am conscious that, in some of what I've written in this chapter, there is a sense that the Highlands and Islands are very much an area apart, almost like a foreign land. This is unfortunate, but it is an understandable impression, especially when you read some of the material that the Victorian evangelists, in particular, produced. In this context, the eminent Scottish historian Professor Tom Devine has claimed that the study of Highland and Lowland history should not have been artificially 'separated' anything like as much as it has been. He reckons that far too much attention has focused on the Highlands and Islands because of all the drama, and undoubted tragedy, in their history. The vast region, he claims, represents in the public mind 'the soul of Scotland' – but this has vitiated Scottish historiography and indeed distorted Scotland's understanding of its past. I heard him make this very point, eloquently and, for some, very provocatively, in the Highlands – from the pulpit of Dornoch Cathedral, no less, when he delivered a public lecture there in 2006.

But, as well as an excessive, and often sentimental, reverence, the Highlands have also been treated with a kind of scathing contempt, partly because the inbuilt sternness occasionally descended to a kind of diseased craziness. Religious zeal was sometimes taken to the point of caricature in a way that inevitably brought mockery, although, as I indicated earlier, I think there has been far too much scoffing about Christianity in this area of Scotland.

As an example of excessive Christian rigour, I could cite the true tale of a preacher on the Isle of Skye who suddenly decided that his flock should renounce all worldly pleasures. Music was one of these. So, as part of his deranged campaign, he organised a mass conflagration in which many musical instruments – mainly fiddles and bagpipes – were ritually burnt. No doubt he thought that the crackle and hiss of this hellish fire was a more beautiful and holy sound than that which all the burning instruments had produced over the years.

But, for every aberration such as that, there were many more episodes of godly conviviality. The famous Johnson family, devout Catholic people across the generations on Barra, were famed for their expertise – and delight – in singing and dancing. And, as a kind of antidote to the grimness, a persistent and balancing quality of Christianity in this part of Scotland has been a sense of mystery. This is most evident on the beautiful island of Iona, just to the west of the much larger island of Mull.

Perhaps more than anywhere else in Scotland, Iona has an elusive, mythic quality. It has been welcoming pilgrims for many generations; and, although these days the tourists probably outnumber the pilgrims, it retains a special sense, intangible yet strong, of past effort and past faith. Some people claim to have been transfigured here; and even the persistently grumpy Dr Johnson was moved to eloquent expression of piety when he visited the island. Famed Scots such as Andrew Carnegie and Thomas Telford have assisted the island's people in various practical ways.

Although Whithorn has a prior and much more valid claim to be the cradle of Scottish Christianity, Iona has now, in the public mind, assumed that accolade. I have visited it three times, and each time I have been struck by an undoubted atmosphere of holiness, a strong sense that this is indeed a sanctified place. That excellent and eloquent celebrator of the abbeys of the UK, the Revd Henry Thorold, wrote simply that Iona is 'the goal of every pilgrim'.

It is a wee island, just over 5 kilometres long and 2 kilometres wide. Some of it consists of arable land, some of coarse pasture; there are splendid bays fringed with white sand. There are several little hills; and some of the island actually consists of beautiful green marble, which was extensively quarried in the early twentieth century.

Here is the centre of the cult of the great warrior-saint Columba, who was a notable diplomat as well as a holy man and a fighting man. He did much to pave the way for the merging of the Pictish and Scottish cultures, and in that sense could be regarded as the father of the kingdom of Scotland. The island was for many generations the burial place of Scottish monarchs.

Why did Columba come to Scotland from Ireland? Was it a voluntary exile, prompted by a quest to evangelise? Or was he sent to Scotland in disgrace, outcast by his royal peers? Probably an uneasy mixture of both. Despite his murky deeds, whatever they were, he had already founded monasteries in Derry and Dunrow. Columba was not an obvious saint, if such a being exists; he was restless and imperious, and his reputation was problematic before he arrived in Scotland. But he possessed both spiritual dynamism and political vision. Iona was, and still is, his place.

He arrived on the island around AD 575 and founded a monastic community that developed into an exceptional Christian power-house and a notable cultural centre, producing beautiful books and distinguished art. But the community was soon to be blighted by irregular but vicious Viking raids. The Vikings have their apologists; some claim they were more interested in trade than rapine. Whatever; their record on Iona was appalling. In their most notorious raid, in AD 806, they massacred around 70 monks.

Slowly, over the generations, the legends and the myths grew. North of Iona is the smaller island of Staffa, famed for its great cave, and to the north of it are yet more little islands, the famed isles of Treshnish. This is where the vast ocean finally reaches the western outliers of Europe, an area that may be particularly perilous for mariners but has become treasured and very precious to generations of tourists.

The composer Felix Mendelssohn visited both Staffa and Iona on his Scottish tour of 1829 (after he had been snubbed by Sir Walter Scott). The overture he was inspired to create on this journey became known as the Hebrides or Fingal's Cave overture, and rapidly established itself as one the most popular pieces of romantic orchestral music ever composed. Even before Mendelssohn visited, Iona had become a major tourist attraction, with the start of timetabled steamer trips in 1826.

Ownership of the island was passed around with something akin to abandon. The Dukes of Argyll eventually became the settled owners, but then the 8th duke donated part of the island to the Church of Scotland. To the alarm of some, the Roman Catholic Church was at one time understood to be a possible purchaser of the entire island. In the late 1970s, the aristocratic Campbell family finally sold the island to the controversial magnate Sir Hugh Fraser. In an act of splendid munifence, he donated it to the National Trust for Scotland. All this combined with a steady growth in tourism.

The Ross of Mull is a long, lovely promontory at the western extremity of Mull, which is a big island. Its main artery is the winding A849. As the single-track road progresses west, the anticipation builds. For a time, the road hugs the glorious sea loch of Scridain; to the north is the wild and spectacular area of Ardmeanach. At the little community of Bunessan the road almost touches the exquisite little inlet of Loch na Lathaich; you are now on the last few furlongs, approaching the busy little port of Fionnphort, where there is provision for the parking of many cars and buses.

In 1990, a new ferry was built; it can carry 250 passengers and several vehicles. It plies frequently across the kilometre of sometimes troubled, and often mist-shrouded, water that lies between Fionnphort and Iona's own well-constructed jetty at the beautiful bay of St Ronan.

Columba's monastic community withered away and was eventually revived by Benedictine missionaries in the twelfth century. They built an impressive abbey on the site of Columba's church. It was a large, cruciform building and was steadily expanded, but was partly destroyed, and then abandoned, at the time of the Reformation. The Episcopalian Bishop of the Isles eventually ordered rebuilding. But it was not until the late nineteenth century that the building was properly reconstructed, on the order of the then Duke of Argyll. Even then, real revival was left to the twentieth century and the sometimes wayward but always numinous genius of George MacLeod.

Major rebuilding work began just before the Second World War, directed by the distinguished architect Ian Lindsay, and was not finally completed until the mid-1960s. Much of the construction was undertaken by craftsmen, artisans and trainee ministers working together under the aegis of the newly formed Iona Community. They worked together and lived together. This rebuilding had, then, considerable resonance as a practical social and religious project.

Now it is a busy church receiving many tourist visitors and groups of pilgrims. It has a full and rich programme of worship and ecumenical religious study, and is a fine testament to the vision of George MacLeod. There can be no doubt that the island of Iona is once again a place of practical and positive faith. The actual site around the cathedral is a little too sanitised for my taste; it is very trig and trim, the stonework is incredibly smooth and the grass is manicured; and you are always conscious of the imperatives of tourism, such as the very large and well-stocked cathedral shop.

You are less aware of the work of the ecumenical Iona Community; but it is good work, and it is going on all the time. The actual members of the Community follow a precise regimen of prayer and communal work for justice and peace. Each year, members of the Community receive guests from across the world, people who have come to pray, work and study, to live together for a time and learn about practical mission and outreach elsewhere.

Wandering around the whole complex, on my last visit, the only things I found that clashed with the pervasive sense of orderliness, quiet purpose and genteel commerce were some fairly lurid and subversive left-wing political literature I found scattered around – and a most incongruous, but utterly magnificent, piece of modern artwork in the centre of the cloister.

My first impression was that it was distinctly peculiar. I gazed at this challenging, and ultimately very moving, bronze sculpture for some time, trying to figure out exactly what it depicted. Eventually, I went to the large cathedral shop, where the two ladies on duty could not have been more helpful; they dug out some material that guided me through the strange story of the creation of *Descent of the Holy Spirit*, for that is what the sculpture is called, by Jacques Lipchitz, an eminent Lithuanian artist who worked with Picasso and Modigliani in Montparnasse, Paris, in the early 1900s.

The work was commissioned by a wealthy French cleric who liked to place numinous creations by celebrated artists in his church. He asked Lipchitz to create a special sculpture of the Virgin Mary. Lipchitz demurred, explaining that he was Jewish. He was told that did not matter. But inspiration took a long time to come.

Indeed, it was while he was in a New York subway that he suddenly had his idea: the Virgin would be placed within a mandala (a Tibetan religious form representing the entire cosmos). There would be a dove above her and a lamb below. When the work was at last completed, in the early 1950s, the artist inscribed it thus: *Lipchitz, Jew, faithful to the religion of his ancestors, has made this Virgin for better understanding of human beings on the Earth so that the Spirit may prevail.* Amen to that.

Three casts were made. One for the French church; a second for the celebrated 'roofless church' designed by Philip Johnson in Indiana in the USA; and the third, whose history was unknown until it was given by a generous anonymous benefactor to Iona Abbey. I needed guidance and help; but, once I realised that the mandala represented the entire cosmos, that the dove was descending on the Virgin's head, and underneath, resting on the plinth, was the lamb – then I understood.

The more I studied it, the more aware I was of its spiritual and political power. It is a most fitting work for the heart of the Iona Community.

As noted above, you travel to Iona across the sea, twice – first to the bigger island of Mull, and then across to Iona itself. Once on the little island, you are always vaguely conscious of the surrounding sea, and its myriad, much-chronicled moods, from beguiling calm to ferocious tempest. About 25 kilometres to the south-west, where the sea has become the ocean, and the great Atlantic swells in all its might, glory and occasional fury, is one of the greatest of the Stevensons' lighthouses, the lonely 45-metre-high Dhu Heartach. Its strength amid the plunder of the wrecking water, its light amid the darkness, serve as symbols of everything that the island to the north-east represents.

✠

These days, it is easy to despair of the constant divisions and splitting that have scarred the development of Scottish Christianity. This tendency has been most marked in the Highlands and Islands. One scattered and lightly populated Highland parish to this day hosts six separate Presbyterian denominations.

I was once asked to explain the difference between the Free Church of Scotland (which is devotedly Presbyterian) and the separate Free Presbyterian Church of Scotland. Pitifully, the best I could come up with was that the Free Church had an honourable tradition of far-flung Christian mission in countries such as India and Peru, while the Free Presbyterian Church had concentrated on a notable mission in Zimbabwe. This was reasonably accurate, I believe; but of course what my interlocutor wanted was a quick explanation of the doctrinal difference between the two churches. This I was wholly unable to provide.

A deprecation of the tendency of Scottish Protestant churches to splinter has occurred from time to time in this book. But, in a country that values individual conscience, the need to split and split again is perhaps inevitable. In the north and west of Scotland where the reading of Scripture was and still is intense, and the meaning taken from that scrutiny is sometimes narrow, fissures and splits among churches are natural occurrences.

They also reflect the extremities of the landscape, much of which is very beautiful but also rugged, harsh and unforgiving. But equally, much of it is soft and benign. The topography of the Highlands is replete with stark contrasts. Most Highland glens are glorious, but in different ways: sometimes the beauty is dark and even baneful, while other glens possess a lovely lightness that makes them seem almost ethereal. But this can be false. The most beautiful-seeming Highland landscape can turn out, on closer inspection, to consist of terrain that is treacherous and almost impossible to cross on foot. And too much Highland Christianity has not been soft, which is fair enough, or benign, which isn't.

Of course, the Highlands of Scotland have been ravaged – and I use the world advisedly. The worst atrocities came in the hideous, extended aftermath of the Battle of Culloden in 1746. But the Clearances, in the next century, while less bloody and vicious, were another passage of Scottish history that has gained deserved notoriety.

The Clearances were all about greed and the enforced eviction of people from the land – from their heritage, their homes and their livelihoods. This was a callous and even wicked process. Depopulation as a result of general social and economic trends is bad enough; the forceful removal of people by brutal, exploiting landowners and their often barbarous agents was inexcusable. And all because greedy, distant men saw sheep as better economic units than people.

The Highland chiefs had become, after Prince Charlie's ill-fated escapades, more and more remote from their clansfolk. Immediately after Culloden, the Highlands knew horror and something not too far removed from attempted genocide; but, long after those vile times, there was a lingering loss of structure and an absence of decent and concerned local authority. Some of those who could and should have provided leadership had been slaughtered. Others had been corrupted.

In the 1830s and 1840s, when the clearing was at its worst, local leaders were too often not to be found. Meanwhile, the Highlands were becoming a sentimental playground for early tourists, folk like the composer Felix Mendelssohn (see above).

At first there was little intention, or need, to get rid of people. At the worst, they would be moved to the coast. Nor was the process unique to the Highlands. But there was soon to be much cruelty in the far north and west of Scotland, and especially in the vast county of Sutherland. The chief, the landlord, had once been the protector; now the landlord, and his agents, who were sometimes scum, was there not to protect but to expel. The sustained cruelty was predicated on the supposed need for new sheep farms; in essence, sheep now had precedence over human beings.

There was resistance, but it was sporadic and disorganised; and the churches did too little to support the folk who were evicted and displaced. As noted above, some clerics appeared to find that their first loyalty was not to their God or to their people, but to their absent patrons. There were of course notable exceptions, but the key point is that Christian ministers were unable to organise mass protest or coherent attempts to achieve collective justice. To generalise, it is probably correct to say that the Free Church ministers come out of the later part of this sorry saga marginally better than their brethren in the national Kirk. As for the Catholic priests, many of them were weak and absent when they were needed most. On the other hand, a society fractured by the Clearances needed to be put together again – and Christian ministers certainly made a considerable contribution to that process.

There was a horrible irony in the story of the Highland Clearances. Much of the rest of Scotland was being, or was about to be, industrialised, with all the brutality and suffering and exploitation that that entailed. The great tracts of the Highlands escaped industrialisation, and yet they had visited on them a parallel social horror. Reflecting on this, Tom Devine believes that the many dispossessions in the Lowlands actually exceeded those in the Highlands. He thinks there is less retrospective anger about appalling events in the Lowlands because the Highlanders have taken 'cultural possession' of their Clearances in a way that Lowlanders haven't.

As for Highland Christian history, too much of it has been a narrative of failed mission, misplaced zeal and botched opportunity. Amid this darkness, it is pleasant to mention that, in more recent times, the Highlands have hosted a splendid development that combines vigorous Christian commitment with practical educational needs. This is the Highland Theological College (HTC) at Dingwall, which is that rare thing, a new and highly successful religious enterprise in Scotland. I'm perhaps not being wholly objective here, for I have received many warm welcomes at the college and have spent many hours working in its splendid library, which now contains around 80,000 books.

This excellent young library has benefited enormously from various judicious acquisitions, including most of the books from the Benedictine Abbey at Fort Augustus; part of the William Temple collection at Manchester University; and the entire library of Rutherford House, Edinburgh. But the rapid growth of the HTC library has brought with it logistical problems; and indeed the college has had, through the 20 years since its founding, to struggle with some of the consequences of its own success.

In spirit and ambience, the college is totally devoid of the harshness that has characterised much Highland Christianity, although the theology taught is evangelical, and I suspect that the staff of the college have little time for some of the modish experimentation evident at the divinity schools attached to Scotland's older universities. Indeed, the foundation of the college was partly motivated by the sense that some of the divinity faculties elsewhere in Scotland were providing what amounted to liberal arts courses as opposed to specific theological training.

The HTC is a friendly institution that happily maintains the age-old traditions of Highland hospitality. It has an intimate ambience; there are no large lecture halls. The students are men and women of varied backgrounds and all ages from their late teens to their eighties, who study on a full-time or a part-time basis. Quite often, theology students, here and elsewhere, are mature; they have developed other careers before deciding to change course in midlife. The college specialises in distance learning.

The HTC was the brainchild of two distinguished Church of Scotland clerics, the Revd Professor Andrew McGowan and the Revd Hector Morrison. Andrew was the founding principal of the college and was succeeded by Hector in 2009. Both of them had been successful parish ministers, and they came to the conclusion that the Kirk had a big problem with pulpit supply. When they combined this concern with their worries about some of the trends in the established Scottish divinity schools, it occurred to them that a new college in the Highlands could become a useful counter-force to some of the tendencies they deprecated. So, they gathered together a group of ministers and Christian businesspeople who gave the nascent project their backing.

The training and provision of new ministers, while important, is however not the sole function of the college. It does excellent work in many academic areas. It also helps people to learn computer skills and the like. But the provision of properly prepared ministers is an area where the national Church has been struggling for generations; and in recent times the crisis would have been even more grave without the HTC, for the college has certainly played its part in providing credible candidates for the ministry. It has also become an established and respected centre for teaching and research in Reformed theology.

Unfortunately, the national Church did not evince graciousness when it should have been welcoming the initiative. When Andrew and Hector were working in a little hut at the back of Moray College, Elgin, to give the infant project initial momentum and credibility, the Church of Scotland was suspicious and even hostile. A large delegation was sent north to investigate. Although the report that was eventually produced was at least partly positive, the Kirk's initial response was that the proposed HTC would not be a suitable body to train ministers. This negativity outraged Andrew McGowan in particular, but he and Hector carried on – and eventually prevailed.

What helped more than anything was that the college was quickly endorsed as a constituent and degree-awarding part of the new University of the Highlands and Islands. The first principal of the university, Professor Brian Duffield, was consistently supportive. Recognition by the University of the Highlands and Islands was every bit as important as recognition by the Church of Scotland, although the Kirk eventually found, as well it might, that it could indeed endorse an institution that has since raised its profile in the Highlands. The Kirk has given the HTC much practical support, although the college is non-denominational.

Inevitably, the biggest continuing task has been fundraising. Although there is a large pool of committed and generous benefactors, the financial health of the college, which remains independent, has always been precarious. There have been several crises, but the college has survived – and I personally hope that it will flourish for many generations to come.

The Ruthwell Cross

Gavin Young, Henry Duncan and John Dinwoodie

The magnificent Ruthwell Cross, about 18 feet high and richly adorned with exquisite Christian carvings that date from the eighth century, is for me the most beautiful and moving artefact in all Scotland.

The cross was broken and buried after an appalling specific edict of the General Assembly of the Church of Scotland in 1642. The cross was condemned as an idolatrous monument; but, thanks to the painstaking and patient efforts of a later Ruthwell parish minister, Henry Duncan, it was – as it were – resurrected and gradually pieced together again. It now stands, in all its numinous splendour, in the little parish church, totally dwarfing the pulpit beside it.

Gavin Young

The General Assembly of the Church of Scotland, convening at Aberdeen in 1640, passed a decree for the demolition of idolatrous monuments. The reformed Kirk was a church of the Word, and was very suspicious of images. Fair enough; but the orgy of destruction that the Scottish Reformation unleashed was inexcusable.

Luckily, Gavin Young, the minister of Ruthwell at the time – presumably backed by his congregation – was quite prepared to defy the supreme sovereign court of his Church, the General Assembly, in order to preserve the great cross for posterity. He believed that there was nothing idolatrous about this extraordinary monument. But he was not allowed to stand firm; two years later, the General Assembly followed up with a specific decree 'anent idolatrous monuments at Ruthwell'.

Gavin Young could hold out no longer. The cross was broken, but carefully; it was broken in such a way that it could, one day, be put together again. Mr Young, working covertly, had a trench dug in his church's clay floor. The shaft was buried in the trench, and other parts of the cross were buried in the churchyard. Mr Young had compromised, with considerable guile; he had obeyed, up to a point, the Assembly's second and more specific decree.

Indeed, Gavin Young was a far-sighted, brave and resolute man. He was also subtle. He guarded the sacred treasure in his keeping, now broken but not destroyed. Had he openly and brazenly defied the highest court of the national Kirk, he would have faced severe punishment; the least of it would have been to be deprived of his ministry. As it was, his ministry at Ruthwell continued until 1667.

About 100 years later, extensive alterations and repairs were undertaken at the church. Some of the fragments that had been buried in the trench were removed and buried outside. Most of the church floor was covered with flagstones. Gavin Young was a hero – but an even greater hero now appears.

Henry Duncan

The Revd Dr Henry Duncan, who was ordained minister of Ruthwell in 1779, is one of the all-time great Scots. It did not take him long to discover that various pieces of beautifully sculptured stone were lying, half-buried, in his churchyard. He asked questions, and was gradually able to piece together the story of the cross. Then he began, literally, to piece the cross together. It took him almost 25 years, but many later scholars have inspected his work and commended it. He got almost everything right.

The reconstruction of the cross was almost as remarkable as its original creation. This is, in a way, a story of resurrection. Only one significant part of the cross was irretrievably lost. But, even as he was engaged in his work of painstaking reconstruction, Henry Duncan knew that he had to proceed cautiously. The General Assembly decree had never been revoked.

The Revd Dr Henry Duncan reckoned that, technically, the command of the Assembly did not apply beyond his actual church. Eventually, as late as 1823, the great cross was erected outside the church; it had resumed its first role as a preaching cross. Henry Duncan understood that he was the custodian of something very special – the finest piece of religious art from the period of the Celtic Church.

It became clear that the resurrected cross had to be protected; it could not be left exposed to the elements. By this time, scholars were coming from across the UK – and beyond – to inspect it. They authenticated it; one of them, an expert from Copenhagen, pronounced that it was a 'matchless northern monument – the finest runic cross in the world'.

To preserve the precious monument, a special pit was created within the church beside the pulpit. (The alternative would have been to raise the roof of the church, for the cross was too high to be placed on the floor.) It was taken inside and placed in its latest, and final, site. Visitors came from afar to inspect it. I'm sure most of them were awestruck. Today the cross, which is over 18 feet tall, can be viewed in all its mysterious glory.

It must surely be one of the finest pieces of Christian art in the entire world. The 16 lines of poetry on the cross are said to be the oldest extant piece of written English. They quote from a mystical poem possibly written by Caedmon in the seventh century, the *Dream of the Rood*. It has been claimed that this marks the beginning of Scottish literature. What is probably more important is that the cross indicates an aspiration to a very high level of art. The sculpture panels depict various scenes; they have a simplicity that is deceptive. The south face is particularly impressive. The artwork on it includes a large section with a very beautiful depiction of the washing of Christ's feet. Christ stands, his broken hand raised in benediction; at his feet there kneels a woman, presumably Mary Magdalene, washing them. Beneath, there is a panel with an even more moving depiction of the crucifixion. Several other scenes are carved, with a simple yet subtle grace.

The Church of Ruthwell stands in gentle pastoral land about 10 miles south-west of Dumfries, a little north of the Solway Firth. It is pleasing that this small, modest but beautifully maintained church is the home of what is without doubt the finest standing cross in the British Isles; in fact, it might well be the finest piece of figurative art in the British Isles. As a piece of early Christian art, it is clearly world-class.

The early sculptors who created these images are of course anonymous, but quite a lot is known about the three outstanding parish ministers of Ruthwell. Two of them feature in the narrative above.

Henry Duncan was primarily a cleric; he was also a polymath, an architect, a notable gardener and an outstanding writer and journalist (he founded the *Dumfries and Galloway Gazette*) as well as an energetic philanthropist. He was active in the anti-slavery movement, and he corresponded with William Wilberforce.

Altogether, he has a claim to being the most impressive individual parish minister the Church of Scotland has ever had, but it might be better to regard him as the exemplar of a special type: a man of God, first and foremost, but with a wide range of interests, many of them temporal. He had a profound commitment to the well-being of his parishioners – a commitment that extended well beyond the conduct of services and the delivery of sermons. He was Moderator of the General Assembly in 1839. He is truly one of Scotland's greatest men.

John Dinwoodie

The third of this outstanding trio was the Revd Dr John Dinwoodie, who, over many years, played host to scholars from literally all over the world who came to inspect the cross. He came from a farming family a few miles north of Ruthwell. He was educated at Dumfries Academy and Edinburgh University; in 1890, he beat an extraordinary 112 other applicants and was elected minister of Ruthwell. He was to serve his parish for almost 50 years.

He soon realised that a full account of the history of the Ruthwell Cross, of which he was to be the honorary custodian for so many years, was required. After much careful research, he published his book on the history of the cross in 1927. The paragraphs above are largely based on this book.

It is now accepted that he got certain things wrong, not least the actual age of the cross; today it is generally believed that the cross was created somewhat later than he suggests. His account of the great monument's history has just a whiff of sectarianism; he is at pains to point out that the 'Church of Rome' could not make a valid claim to 'the authorship or erection of the cross'. To ram home the point, he asserts that it is to the 'Celtic church – the church of Columba' that the cross owed its existence, not the Roman Catholic Church.

He is also prepared to excuse, and even justify, the action of the General Assemblies in 1640 and 1642, whose members were so concerned that the cross should be destroyed. He imputes to these Assemblies only 'the highest religious motives'. He tries, earnestly, to justify 'the ineradicable dislike of the use of the sign of the cross in any part of the Presbyterian service' – and, in that context, he tries to explain why, at the time, the exhibition of a high standing cross could not be allowed. This is special pleading, and he does not manage to carry it off.

But, overall, we owe him a huge debt: more than anyone else, he is responsible for our appreciation of its greatest custodian and protector, his predecessor the Revd Henry Duncan.

Saints

St Margaret, St Andrew, St Mungo and St John Ogilvie

Scotland has a rich religious history but can boast relatively few saints. The chronicler Walter Bower, writing in the fifteenth century, and conscious of this paucity, found it necessary to 'borrow' various Irish saints.

St Margaret

Chief among the Scottish saints is Margaret, the wife of King Malcolm III of Scotland, known as Canmore or the Bighead. Margaret's life was written, enthusiastically, by her confessor, Prior Turgot of Durham and later Bishop of St Andrews. Turgot presented Malcolm as an illiterate boor who was besotted with his saintly wife. Malcolm could not understand the books that Margaret was constantly reading. He showed his devotion to her by kissing the books and then adorning them with gold.

Margaret's influence was multi-faceted. She was only Scottish in the adoptive sense; she was half-English, half-Hungarian. She came from English royal stock, but her family was exiled during one of the regular upheavals at the English court. She was born in Reka in southern Hungary, and brought up in the court of King Stephen of Hungary, which had recently converted to Christianity. After the Norman Conquest of England, she was supposedly in serious peril as one of the extant members of the Anglo-Saxon royal line.

She eventually found refuge at the court of King Malcolm of Scotland – and by all accounts Scotland was lucky to receive her. Even allowing for subsequent hagiography, she appears to have been a notably devout, intelligent, kind and altogether special woman. It has, however, been suggested, possibly in a somewhat sexist way, that she was rather officious and domineering.

Her union with Malcolm – she was his second wife – was without doubt both fecund and happy. She rendered the hitherto somewhat obscure and unsophisticated Scottish court a place of civilisation and enlightenment. More significantly, she transformed the Scottish Church, which had been stagnating; she introduced the practice of Easter communion, and founded various monasteries and refuges for pilgrims. She revived Christian life on Iona.

She undoubtedly brought a certain subtle English influence to the Scottish court and indeed to wider Scotland. She never learned Gaelic; and many in the court followed her example and spoke English. She imported Benedictine monks from Canterbury to serve at her new religious foundation at Dunfermline.

While it would be wrong to suggest that she was intent on a creeping Anglicisation, there is no doubt that, like John Knox later, she was something of an agent for Anglicisation. There is in the overall picture – boorish, belligerent Scottish monarch civilised by much more gracious lady from foreign parts – something that seems marginally patronising; certainly, some Scots have been somewhat sniffy about her extensive achievements.

Her devotional life included much prayer as well as (rather showy) almsgiving. This included having 300 of the poor rounded up to be fed under her benevolent gaze. She also washed the feet of the poor during Lent, and personally looked after young abandoned orphans.

Her religious reforms helped to bring Scotland more into line with conventional practice in the Roman Church – and this too has been regarded as a kind of dilution of Scottishness. There is perhaps a legitimate grievance insofar as she helped to end the sway of Celtic Christianity; she was in that sense something of an agent of Rome.

Her piety left a strong imprint on her eight children. Two of them became kings of Scotland; and her daughter Matilda married Henry I of England. Today, she is best remembered for endowing the pilgrims' ferry that plied between South and North Queensferry, near where the road and rail bridges across the Forth now stand.

Margaret died in 1093, not long after hearing of the deaths of her husband King Malcolm and also her eldest son. She is supposed to have died while holding a cross and praising the Lord. She was buried in Dunfermline Abbey; the Canmore dynasty, understandably, were delighted when she was canonised in 1250, 157 years after she died.

In the Reformation period, her body, and that of her husband King Malcolm, were removed from Scotland and eventually taken to Spain. There is a beautiful stained-glass portrait by Lalia Dickson of St Margaret, complete with the arms of Edinburgh, in the kirk of Dalmeny, a mile south of South Queensferry.

St Andrew

St Andrew, fisherman and brother of Simon Peter, was a disciple of John the Baptist and then one of the four key apostles of Christ. He was crucified in the Achaia region of Greece on a diagonal cross. As far as we know, he never came anywhere near Scotland. So, why did he become the nation's patron saint?

There are two main reasons. Both may well be legends, but they are pleasing legends. The first concerns another saint, St Rule, who supposedly took Andrew's relics to the east coast of Fife, where he founded a church. This became the site of the town of St Andrews, and a celebrated place of pilgrimage. The other, even more pleasing, legend concerns the trim and trig village of Athelstaneford, 2 or 3 miles inland from the coast in East Lothian.

In AD 832, a small army of Picts under Angus, the High King of Alba, aided by Scots led by Eochaidh, King of Dalriada, were trying to exact retribution on Northumbrians who had been raiding Scottish territory. (Lothian was then part of Northumbria.) The Scots were trapped by a larger army of Angles and Saxons on unsuitable ground somewhere between Athelstaneford and East Linton, near the Peffer Burn. King Angus prayed that he and his men might be saved. At this very moment, there appeared in the azure sky overhead a white cloud in the strange shape of a diagonal cross or saltire. The king there and then decided that if he and his men were, against the odds, victorious in the coming battle, then St Andrew would become the patron saint of Scotland. The Picts and Scots duly prevailed, and the saltire – a white diagonal cross on a blue background – became the flag of Scotland. It is reputed to be the oldest flag in Europe.

In the grounds of the parish kirk of Athelstaneford (itself a fine building that dates from the 1780s, although the first church on this historic site was founded in the twelfth century by Countess Ada, mother of William the Lion) is a dovecote that contains the Small Flag Heritage Centre. Next to it is a fine viewpoint, with of course a high flagpole and the saltire flying proudly. On the other side of the churchyard, you can inspect the Saltire Memorial, built in 1965.

St Mungo

Glasgow's most celebrated saint is Mungo, or Kentigern. The city's early history – and the myths surrounding it – is inextricably bound up with this man. Many buildings in the city carry the Glasgow coat of arms. The main features are the city motto: *Lord, let Glasgow flourish through the preaching of thy word*; a depiction of the city's patron saint, Mungo; and four objects associated with him – a fish, a bell, a tree and a bird. (In our secular times, the words are now often abridged to just three: *Let Glasgow flourish*.)

Mungo was born in the sixth century, the son of a princess; there are many legends about him, and probably most of them are untrue. In his early life, he was associated with Lothian and Fife rather than what is now Glasgow. What does seem to be factual (more or less) is that later he built a little wooden church beside the Molendinar Burn on what is now the site of the magnificent cathedral of Glasgow. How did Mungo come to be there?

The young Mungo was supposedly tutored by St Serf, who worked in various places in Scotland, notably Culross in Fife. Mungo became a missionary and was led by two wild bulls to a place called Cleschu. There he was, in time, consecrated bishop; and he established his church by the Molendinar, and soon added a monastery. St Serf was supposed to have visited him there more than once, and encouraged him in his evangelising. There are myriad tales about Mungo, including different ones featuring a salmon, a tree, a ring and a robin.

The robin will suffice here, for it's the shortest story: Mungo was supposed to have restored a pet robin to life after it was stoned to death by some young hooligans. (Some in the east of Scotland would say that Glasgow started off as it was to continue.)

Christianity was already reasonably well established in Scotland by the time St Mungo arrived at Cleschu. As the religious community grew, he was supposed to have performed many miracles. His tomb is now splendidly situated in the lower part of Glasgow Cathedral.

St John Ogilvie

If Mungo remains Glasgow's patron saint, the city is now also famed for a more recent saint: John Ogilvie. He was brought up as a Protestant in the north-east of Scotland in the late sixteenth century. His family were rich and respected, and owned a fair amount of land. John went abroad around 1591, converted to Catholicism and was educated by the Jesuits at various colleges and seminaries. He taught in France, and then returned to Scotland as a covert priest. He was arrested in Glasgow in 1614, subjected to lengthy interrogation, condemned as a traitor, and was eventually hanged at Glasgow Cross in March 1615 for 'heinous, detestable and unpardonable treason'.

He was beatified in 1929 and canonised in 1976. He is reputedly the only Roman Catholic to have been officially executed in Scotland for his religion, although this is not absolutely certain. There were many Protestant martyrs in Scotland in the period preceding the Reformation, notably Patrick Hamilton in 1528, George Wishart in 1546, and the 82-year-old Walter Myln in 1558; so it is surprising that later Ogilvie was the only official Roman Catholic martyr.

These are the bare bones of Ogilvie's story; what is fascinating is the process that led to his canonisation well over 300 years after his martyrdom. It features what seems to have been a genuine miracle, a very painstaking investigation by the then Archbishop of Glasgow, Tom Winning – and, this being Scotland, a whiff of sectarian controversy.

At the centre of the story is the subject of the miracle, who was by all accounts a decent Glasgow working man, one John Fagan. In the mid-1960s, he became seriously ill with cancer, and death seemed imminent. Mr Fagan's local church was dedicated to the Blessed John Ogilvie, and his parish priest suggested to the family that they should address their prayers to the martyr.

In early 1967, it was obvious that Mr Fagan was desperately ill and about to die. The family doctor, who was not a Catholic, visited Mr Fagan frequently; eventually, he declared that his patient had only hours to live. An hour or so after that, Mr Fagan recovered in a way that can only be described as miraculous. However, it was to take almost a decade before the Vatican – generally and commendably cautious in such matters – agreed that John Ogilvie should become a saint because of the miracle of Mr Fagan's revival.

Archbishop Tom Winning had carefully interrogated all the participants in the drama. At the start of the process, he was openly and profoundly sceptical. While the archbishop pursued his inquiries, three senior doctors trawled through all the medical evidence. No acceptable medical explanation for Mr Fagan's recovery was found. Tom Winning was finally persuaded, as was the Vatican; and Scotland had a new saint.

The surprise and delight that attended the announcement was immediately shadowed by a cloud of sectarianism, for the Church of Scotland's official magazine, *Life and Work*, suggested that the canonisation was a threat to ecumenism. This dubious proposition was surprisingly endorsed by Professor William Barclay, but was not backed by the then Moderator of the General Assembly, Dr James Matheson.

Meanwhile, Tom Winning – not always the most diplomatic of men – maintained a dignified detachment and merely stated that he did not want to be drawn into any kind of public dispute. The controversy petered out. Pope Paul VI officially confirmed Ogilvie's sainthood in October 1976. Mr Fagan lived for another 17 years.

In the refurbished, and genuinely ethereal, St Andrew's Cathedral, by the Clyde in central Glasgow, there is a splendid portrait of the saint by the man who is arguably Scotland's greatest living artist, Peter Howson. It is a most powerful piece of art, and Howson manages to convey, in Ogilvie's face and his pious posture, something that combines strength, suffering and Christian yearning.

There is a fascinating back story to this wonderful piece of contemporary religious art. The painting was commissioned by Archbishop Mario Conti, and it was a commission that Howson treated with great respect and care. His research was extensive, and he produced many preparatory sketches (one of these now hangs in the Glasgow archdiocesan offices). At first, he intended to paint a huge panoramic picture of the scene at Glasgow Cross when Ogilvie was martyred.

During these prolonged preliminaries, Howson suffered a personal crisis. He had a breakdown, and he feared that he would not be able to complete the commission, which had become so important to him. He decided that the huge crowd scene was not going to achieve the numinosity that he sought. After enduring something of an artistic crisis, he destroyed what he had painted of the scene at Glasgow Cross, and started again. This time, he concentrated on the single figure of the saint, in a posture of sublime holiness.

The result is magnificent.

Jacobitism, sectarianism, state-sponsored slaughter, and industrial exploitation

Bonnie Prince Charlie and Post-Culloden

Jacobitism was a religious rather than a political movement that was nonetheless to be a huge threat to the safety of the Scottish people through the first half of the eighteenth century.

The Scottish Parliament in 1689 decreed that James VII had forfeited the crown and that it should be held jointly by William of Orange and his wife Mary (James's daughter). William was of course one of Europe's most prominent Protestants. This was too much for Viscount Dundee – ironically, he had presided over the hunting down of the last Covenanters – and slowly the rebellious movement of Jacobitism took shape. The standard of King James was raised, fittingly at Dundee; a minor battle took place at Killiecrankie (where Dundee died), and a lesser one at Dunkeld. The rising was thwarted easily enough, but the movement grew.

Perhaps surprisingly, many Scottish Protestant clergy sincerely felt that they could not glibly transfer their allegiance from the Catholic James to the distinctly Protestant William. As for Catholics and Episcopalians in Scotland, they felt they had plenty of reasons for disillusionment. So, these were even more difficult times than usual for Scotland, what with a series of very bad harvests and two notorious debacles: the Massacre of Glencoe and the more significant collapse of the Darien Scheme. (The small-scale massacre was an attempt, partially successful, to eliminate the MacDonalds of Glencoe, allegedly for being tardy in expressing allegiance to William; the Darien Scheme was a bungled colonial venture on a grand scale.) The general climate was clearly not conducive to confidence and the enthusiastic embracing of a new era.

The Union with England of 1707, controversial then and to a greater or lesser extent controversial ever since, was regarded with special suspicion by the Jacobites. Many Scots were reluctant to endorse it. Those who felt really strongly could find in Jacobitism a useful channel for their discontent. In that sense, the movement was political; but a series of botched rebellions made it clear that it was really about the religion and the restoration of Roman Catholicism.

There was also a kind of romantic ardour about the Jacobite cause; even hardbitten Presbyterians could find in the later adventures of Bonnie Prince Charlie, in 1745, a marvellous, if doomed, narrative. Lost causes often confound rationality. The Liberal prime minister Lord Rosebery, an eager amateur historian and, according to John Buchan, a man whose outlook was essentially Calvinist, nonetheless thought that every Scot was 'at least half a Jacobite at heart'. And he may well be right, even now.

A few Scots Jacobites rallied directly to the cause of James's son, James VIII; in 1708, the French king provided a small fleet to take James to Scotland, where he was to launch a rebellion. His tiny fleet was intercepted by the English navy, and it never reached Scotland. There was a more serious attempt at rebellion in 1715: the Jacobite forces were checked at the indecisive battle of Sheriffmuir, in the Ochil Hills, while various Jacobite factions proved unable to link up. Had they managed to do so, the rising might have developed into something far more serious.

Four years later, Cardinal Alberoni in Spain tried to organise a force to invade England. A tiny expeditionary army did land in northwest Scotland, at Loch Duich, but it was easily and swiftly defeated.

Bonnie Prince Charlie

Then, in 1743, James Stuart, the Chevalier de St George, declared that he had appointed his son Charles as Prince Regent of Britain. Charles promptly left Rome for France, where he set about raising troops and funds for an invasion of Britain. It duly took place in

1745, and it has been the stuff of myth, legend and fantasy ever since. Whatever happened and did not happen, one thing is clear: the British state, just 38 years old, was very severely tested, by Jacobites led by one of history's most flawed but most romantic heroes.

Charles Edward Stuart, generally known to posterity as Bonnie Prince Charlie, and to some as Charles III of Britain, was young, courageous and charismatic, but he was also a fool. He was no leader, and certainly no politician. Born in Rome in 1720, he was the eldest son of the exiled James VIII and Clementina Sobieski. He has become one of the most romantic characters in British history, but it is also possible to regard him as a mindless adventurer.

He certainly worked hard in France and Italy to raise funds for his invasion. He pawned valuable jewellery; he raised loans from the Pope. Meanwhile, the Jacobite clan chiefs in Scotland knew what was going on but were unenthusiastic.

Charles eventually gathered around 4,000 guns, some heavier artillery, many swords and a lot of gold. His 'invasion force' of two ships set sail for Scotland in July 1745. One of them encountered HMS *Lion* of the British Navy, and had to turn back. So, Charles was left with one ship, a few troops and a few fellow adventurers. It seems ludicrous that one man in one ship should have seriously considered overturning what was then one of the three greatest powers in Europe. To be fair to him, he had a darn good go.

He landed at Eriskay in the Hebrides, the beginning of a madcap enterprise that nonetheless soon had the supposedly mighty British state in serious peril. From the beginning, Charles encountered negativity and suspicion, even from those who might have been expected to back him enthusiastically. The first leading Jacobite he met, MacDonald of Boisdale, promptly told him to go home. Charlie replied with some spirit: 'I have come home, sir'. Next to greet him in Scotland was Bishop Hugh Macdonald, the (unofficial) Roman Catholic vicar-apostolic of the Highlands, who simply repeated Boisdale's advice.

Undaunted, the prince crossed to the mainland and raised his standard at Glenfinnan in August. A few hundred Gaelic-speaking clansmen, led by their chiefs, appeared – and the so-called 'royal standard' was raised. The rebellion was on. The clansmen marched south to Edinburgh, encountering little opposition but not gaining many supporters either. The prince managed to take over the royal palace of Holyroodhouse with his retinue, but he lingered far too long in the capital. His father was proclaimed king, and he was proclaimed 'regent'. The 'pretended union' of Scotland and England was declared to be null and void.

Charles then defeated the British state's inadequate army, led by Lord John Cope, at Prestonpans, just east of Edinburgh, and at last headed south. He assured his men that they would gather support as they marched south; but this proved to be nonsense. Even so, he and his ragged army got as far as Derby; and some historians have suggested that, if they had proceeded on to London, the forces of the British state, despite its various armies, were in no condition to defeat them. Whatever; Charles's most senior commander, Lord George Murray, had decided to turn back. That Murray could overrule Charles says much about Charlie's stature as a leader.

The rebels had been grievously let down, particularly by the frivolous French, who had promised generous assistance that never materialised. They had attracted little support in England on their march south, but they had encountered little effective resistance either, although now it was reported that no fewer than three separate British armies were advancing towards Derby.

The retreat – and retreat it was – could have been better managed. Charles, ardent and brave up to this point, was now disgruntled. He sulked and left the organisation of the retreat to Murray – but, even so, back in Scotland in January 1746, Charles and his tired army were able once more to defeat the forces of the British state, led by the brutish General Henry 'Hangman' Hawley. General Hawley was then replaced by the man who was to become, justifiably, one the most despised figures in British history – the king's son, George, Duke of Cumberland.

Cumberland may be despised now, but in his day he was very popular. That should not be forgotten. Anyway, despised or popular, he was able to defeat the Jacobite army – by now terribly weary and thoroughly dispirited – at Culloden Moor, a little east of Inverness. The battle did not last long – just a few minutes.

Cumberland had well-trained professional troops and considerable artillery.

This was the last set-piece battle to be fought on British soil, and probably the most shameful. Indeed, the immediate aftermath of the battle must be regarded as one of the most lamentable and ignominious episodes in the entirety of our history. The multiple atrocities that ensued had a sectarian tinge, though this is rarely discussed. Two points can hardly be disputed. Most of the defeated army were either Episcopalians or Roman Catholics. The Episcopalians were in the majority – and, although they were theoretically Protestants, this counted little with many Presbyterian Scots, some of whom chose to regard them as tepid Catholics. And the memories of Archbishop Laud's Episcopalian arrogance lingered on from the previous century. Yet, for a time, Episcopalianism had been the 'official' national religion.

Charles's army was well beaten on the battlefield; those who survived were subjected to merciless and sustained barbarity. In the eighteenth century, wars and battles were supposed to be conducted in a gentlemanly fashion. The great historian Edward Gibbon noted that armies were given to 'temperate contests'. This may have been fanciful, yet an informal convention without doubt existed. The Duke of Cumberland himself had previously shown compassion to prisoners and defeated soldiers.

On this occasion, for whatever reason, Cumberland allowed his men to behave like savages. The defeated clansmen, many of them wounded, all of them exhausted, were butchered without mercy. Spectators who had wandered up the hill from Inverness to view the battle were also slaughtered, as were some innocent local bystanders and their children whose sole crime was to live in the vicinity. The only thing to be written in extenuation of Cumberland is that it is not certain that he actually commanded this systematic post-battle bestiality. The response to that is that he did nothing to stop it.

The indiscriminate killing and raping and, almost as bad, the persistent evicting – from shacks, sheds, cottages and even hovels that were torched and destroyed – continued for weeks. Much of the Highlands, particularly to the north and the north-west (the far west, where the fugitive prince now sought refuge, suffered a little less) were scoured and swept by out-of-control, feral troops intent on a vicious and contemptible orgy of vengeance. Many of those who were not murdered or seriously wounded or left to long, lingering deaths of hunger and fever were transported south and condemned to rot in the Tilbury hulks on the Thames.

Charlie himself managed the great escape, not least because he was protected and aided by some notably brave and devoted Highlanders, including the famed Flora MacDonald. Eventually he escaped to France, and the rest of his sad life petered out painfully and pitifully, a protracted anticlimax. He became an Anglican, briefly, before converting back to Roman Catholicism. Seven years after the disaster of Culloden, he took as his mistress Clementine Walkinshaw, whose sister was a leading member of the Hanoverian court in London. Clementine was almost certainly a spy.

When his father died in 1766, it is significant that neither the papacy nor the French monarchy, who were nothing if not realistic, acknowledged Charles as king of Britain. In 1772, he married a minor European royal, Princess Louisa of Stolberg; but the marriage was barren and bitter and did not last long. Charles moved around Italy, a sad and pitiful figure; eventually he settled in Florence. He died in 1788, 42 years after his great adventure had ended so terribly.

Post-Culloden

The British state made no attempt to stop all the rapine and carnage that followed the rout of Culloden. Indeed, its various satraps were happy to treat Cumberland as a hero. In much of lowland Scotland, there were extravagant outpourings of relief, joy and gratitude. In Glasgow, there was sustained celebration: the 'greatest rejoicings that had ever been known', according to one newssheet.

Professor Tom Devine has pointed out that many of the Presbyterian clergy of the Lowlands were already in effect 'propaganda agents' for the British state. Certainly, the voices of Scottish Presbyterianism were not raised in protest against the sustained savagery. Quite the opposite. Disgracefully, the General Assembly of the Church of Scotland stooped to the occasion with a grovelling and utterly shameful letter of gratitude to Cumberland, praising his 'generous resolution in coming to be the deliverer of this Church and Nation'. Deliverer? The devil's deliverer, perhaps.

It is significant that Cumberland and his troops had been acting on behalf of the relatively new British state. They had constitutional and political – if not necessarily religious, and certainly not moral – legitimacy. But the British state, only two generations or so old, was already mired in grievous corruption and incompetence. It lacked, to use the old phrase, any kind of moral compass. It was soon to lose its American colonies in an exemplary masterclass of political and military bungling.

Scotland's creative writers have been, for the most part, surprisingly (and shamefully?) quiet on this ghastly period of horror, retribution and bloodlust. The underrated but very distinguished novelist Violet Jacob did write a superb but little-read novel called *Flemington* (published in 1911), which is mainly about the '45 Rising as it affected the east coast of Scotland. Towards the end, there is an absolutely magnificent set-piece in which the titular hero Flemington's mother confronts the triumphant Cumberland at Holyroodhouse in Edinburgh. This passage contains some of the best dialogue I've ever come across in a Scottish novel. The book ends with a very moving description of Flemington's execution; this fine passage serves as a noble epitaph of all those who died in this most curious and futile of misadventures.

The killing, raping and looting eventually ended, but there followed not at last an attempt at peaceful renewal and reconciliation, but rather a systematic and cynical attempt to destroy Highland culture. The clan chiefs were replaced by state 'factors' – managers who, to be fair to them, in some ways proved to be more efficient and businesslike than the chiefs had ever been. A necessary and reasonable reform was the removal of the right of the clan chiefs to dispense justice.

As for the ordinary clansfolk – those who were left – they suffered from a systematic attempt to expunge their entire way of life. Ludicrously, bagpipes were banned as a weapon of war. The language of the Highlands, Gaelic, was also banned. The wearing of anything tartan was proscribed. Cumberland himself arrogantly proposed the wholesale transportation of errant clans (with the exception of the Campbells, consistent foes of the Jacobites). Around 1,000 clansmen were sent to the West Indies to be sold as slaves.

As for Presbyterianism, it had never really taken root in the Highlands. Since 1725, the so-called 'Royal Bounty' had been dispensed, supposedly to extend Presbyterian influence and culture. The real purpose was to weaken what were known as the 'Papish parts' of the vast area. Itinerant missionaries and ministers were granted stipends from the Bounty, but they lacked parishes, manses or churches, and they struggled to make much impact, although they had some success in the Caithness area.

What happened after 1745 was a renewed effort to eliminate Roman Catholicism altogether, and a marginally less fervent effort to destroy Episcopalianism. In that sense, it was a particularly dark episode in Scotland's long and often tormented religious history. To a limited extent, the programme of elimination was successful: the Catholics went underground but kept going; the Episcopalians struggled.

But there was scant evidence of any great awakening of Presbyterianism. Jacobitism was not completely obliterated. There were brave, if uncoordinated, outbreaks of defiance for several years. But the reality was that the spirit of the Highlands had been broken, and most of the rest of Scotland was quite relaxed about the breakage.

The horrific wickedness of the agents and soldiers of the British state at this terrible time cannot be justified, even in terms of hard politics. Is there any rational explanation for it?

One of the most powerful states in all Europe had been in danger of being overthrown by a handful of Highlanders marching deep into England. Was this affront to British security and self-esteem the reason for the grotesque over-reaction after Culloden? Or were the reprisals driven by an insidious undercurrent of sectarian fear? Certainly, neither Scotland nor England was yet relaxed about what was still known as the Popish Danger. The ferocious attempt to destroy Highland culture was in part the result of deep loathing and funk.

A persistent, nagging worry about Roman Catholicism continued to fester right across the British state. As late as 1780, London suffered a wretched and utterly horrific week of anti-Catholic rioting which resulted in hundreds of deaths. Churches were burned, and many Londoners – the majority of them non-Catholic – lived in fear. (This outbreak of vicious and intense, if short-lived, sectarianism was the subject of a fine novel by Charles Dickens, *Barnaby Rudge*, one of his more concise and carefully constructed works. Although Dickens personally disliked the Catholic Church, this animus does not inform the novel.)

The riots were led by a grotesque establishment figure, Lord George Gordon, who had been incensed by proposals for a very moderate measure of Catholic emancipation. The splendid historian Edward Gibbon opined that the 'disgrace' of the riots would be long-lasting. He said London had witnessed 'a dark and diabolical fanaticism', which he had wrongly understood to be extinct.

Gordon was one of history's creeps: a dangerous and deluded fantasist who claimed, ludicrously, to have 160,000 men at his command in Scotland. But even if you divide by ten, the statistic is worrying. Gordon was convinced that the British King George III was a closet Catholic. He reckoned that the highest levels of the British state had been infiltrated by subversive Papists and that Britain's ongoing war with its American colonies was sectarian, a war against brave 'American Protestants'. This mixture of political paranoia, religious hatred and sheer stupidity was very dangerous.

The American war had admittedly been an indirect cause of the Gordon Riots, for the British government, determined to strengthen its armies, needed to conciliate its Roman Catholic subjects. Parliamentary attempts at emancipation merely provoked Gordon to rabble-rousing fury. In Scotland, the Highlands were seen as a likely recruiting ground for new Catholic troops. The British government's intention to apply 'relief' to Scottish Catholics led to serious riots in both Edinburgh and Glasgow. In Edinburgh, at least one Catholic church was set ablaze, and people who were Catholics, or were suspected of being Catholics, were attacked. Some prominent Catholics had to take refuge in Edinburgh Castle. This, incidentally, was the time of the much-lauded Scottish Enlightenment.

⊠

Hideous and unforgivable as the extensive post-Culloden reprisals were, it should be stressed that there was no concerted attempt by the British state at a kind of 'final solution', the wholesale and systematic eradication of a particular group of people. Many of those who fought on the Jacobite side managed to escape, or were imprisoned only briefly. Some of them went on to have successful lives and careers in late eighteenth-century Scotland. A case in point is Gordon Hay, a young Episcopalian who had been attached to the Jacobite army as a kind of informal medical auxiliary. After serving a short prison sentence for his part in the rebellion, he converted to Roman Catholicism and eventually became a priest.

He worked in Banffshire – for a long time the most Catholic county in Scotland – and was consecrated bishop in 1769. He did much to rehabilitate Catholicism, and wrote two bestsellers, *The Pious Christian* and *The Decent Christian*. (I suspect that most Scottish Christians have, over the years, been decent rather than pious.) Hay moved to Edinburgh, where he was one of those who suffered from anti-Catholic fury stirred up at the time of the Gordon Riots; his house was burnt down. He is not a major figure in Scottish religious history, but his career points to the progress that was steadily made in bringing Catholics back into the fold, though there were to be very many bumps and pitfalls along the way.

Henry Dundas, a senior and powerful fixer who effectively ran Scotland for the British state towards the end of the eighteenth century, was a perennially controversial figure. He controlled much ecclesiastical patronage in Scotland – and, to be fair to him, he played his part in reconciliation by supporting the creation of seminaries and stipends for Scottish priests. He also worked to have forfeited estates restored to their former Jacobite owners.

In 1800, there were only around 30,000 Catholics in Scotland. A century later, the figure was over 500,000. In nineteenth-century Scotland, the rapid process of industrialisation required labour, although ludicrously there was also chronic unemployment. Similar tensions are found in much of Western Europe today. Immigrant workers are often very unpopular; and cynical politicians whip up animus against them. They arrive in the host countries at a time of serious unemployment, yet there is a conundrum: there are also very many job vacancies, and they often find it surprisingly easy to find employment.

Much of the 'new' labour that arrived in Scotland came from Ireland, in ever greater numbers from the late 1820s onwards. Indeed, by the early 1840s – before the terrible Irish famine – it was reckoned that as many as 75 per cent of the miners in Lanarkshire were Irish. The Catholic priests – though there were not very many of them – who were already established in west central Scotland regarded this influx as a very mixed blessing. Some of them strongly opposed any incipient political agitation by incoming Catholic workers.

Many of these Irish folk found work as itinerant navvies – notably in building the new railways – but even more of them settled in their own communities in Lanarkshire, Ayrshire and the rapidly expanding city of Glasgow, and in Dundee as well. 'Their own communities' is the appropriate phrase. There was some integration, but not nearly enough. Religion was undoubtedly one of the problems. The Church of Scotland may have been grievously divided in the mid-nineteenth century, but most Scottish Presbyterians managed to agree on at least one matter: the 'menace' of Roman Catholicism.

Further, Scotland may have been a nation, but it was by now well integrated as part of the British state – and that British state had little understanding of, or wish to understand, the tensions that arose when thousands upon thousands of humans with wholly separate social and religious identities were living in close proximity.

Yet more Catholic immigrants arrived as the century wore on. There was, if anything, even less integration, but that should not obscure the fact that the Irish immigrants played an indispensable part in the spectacular growth of the Scottish economy.

Indeed, without Irish labour, the process of industrialisation – and wealth-creation – would have been far less impressive.

The real tragedy was that most of the Irish workers – like their Scottish counterparts – did not benefit from their efforts. The new prosperity was for the few. Most of the workers were more or less systematically denied the fruits of their labour. There was growing trade-union activity – and this was certainly one area where some of the Irish workers and their Scottish counterparts could co-operate – but overall there was far too little concerted organisation. As I note at length elsewhere, it took the great vision-ary Keir Hardie, with his prophetic linking of Christianity to social-ism, to lead a sustained assault on the processes of exploitation and alienation.

Indigenous Scottish antagonism to the Irish was based on various factors, but all too often it took on a religious tinge. It did not help that many of the Irish immigrants were committed to Irish national-ism. Evangelical Protestantism, as a social and political movement as well as a religious one, was obviously not going to be sympa-thetic to Irish nationalist aspiration.

Some Scots viewed the new Irish workers not just with suspicion, but with downright, blatant antagonism. At times, it was almost as if there were two separate proletariats. Even the establishment of a proper school system by the British state in 1872 did not help matters. Indeed, it possibly exacerbated existing divisions; and Catholic parents preferred to send their children to the local 'infor-mal' Catholic schools.

The founding of Celtic Football Club in 1888 was an assertion – a very understandable assertion – of separate identity. Meanwhile, the growing number of Protestant Irish immigrants arriving from Ulster did nothing to ease the pervasive social and religious nasti-ness and suspicion.

The Scottish Protestant mindset was frequently confused. There was certainly some overt and bitter hostility. The Scottish Reformation Society was actually founded to resist 'Popery' rather than to celebrate the many positives in the actual Reformation. Some Irish were actually shipped back home. There were serious anti-Irish riots in Greenock and in other, smaller, towns. Yet the tensions between the two religious communities did ebb and flow and were certainly not characterised by organised, permanent hostility. Possibly this was because the Scottish Protestants, as ever, were much animated by internal divisions, doctrinal ones and, in the case of church-building, physical ones; and, importantly, it was increasingly understood that a grievously exploited worker was equally exploited whether he or she be Protestant or Catholic.

Some Protestant workers were often impressed by the lives of the Scottish and Irish Catholic priests, who generally lived among their own people; there was a feeling that too many Church of Scotland ministers preferred 'west-endy' parishes, and consorting with the middle or boss class, instead of actually ministering to the workers. Professor Tom Gallacher has reminded us that Catholic priests lived on the same scale as their working-class parishioners.

⊠

It must never, ever be forgotten that in the mines, the factories, the warehouses and the sweatshops, Scots and Irish, Protestants and Catholics, males and females, young and old, all experienced the same hellish conditions and suffered the same wretched exploitation. When chained boys have to drag heavy carts of coal through long, dark, dripping underground tunnels, when stunted, injured, hungry and ill-clad workers have to work 12- or 14-hour days in vile conditions and then return to totally inadequate housing devoid of heating and sanitation, their religion or ethnicity can become a fairly irrelevant issue.

At this time, Glasgow's boss class, and their lackeys in the growing middle class, most of whom were Protestant, certainly knew how to party. Sir Robert Peel, who, to be fair to him, was by far the most socially responsible of all the leading nineteenth-century UK statesmen, was elected Lord Rector of Glasgow University in 1837. To celebrate this event – which of course had little resonance for the actual workers of Glasgow – a huge banquet was held. No building big enough to hold the 3,500 invited guests could be found, so a special temporary hall was erected. Turtle soup and venison were served to the platform party; the rest had to make do with chicken and lobster. Copious quantities of port and sherry were available for all; the guests could drink as much as they wished over many hours.

Peel was a Tory politician who had controversially – and against his own instincts – decided to endorse the cause of Catholic emancipation. He was a good friend of Thomas Chalmers, the leading Scottish cleric of the period, and he praised 'the consoling power of religion' in his rectorial address. At the banquet, Peel defended the rights of the established Church of Scotland. Many toasts were drunk. The banquet began at 5pm; carriages were called eight and a half hours later.

Peel had already served a short stint as the British premier; then, between 1841 and 1846, he was to lead an administration that introduced significant legislation to ameliorate and regulate the wretched working conditions of the new proletariat.

Sadly, progress depended on top-down concern from the rich and privileged; the workers had not yet learned how to combine and organise effectively. What agitation there was – for example, through the Chartist movement – tended to be concerned with political progress rather than the specific improvement of working conditions.

But, of course, there was the consoling power of religion.

George Buchanan, the unwitting father of the National Covenant

Scotland has produced far more than its fair share of world-class intellectuals and thinkers. Some of these formidable souls – Adam Smith, the economic philosopher, is a classic example – were pleasant and gracious men. Perhaps the most ferocious intellect of them all belonged to George Buchanan, the sixteenth-century sage. He was probably the most clever Christian that Scotland has ever produced. He was neither pleasant nor gracious. Rather, he was extremely severe and disputatious.

Martin Luther's Reformation led to division, war and constant cerebral dispute. The sixteenth century was, in Europe, marked by intellectual and religious ferment that often led to extreme turbulence. Debates about the nature of Christianity were fiery and involved secular intellectuals every bit as much as clerics and theologians. Buchanan in some ways typified the century. As an intellectual, he was in the very first rank. He merged religious and political thought in a way that was typical of the century.

Buchanan had a profound influence on Scottish religious thought. He also had a profound – and negative – influence on King James VI of Scotland and I of England, unsurprisingly as he became James's tutor when the boy was just 4. Buchanan was in his mid-sixties by then, and age had not mellowed him. He was cantankerous and stern, very short-tempered, and full of (at least partly merited) contempt for James's mother, Mary Queen of Scots – contempt that he was not slow to communicate to her son. He took matters too far, insisting to the child that his mother had been a whore. This must have been psychologically damaging, especially as, for most of James's early life, Mary was a prisoner of the English Queen Elizabeth. When Elizabeth eventually and reluctantly agreed to Mary's execution, James was apparently unmoved.

The royal child was a precocious pupil; and you might have thought, despite Buchanan's harsh views on James's mother, that the two of them would have got on reasonably well. But James needed kindness and understanding; Buchanan was rigorous to the point of cruelty. So, the boy grew into adolescence unhappy and lonely, surrounded by books rather than friends. Buchanan hectored him and inflicted his ideas on him. These were both democratic and authoritarian.

He was an obsessively cerebral man who had swallowed Calvinism whole; he was, however, unable to wash the theology down with what his contemporary William Shakespeare called the milk of human kindness. Many of his political views were far-sighted and commendable, but he was not well suited to preside over James's education. Unsurprisingly, James grew into adulthood hating Scottish pedagogues (as many others have down the generations) and hating strong-line Presbyterianism even more. He soon came to detest the new national Church of Scotland and all it stood for.

As he grew up, James worked out his own views on kingship – and they clashed directly with those of his tutor. He reacted against Buchanan's excessive severity, both mentally and emotionally. He developed ideas on the divine right of kings, particularly in his book *The True Law of Free Monarchies*. On the other hand, under the over-strict discipline of Buchanan, he received a splendid education – not only in Greek, Latin and theology, but also in geography, history and arithmetic. James may well have been the best-educated monarch in the entire history of the British Isles; but perhaps there was not that much competition.

※

As you approach the west Stirlingshire village of Killearn – now expanded into a flourishing community for commuters to Glasgow, and more of a little town than a village – you are aware of a magnificent (for some, overpowering) 105-foot-high obelisk. Designed by James Craig and erected at the end of the eighteenth century, it is situated on a fine site near the highest part of the town, and it commemorates Killearn's most famous son – George Buchanan.

. In 1976, Thomas Downie of Killearn delivered a public lecture that was later published by the Buchanan Society and the Killearn Trust. It was a magnificent lecture, at once scholarly, proud and realistic. He was as aware of Buchanan's faults as much as his virtues, but he also emphasised the man's integrity: he could not be bought either by money or by favour. Buchanan may still be remembered in Killearn, but in most of contemporary Scotland he is forgotten. The Victorian novelist and social reformer Charles Kingsley regarded him as the father of political liberty no less.

After his infancy and childhood at Killearn, Buchanan was educated in Paris and then back in Scotland, at St Andrews. In the pre-Reformation period, he incurred the considerable enmity of Cardinal Beaton for his fierce condemnations of corruption in the Scottish Church. He was jailed for heresy, but escaped to France, where, for a time, he was tutor to a youth who was to become one of the very greatest of all French writers: Montaigne. He moved on to Portugal, where history repeated itself. He condemned the Roman Catholic Church and was once again imprisoned for heresy. No-one could dispute his bravery, both intellectual and physical. He always told it as he saw it; he was never one to trim or prevaricate. He was well used to physical suffering; he stood up for his ideas.

He returned to Scotland; initially a friend and confidant of Mary Queen of Scots, he quickly turned against her and became a leading reformer. He wrote a dramatic life of John the Baptist and a partisan history of Scotland, and – most importantly – a treatise on *The Right of Kingship among the Scots*. Buchanan insisted that monarchs were chosen and kept in power by the people, and were subject not just to divine law but also to temporal law. He reckoned that the Scots had always called bad rulers to account. A tyrant, then, might be judicially and correctly executed. These ideas were admired across much of the Continent, although not at Oxford University, where the treatise was ceremonially burned.

A century or so later, his political theory was taken up with enormous enthusiasm by the Covenanters. Indeed, Buchanan was the great intellectual forerunner of the Covenanters. He was a distinguished and very influential Christian thinker. But his personality was unpleasant; he was too harsh, and lacked grace.

Buchanan was Moderator of the General Assembly of the Church of Scotland in 1567 – probably both the most intelligent and the most rebarbative figure ever to have held that august office. He wrote mainly in Latin – and one Scottish scholar has claimed that his verse is much better than Cicero's, while his prose far surpasses that of Seneca. On that, I cannot comment. Dr Johnson, no friend of the Scots, asserted that Buchanan was Scotland's only man of genius. My comment on this would be that he was merely one of many Scots geniuses. What I would aver with some confidence is that, overall, through the various effects of his ill-treatment of young James, he probably did Scotland more harm than good.

✕

James was to be the first British king. When he left Scotland for London, he relished the wider, less constricted scope of the English court. He had gained much, possibly overmuch, intellectual confidence from his rigorous cerebral upbringing, and he was now concerned to show English bishops and assorted divines how clever he was. He also seized the opportunities he had to exact a slow and cautious revenge on much that his fierce tutor had held dear, though his first initiative was most propitious.

He had noted that the General Assembly of 1601, meeting in Burntisland, had resolved on a major new Bible translation. He took the idea south, and convened a conference at Hampton Court in 1604 to set the project in motion. The resultant King James Bible, of 1611, was to become the best-known, most influential and most cited book in the English language. The team of scholars charged with the work of the new translation drew heavily, and rightly, on the work of earlier scholars, in particular William Tyndale.

Partly as a result of the overzealous tutoring of Buchanan, and partly because of his own temperament, James had come to loathe Presbyterianism. Andrew Melville, the greatest Scottish Reformation figure of the generation following John Knox, had contemptuously told him that he was just 'God's silly vassal'.

James reckoned that an Episcopal polity was much easier to control, more likely to be deferential and certainly less likely to be infected with the radical, almost republican, tendencies that he discerned in Presbyterianism.

His new role as king of Britain (technically, the king of two kingdoms) made it possible for him to pursue an anti-Scottish agenda, which he certainly did where religion was concerned. From a distance, he meddled with – rather than assaulted – Scottish Presbyterianism (even so, some in Scotland thought that, from his London base, the monarch was embarking on a process not so much of Anglicisation as of sleekit Romanisation). Yet James never really took on the national Kirk. North of the Border, there was a strong sense that real confrontation was in no-one's interests – and how prescient this was.

The full-scale attack did not come until James's crass son, Charles I, became the British king; and, even then, the assault did not come immediately. There was an awkward stand-off before Charles allowed his ecclesiastical hatchet-man, Archbishop William Laud, to take on the Scots. Not that Laud required much encouragement. This English interference in the religious affairs of Scotland was met head-on by two exceptional Scots who are not as well remembered as they should be: Archibald Johnston and Alexander Henderson. They led Scotland into the mother and father of all religious confrontations. This was, for most of the Scottish nation, a splendid fightback; it culminated in the magnificent National Covenant of 1638.

The Covenant is an extraordinary document that somehow manages to be at once noble and tedious. The authors were concerned to emphasise that the Scots remained loyal to the British crown in general and to Charles, the current British monarch, in particular. Yet, for all that, it was quite obviously a statement of rebellion.

The Scottish people endorsed the Covenant enthusiastically. It is estimated that more than 300,000 people signed copies of the document in kirks across the country after the first grand signing at Greyfriars in Edinburgh. Clearly implicit in the document is the idea that, if need be, the national Church of Scotland could operate independently of the monarch.

What followed was enormously complicated; in effect a series of bloody civil wars affecting Scotland, England and indeed Ireland. The key point came when the Scottish Covenanters and the English parliamentarians joined to fight their common enemy, the British king, Charles. There is very little to be said in favour of Charles. As the king of Scotland and England, he was an unmitigated catastrophe; he ended up doing the worst possible thing any monarch can do – making war against his own people.

Scots armies rampaged through England; the English army of Oliver Cromwell, who was the outstanding figure of sixteenth-century Britain, was later to rampage through Scotland. In mid-century, everything seemed to turn on its head, and then turn upside down again. It was a confused and terrible time, but perhaps all the bloodshed and fury was required for the Scots and the English to work out their religious destiny and learn how to live together (the two outcomes were closely linked).

Cromwell was a military genius, a far-sighted political thinker, a parliamentarian of brilliance and the most staunch and fervent of Protestants. Yet it is hard for Scots to approve of him, even now, as he created much bloody mayhem north of the Border. Though these were terrible times, they produced plenty of heroes – not least the Marquis of Montrose, possibly the most romantic figure in Scottish history, an adventurer who as a guerrilla leader possessed extraordinary skill and daring. Originally a Covenanter, he dramatically changed allegiance and became the leader of the Royalist faction in Scotland. It is no exaggeration to write that he was one of the most brilliant tacticians in the history of warfare.

As for Charles I, he was eventually executed after having been tried in what was undoubtedly something of a kangaroo court. But he had wreaked appalling damage in the kingdoms he was supposed to protect – and I for one cannot see that the sentence was unjust, no matter the invalidity of the court. Matters became even more confused, and yet more bloody, after the king's death. Cromwell was soon waging war against the Scots; his army came across the Border and inflicted a grievous defeat near Dunbar. Scotland was now being subjugated, brutally – and all because of religion. For a time, it was ruled not by a king but by an Englishman who was, *pace* Montrose, the most brilliant general of his day and also a committed republican.

Cromwell's republic did not survive his death for long. By 1660, there was a reversion to the previous dispensation of a British king and two British kingdoms (technically, there was a third: Ireland). The new king, Charles II, had himself earlier signed the Scottish National Covenant, but this was to prove irrelevant in the troubled decade – yet another troubled decade – of the 1660s. The king was a cynical and unpleasant man; he glibly reneged on his past commitments and sought to restore Episcopacy to Scotland. He also made it abundantly clear that he now had a very strong distaste for Presbyterianism.

While most Scots remained Presbyterian, their version of Protestantism was perceived elsewhere to be raw, egalitarian and chippy. And the key question was this: after two generations of bitter turmoil, were the Scots prepared to compromise? Most were. The hardline Covenanters were now a rump, albeit a sizeable one, who acknowledged 'No King but Jesus' in one of their most noble rallying cries.

Most of Scotland had endorsed the Covenant in a magnificent show of national solidarity; now, a mere two generations later, the Covenanters were a minority, persecuted, outlawed and hunted down with vicious contempt as if they were wild animals. Yet they were determined to sustain. Some of the remaining Covenanting ministers were purged; and a few of them took refuge in Holland, where the Parliament passed a resolution to help them with both arms and money. But most of the Covenanters were now regarded by the powers-that-be in Scotland as dangerous enemies of the Scottish state rather than mere religious dissidents. Scotland, after two generations of struggle and war, was politically, militarily, economically, socially and spiritually exhausted. Yet, here and there, the Covenanting flame still burned. At a parish in Dumfriesshire, the congregation attacked their new, imposed minister with a hail of stones.

Increasingly, the Covenanters could be regarded as fanatics in this new era of settlement and compromise – yet, by their own belief, all they were doing was honestly maintaining their Christian convictions.

Further, they mixed these convictions with the certainty that they were fighting for Scotland's national identity and integrity. This was a very potent mix.

And there were still some huge conventicles. In 1670, John Blackadder preached to a 'great multitude' on the Hill of Beath near Dunfermline, protected by fierce 'irregulars' from Galloway. Some of those present were later rounded up and transported to Virginia. At Skeoch Hill, near Dumfries, a crowd estimated at 15,000 gathered to hear Blackadder preach. The Covenanters actually won a set-piece military battle at Drumclog, though they were later defeated at Bothwell Bridge. After that fight, the authorities tried to evince leniency. Open-air conventicles were still suppressed, but 'house conventicles' were allowed.

A new leader emerged: Richard Cameron, who was more extreme and fiery than the likes of Blackadder. Cameron and a small band of supporters arrived in Sanquhar, where they pinned a declaration to the town cross: 'under Lord Jesus, Captain of Salvation, we do declare a war'. The government panicked and perhaps made Cameron more significant than he really was by offering a huge bounty for him, dead or alive. An intense manhunt then took place. Cameron and his supporters – probably about 80 of them – were heading over the moors towards Muirkirk when a large contingent of government troops saw them. In the ensuing fight, Cameron and his men showed exceptional courage, but to no avail.

Around 20,000 Covenanters are reckoned to have died for their beliefs in various military encounters and assorted brutal persecutions over a period of 25 years or so. Men, women and children constantly risked death as they worshipped Jesus Christ in open-air conventicles, mainly across the wilder uplands of south-west Scotland. The Royalist soldiers and agents of the state, brutally deployed by hard men such as Claverhouse, Viscount Dundee, hunted them across the heather, the bogs and the moors, and then slaughtered them as if they were vermin. They suffered atrocity after atrocity.

Latterly, the Covenanters had lacked serious intellectual leadership. The man who should have been their cerebral, if not military, leader was the great writer and preacher Samuel Rutherford.

Although he is described in his memorial plaque at the picturesque, ruined churchyard of Anwoth (near Gatehouse of Fleet) – a site that featured in the cult film *The Wicker Man* – as 'the Preacher of Permanent Renown', it has to be admitted that, even in Scotland, his renown has slumped to negligibility.

Rutherford was a theologian and political theorist who almost equalled Buchanan in scholarly stature. Born in the Borders, near Roxburgh, he studied at Edinburgh University and then worked as a tutor. He soon embarked on a religious career, and proved to be a precocious theologian and a supremely eloquent preacher. He was called to the parish of Anwoth as minister in 1627. It was an obscure, if large, rural parish, yet his preaching soon attracted much attention. He was eventually summoned to Edinburgh to account for his outspoken anti-Episcopalianism. As an outspoken critic of Laud, he was now playing with fire. His ministry at Anwoth was abruptly halted, but after the signing of the National Covenant in 1639 he was able to return.

In the 1640s, he went to London and preached before the Long Parliament. He was now writing forcefully in the manner of Buchanan, arguing that a monarch is only allowed to rule by the consent of the people, and further that the people had a duty to resist tyranny. In 1647, he was given high office at St Andrews University.

When Charles II was restored as monarch in 1661, Rutherford's books were burnt publicly. He was ordered to attend the Scottish Parliament, now subservient to the monarchy, to justify his views on kingship and generally to account for his 'treason'. But, by now, Rutherford was dying, and he sent word to Edinburgh that he had already been summoned by a 'Superior Judge'. He was going, he said, where few kings and 'great folks' went. His death, at the age of 60 in 1661, denied the Covenanters the intellectual authority and leadership they were to require in the next two decades.

Enlightenment

For much of its modern history – that is, from the end of the medieval era – Scotland has been looked on askance. At best, the country has been patronised (most notably by Dr Johnson), at worst neglected. It was often regarded as a remote wee country on the periphery, both intellectually and geographically. At other times, it was regarded (thanks mainly to the fictive efforts of Sir Walter Scott) as a romantic wonderland.

Scotland was actually in a condition of almost perpetual cerebral ferment. Much of this intellectual activity was inward-looking, and a lot of it was excessively religious for external tastes. Scotland's relationship with Christianity had been exceptionally intense, but in the eighteenth century this intensity began to be distinctly unfashionable.

Indeed, some believe that Scotland began to reinvent itself sometime in the course of the eighteenth century. I'm not so sure. Certainly, Scotland did rapidly come to be regarded internationally as a country of high culture and deep learning. Part of this process was simply linguistic. For many centuries, Scotland had had three languages. Gaelic was now disappearing slowly but surely; Scots was also being steadily eroded and – worse – was becoming, for snobbish Scots, a source of embarrassment and even shame. Then, after Culloden, Highland culture was nearly obliterated – partly because of a deliberate effort by the British state, partly because of other factors.

Meanwhile, intellectuals like David Hume – perhaps the greatest figure of the Scottish Enlightenment – were embarrassed by aspects of their Scottishness, in particular the Scots language. Hume tried to cleanse his written work of Scottishness. He and his like tired of the Scottish propensity – often driven by the Presbyterian culture – to nurture an intellectual life that could be bruising and inhumane.

The long legacy of the Reformation was never wholly rejected, but there was undoubtedly a new – and, for many, refreshing – emphasis on secular speculation, linked with a flourishing of artistic, philosophical and scientific achievement that appeared to be free of Scotland's old religious tensions. Hume – in persona the most amiable and pleasant of men – was quite relaxed about rejecting Scotland's fierce religious inheritance. He undermined the basis of faith by elevating rational inquiry and questioning how reasonable people could believe in what went against both practice and personal experience.

Indeed, he came to regard faith as literally incredible. Yet, this did not prompt the fury that would have been inevitable earlier, for two reasons. First, Hume was such a polite and gracious man that it was difficult to get angry with him; and second, many Scottish ministers were at this time themselves becoming deeply worried about aspects of Scottish Christianity.

Of course, the hardliners remained, and they were as loud as ever. However mildly expressed and carefully presented, Hume's notions provoked predictable fury among this group. He was attacked at Kirk General Assemblies. Yet – and this was even more worrying for the old guard in the Kirk – many of the more liberal spirits in the national Church were now happy to be regarded as 'enlightened' figures. The most prominent of these was one of the greatest Scots of the eighteenth century, William Robertson – a man who did an immense amount to build the reputation of Edinburgh University.

Robertson was the son of the minister of Borthwick, south of Edinburgh; he moved to Edinburgh when his father became minister of Old Greyfriars. He also served as a minister in East Lothian, and then moved to a charge in Edinburgh in 1756. He was very much attached to the Moderate party in the Kirk; that is, he was reluctant to condemn the current intellectual trends.

Robertson had many faults. Assertive, excessively ambitious, pompous – his sisters had to call him 'sir' – and in time very rich, he was a superb ecclesiastical politician. He accumulated important offices with ease. He was a royal chaplain (a post that carried more prestige then than it does now) and Historiographer Royal for Scotland. He was a much-admired and long-serving principal of Edinburgh University. His *History of Scotland* was, for militant Presbyterians, offensive; Robertson had little time for the Covenanters, and his urbane, sophisticated soul shivered with distaste at the more bloodthirsty episodes in Scotland's Christian past. He cherished his own liberal values, and was not slow in defending them. For example, he espoused the cause of relief for Catholics in Scotland (when Catholics were very much in the minority). This triggered some sectarian rioting.

Robertson was unique in the extent of his worldly success and influence, but he was not isolated. There were other prominent liberal churchmen, such as Alexander 'Jupiter' Carlyle, who claimed that his own parishioners in Inveresk distrusted him because he was 'too young and too full of levity'. Carlyle also boasted about dancing frequently 'in a manner prohibited by the laws of the church'. Yet, despite such men, there was still a lot of prejudice around. Robertson's influence can be exaggerated; and no Scottish university gave David Hume the professorship he so eminently deserved.

Hume was not particularly interested in challenging the national Church; he no doubt thought he had more pressing intellectual business to attend to. But there were plenty of folk in the national Church who wanted to challenge him. Robertson, however, had the ascendancy. He was more of a careerist than a combative defender of liberalism; and, as for Hume, he was not personally suited to leading a sustained assault on the religious verities of the day. So, the Scottish Enlightenment was characterised by an uneasy stand-off between moderate churchmen like Robertson and civilised sceptics like Hume.

Hume was championed by an ambitious young lawyer called Alexander Wedderburn, who defended him when the Kirk got seriously uppity. But there were also many senior clerics who reckoned that the General Assembly of the Kirk would be better employed attacking professional robbers, brothel-keepers and other patent rogues instead of taking on contemplative if wrong-headed intellectuals. And the opposite was true too. Why indeed should the likes of Hume bother with the Kirk? He was a gracious, easy-going man, and he had neither the inclination nor the stomach for taking on firebrands, religious zealots and hardline preachers.

When Hume was dying, James Boswell, the Scottish man of letters and renowned biographer of Samuel Johnson, and a man who had found the rigorous Calvinism of his mother so constricting that he had converted to Roman Catholicism, went to visit him. Hume told Boswell bluntly that he was near the end. When Boswell then pressed him as to his religious views, Hume replied that, since he had read John Locke, he had never entertained any belief in religion. Hume told Boswell 'flatly' that the morality of every religion was 'bad'. Indeed, when he heard a man was religious, he concluded he was a rascal. On the other hand, he had known instances of good men being religious. He himself had been religious when he was young.

In this deathbed scene, we can see the balanced cerebral serenity with which Hume rejected Christianity at the very time in life's cycle when many might have been tempted to embrace it.

✠

A notable precursor of the Scottish Enlightenment was Francis Hutcheson, who held the chair of Moral Philosophy at Glasgow University for 17 splendid years. In 1738, he was humiliatingly asked to explain himself to the Presbytery of Glasgow for teaching that it was possible to understand good and evil without having knowledge of God. Although he inspired many of his students to become ministers of the Kirk, he himself was a sceptic. Here again, we have the paradox of the Scottish Enlightenment. It was more notable for religious men who could question their own religion than for anti-religious men who totally rejected Christianity.

The Scottish Enlightenment mindset was too confident of progress and of order. At this time, Scotland was experiencing the early stirrings of industrialisation. For those with eyes to see ahead, there were going to be huge problems caused by excessively rapid urban growth and the creation of what would later be called a proletariat. Scotland was about to become considerably wealthier, but the wealth was not going to be fairly distributed. There was going to be grievous division and cynical exploitation.

But, before Scotland was ravaged by industrialisation, the country became famous, intellectually, thanks to the efforts of Hume and his fellow savants. It became a cultural and cerebral hothouse. The Scottish universities gained greatly in international prestige. And so Scotland became, for a time, the perfect place to live the life of the mind. But rapid and difficult social change was to challenge all that.

There was also to be a kind of semi-intellectual reaction against the Enlightenment notions of progress and rationality – what might be called a romantic or sentimental backlash. John G. Lockhart, Walter Scott's son-in-law and biographer, noted that the geniuses of the Scottish Enlightenment – the likes of Adam Smith and David Hume – showed the 'great force' of their intellects in reasoning but left matters of feeling 'very much unexplored'.

This was also true on the Continent. Some thinkers, partly influenced by Rousseau, believed that the Enlightened mindset analysed overmuch. There was too much emphasis on explanation and not nearly enough on understanding. One Continental sage declared that religion had been stripped of all its sensuous elements (not that these had been much to the fore in Scotland) and all its relish. Or, as an eminent English historian put it, reason had looked like a liberator but had turned out to be a tyrant.

Walter Scott was partly responsible for the response, even the revolt, that accentuated feeling – and he celebrated a semi-invented, mystic, wild, Celtic Scotland, peopled not so much by urban thinkers as by rough poets. Robert Burns, who was actually a well-educated and very sophisticated poet, had been presented to the wider world as a 'natural', an untutored rustic from a simple farming background who possessed an almost miraculous gift for song and satire. But it was later that Walter Scott, in the Waverley novels, portrayed Scotland not as a nation struggling with nascent industrialisation but as a wonderland of historical romance.

For a time, the civilised world found Scott irresistible. In the first half of the nineteenth century when the process of industrialisation was tearing the social fabric of Scotland apart, genteel visitors came from far and wide to gape, not at slums and the exploited, but at romantic castles and misty mountains. This, in some ways, was the time when Scotland went wrong: neither her writers, nor her politicians, nor indeed her clerics, seemed able to attend to the Scotland that really mattered, as opposed to some newly concocted and undeniably potent romantic myths.

In a footnote to this, it is useful to recall the brouhaha that attended the first public performance of a tragedy, *Douglas*, by a kirk minister, John Home of Athelstaneford. (Despite the different spelling, he was a relative of David Hume.) Home intended it as something of a morality play, but it offended some bigots in the national Church, who claimed that – among other faults – it glorified suicide (the machinations of the principal villain in the play, one Glenalvon, prompt the suicide of Douglas's distraught mother).

The play was ecstatically received by the Edinburgh audience, one of whom actually shouted 'Whaur's yer Wullie Shakespeare noo?' The Presbytery of Edinburgh was less impressed. It ordered admonitions against *Douglas* and other plays to be read from every pulpit in Edinburgh. The tone of 'exhortation' was pompous, but possibly not as fierce as has sometimes been suggested. There was a distinct feel of 'more in sorrow than anger' about it.

Here is a short extract: 'Taking into serious consideration the declining state of religion, the open profanation of the Lord's Day, the contempt for public worship, the growing luxury and levity of the present age; in which so many seem lovers of pleasure rather than lovers of God' . . . and so on. The Presbytery then expressed, openly and solemnly, its 'deep concern'.

The moderates among the Scottish clergy rallied to Home's defence – he was, after all, one of their number – but the minister-playwright was dismayed. The case came before the General Assembly of 1757, when William Robertson used his considerable skills as a manipulator of his colleagues to defend the play. He persuaded the commissioners that it was neither inconsistent with Christianity nor encouraging to vice.

The writer and critic Alan Bold once told me that it was the lingering residue of this somewhat ridiculous episode, a sourness that he thought had lasted for two centuries and more, that gave the Church of Scotland its continuing and unfortunate reputation for being mean, spiteful and bigoted when it came to literature and the arts. Bold insisted that it was the treatment of Home's play, and not any much earlier outburst from John Knox, that made artistic and creative Scots so suspicious of the Kirk. He may well have been right – and, if he was, this was grossly unfair, as the Kirk's sovereign body had, thanks mainly to its leading figure, William Robertson, effectively endorsed the controversial play – and by extension all serious literature and artistic endeavour. In a way, the national Church came out of the controversy rather well.

But Home had had enough. He might have been vindicated by the General Assembly, but he still thought it best to quit his ministry at Athelstaneford and retreat south, where he worked as a secretary and adviser to his patron, the Earl of Bute, who was to become, briefly, prime minister of Great Britain.

Methodism and socialism

John Wesley, and David Dale and New Lanark

John Wesley, the founder of Methodism, was the most charismatic and influential Christian in eighteenth-century Britain. Yet he made scant impact in Scotland. He preached more than 40,000 sermons and wrote over 400,000 tracts, treatises and texts. Described by one historian, himself a Methodist, as 'a Tory, a very English figure who never really wanted to quit the Church of England', he fell out spectacularly with the Anglican establishment. Church of England pulpits were denied to him, but that in itself hardly mattered, for he was more than happy to preach in the open air. There was something of the Covenanter in his personality and style, though not in his theology, for he totally rejected the notion of the Elect.

In his time, he was accused of fanaticism, superstition and excessive emotionalism. He preached a religion of the heart, not the head – yet, despite his forceful and potent appeal to feeling rather than thought, he was obsessed by what he regarded as the dangers inherent in human sexuality. He had a considerable influence on the early and rapidly growing industrial proletariat in England. This was partly predicated on the work of the Methodist Sunday Schools. Like the Jesuits, Wesley believed in getting at young souls.

Methodists also believed in work – very hard work, and plenty of it. Was he a godsend to employers? Possibly; yet eventually Methodism was to spawn a fair number of agitators, eloquent radicals and subversive activists. When new industrial communities, and indeed whole new towns and cities, were sprouting across northern England, the Methodists were there, providing powerful spiritual succour and a much-needed sense of community. For workers who had come from an agrarian background to an alien, dirty and often hellish environment, Methodism provided something that was at once physically comforting and spiritually consoling – despite the element of grimness that was always paradoxically present in Wesley's religion of the heart. He certainly provided something that the Anglican Church could not provide.

Wesley's version of Christianity was perfectly acceptable – indeed, you could argue, rather too acceptable – to the new breed of hard-faced industrial employers. Whether or not Wesley himself intended it, Methodism became associated with a certain submissiveness and an endorsement of hard work for its own sake. When political action was clearly required, Methodism sometimes seemed to promote the Christianity of non-resistance.

Wesley was a confused man of many apparent contradictions. As with John Calvin (whose theology he completely rejected), he wrote and preached so much that it is possible to find inconsistencies in his thought. He believed in witches. He condemned, with exceptional eloquence, the slave trade. He detested the amassing of vast personal wealth, yet he was often seen as the ally of factory-owners and mine-owners.

Wesley's declining years – the evening of his life of superhuman effort, of constant preaching and evangelisation – were the years when grievous and reckless industrialisation was scarring formerly rural landscapes. At this time, Methodism was weakening the Church of England, reviving Puritanism and – to some extent – giving succour to the new boss class.

Why did Methodism never take root in Scotland? One answer is that Wesley was a man who always needed to be in control. He could be excessively dictatorial. He sought to encourage Scottish Protestantism, but he also sought to manage it and mould it to his tastes. Scant chance of that. He did not accept the Scottish Protestant tradition of elders and kirk sessions.

More significantly, he was a strong opponent of the Calvinism that had been so influential in Scottish Christian thought; Wesley believed that Christ could love and save all, and not just the predetermined Elect. He consistently and fervently denied the doctrine of predestination. Although he visited Scotland more than 20 times, and felt that he was generally well received, he made very little difference to the spiritual life of the nation. At the time of his death in 1791, there were only about 1,000 practising Methodists in Scotland.

He had, naturally enough, been rejected by prominent Scottish Calvinists; and he had also provoked the notable enmity of a lady of considerable religious influence, the prominent evangelical aristocrat Lady Willielma Glenorchy, who had initially seemed well disposed to him. One of the few women to have influenced the development of Christianity in Scotland, this wealthy and determined aristocrat cultivated a retinue of personal chaplains, some of whom went on to careers in the Church of Scotland. Although gently ecumenical in disposition – her chapel in Edinburgh was theoretically open to Presbyterian and Methodist preachers – she soon became a foe of Methodism. After a difficult meeting with Wesley, Methodists were banned from her chapels.

She had founded these chapels to pursue her personal view of Christianity. When she died, she left a large bequest to the Society in Scotland for Propagating Christian Knowledge, which was particularly active in the Highlands – with mixed results. It was hostile to the use of Gaelic (although it did eventually accept the need for a Gaelic Bible) and to much of Highland culture. Its work could almost be regarded as a continuation of the British state's attempt to eradicate traditional Highland culture in the aftermath of Culloden. It does not say much for the supposedly democratic nature of Scottish Christianity that an aristocratic lady, however well intentioned, could exercise such eccentric and officious personal influence.

✄

The Wesleyan response to the incipient industrialisation in England was much better than that of most other Christians. To be fair to the established Anglican Church, it was out of its depth, not least because the rigid system of parishes proved wholly inadequate when so many towns were expanding so quickly. But that was essentially a technicality; overall, there was grievous indifference to the exploitation of the new proletariat. The Christian response to the march of industrialisation was far from impressive. In Scotland, there was one spectacular and early exception – in a most unlikely place.

David Dale and New Lanark

In the eighteenth century, some of the beautiful waterfalls on the River Clyde, in the vicinity of Lanark, were featured as scenic delights on the aristocratic Grand Tour. An 'aristocrat' of a very different kind from Lady Willielma, a Scottish industrial baron called David Dale – who was a good friend of the great Lancashire pioneer of cotton-spinning, Richard Arkwright – realised that this splendid section of the Clyde valley would be an ideal site to exploit water power for a new series of mills. In the 1780s, the two men embarked on a huge project to build what were to be the largest cotton mills in Britain and the most significant single industrial development in Scotland. Arkwright soon dropped out, but Dale built not only mills but also workshops, dyeworks, warehouses, accommodation for his workers and a model school.

By the 1790s, there were around 1,200 employees at Dale's site, hundreds of them children. As well as being an entrepreneur of genius, Dale was a benevolent and enlightened employer by the standards of his time. When there was a serious fire at one of the mills, he continued to pay the workers who were laid off until it had been rebuilt.

There is no doubt that Dale worked the children – many of whom were orphans – hard in his mills; but he also saw to their education and general welfare. They were well fed and clothed and were at school for at least two hours every day.

One view of David Dale is simply that he was the archetypal entrepreneur. He began as a weaver, built up a linen business and amassed enough capital and creditworthiness to embark on his great project. He was also a pragmatic Christian visionary, despite his refusal to allow religious teaching in his school. He always regarded the overall well-being of his workers, and their families, as a key priority.

In his own way, he was devout. He could read the Bible in Hebrew. He was an occasional lay preacher. He had quit the Church of Scotland to join one of the many minor independent secession churches. He was a pioneer of a model of practical Christianity that was ahead of its time; he was far more concerned with the welfare and well-being of his workers (and of course he had an economic interest in these; he was not a starry-eyed altruist) than with ensuring that they were subject to religious indoctrination. He might just have prevented the need for socialism – and indeed Christian socialism – had more factory and mill-owners followed his humane lead.

Dale showed that it was possible to be an innovative entrepreneur, a driver of industrial revolution and at the same time an effective Christian. Unfortunately, he was exceptional. As the eighteenth century closed and the nineteenth century – which saw Scotland transformed into a major industrial nation – began, there were all too few employers who were benign or progressive. Somehow, when it came to industrial development and expansion, Christianity went missing.

At New Lanark, however, the project continued. Dale's son-in-law, a Welshman called Robert Owen, took charge of Dale's growing business in 1800. Owen was not a Christian, though he eventually formed an interest in spiritualism. But his principles were similar to Dale's; he worked even harder to 'improve' his workforce, and he experimented with a kind of early, and almost utopian, socialism.

He took hold of his father-in-law's experiment and developed it with zest. He raised the starting age for full-time employment to 12, which allowed his young employees to be brought up on principles of encouragement rather than punishment. Also, with considerable social foresight, he opened a crèche, one of the world's first. In 1824, he left for America, leaving behind a remarkable project which, alas, was not copied elsewhere in Scotland.

New Lanark remains today a well-preserved tourist site that is one of the most fascinating visitor attractions in all Scotland. But the lingering sense of a lost opportunity permeates it. How was it that the great work of Dale and Owen did not lead to similar progressive projects elsewhere in Scotland? It was not as if the two men had not been successful in economic terms.

Too many Scottish mill-, mine- and factory-owners through the nineteenth century were nasty, cynical men who exploited their workers with a determination that bordered on organised cruelty.

And yet many, possibly most of them, claimed to be Christians. It took the great Keir Hardie, towards the end of the century, to fuse Christianity and socialism. His great political work might not have been necessary had more of the new capitalists followed the lead of Dale.

✠

At the time that Dale was doing great things at New Lanark, some Scots were involved in political agitation, prompted in part by the French Revolution. They tended to be middle-class intellectuals rather than members of the new proletariat. The most celebrated was Thomas Muir of Hunterhill, who was an advocate and came from a middle-class family. He was transported to Botany Bay, Australia, after a trial in which the celebrated judge, Lord Braxfield, was hardly a model of impartiality. Ironically, Braxfield owned some of the land on which Dale had built his mills; and the two men did various property deals.

Braxfield was hard-drinking and roughly spoken – indeed, he was later admired by Scott because he addressed his court in Scots. He was hardly an exemplar of Christian modesty and sobriety, yet he regarded himself as an excellent Christian man. His career was something of a crusade to puncture any notion of judges being austere figures of impeccable virtue. He swore in court, caroused out of it and was later used by R. L. Stevenson as the model of the 'bad father' in his unfinished novel *Weir of Hermiston.*

While the authorities were worried that the ideas of men such as Muir might be taken up by the workers, Scotland was hardly in a state of revolutionary fervour. But there was sufficient potential danger for the establishment to over-react. One of the key Crown witnesses against Muir was a kirk minister, James Lapslie, who was given a government pension for his pains, although in the event his evidence was disallowed.

The national Church was, at this stage in Scotland's history, fearful of revolution. The fresh air of the Enlightenment had given way to the fetid air of disillusion and fear. Ministers of the Kirk were among those who spoke out against political reform, which was somehow seen as un-Christian.

Of course, there were exceptions. An English Unitarian preacher, Thomas Fyshe Palmer, was convicted of serious sedition at Perth in 1793. But, for the most part, the forces of Christianity were very much on the side of the establishment, which was in a state of (unnecessary) near-panic.

The Disruption and the destruction of old Scotland

The Disruption of 1843 is one of the great set-piece events in Scottish Christianity, an event that somehow contrives to be largely forgotten while at the same time being a key component in how we Scots sometimes think of ourselves (that is, a people who will determinedly put principle before our own short-term interests).

In 1843, the General Assembly of the Church of Scotland was held in the Church of St Andrew in George Street, Edinburgh. It was disrupted – spectacularly and, many would say, magnificently – on 18 May, when nearly half of the ministers present walked out and processed northwards, down the steep hill to Canonmills, all the way cheered on by enthusiastic crowds, and there reconvened and in effect decided to found a new church.

In the course of a few hours, the official established Church lost around 40 per cent of its ministers; and it was soon to lose about a third of its congregations. The new 'free' church had no obvious funds, apart from the generosity of its members, many of whom were not particularly wealthy. It had to build new churches, create schools and – not least – provide for its ministers. It did so with spectacular speed and zest.

This was a cataclysmic moment in the religious life of Scotland. For many generations, the organised education of young people, the more general religious education of most of the population, social welfare and poor relief – all of these had in effect been the responsibility of the national Church, albeit at local level. The basic unit in Scottish society had been the parish church, with its minister and kirk session. Suddenly this national framework was smashed, and a new more pluralist dispensation arrived. Although for a few more generations Scotland was to remain, for the most part, a

Presbyterian nation, the country's rapidly growing population was now presented with much more choice in what remained, for so many Scots, the most fundamental issue of all: religion. As a result, Scotland became much less communal and less able to respond to the huge social pressures presented by mass industrialisation.

At the same time, we should remember, as ever, the chronic fissile tendency of Scottish Protestantism. Secession was hardly a new phenomenon. Exactly 100 years earlier, there had been a significant secession from the national Church, led by Ebenezer Erskine. And, 43 years prior to that, at the time of the formal restoration of Presbyterianism, both the Episcopalians and the remaining Covenanters had, from very different standpoints, refused to have anything to do with the new official brand of Protestantism. Rupture, secession and disruption were not new. But what happened in 1843 was both spectacular and calamitous.

The issue that prompted the dramatic – and undoubtedly honourable – walkout was the vexed one of patronage, which had scarred and divided the national Kirk for a long time and was to continue to do so. In essence, the great issue was whether ministers were to be appointed democratically by the congregations, or non-democratically by a patron, which generally meant a local bigwig such as the principal landowner. Sometimes these landowners flaunted their influence in an unseemly and ungodly way by building special extensions and showy appendages to the local church, so that they could enter separately and could worship in considerable comfort, which was denied to other Christians lower down the social pecking order.

There had been a series of disputes about the ending of this patronage – something the early reformers had certainly not wanted – but it had been legalised in 1712 as an unfortunate amendment to the Act of Union of 1707. Eventually, in the 1830s, the issue became, in effect, a rancid row between the national Church, which increasingly wanted to end patronage, and the British state, through the London Parliament, which insisted on maintaining the principle of patronage. The struggle within the Church itself was between the conformist, politically conservative supporters of the state, and the ever more vocal radical wing led by the charismatic Thomas Chalmers, who had at first been a somewhat lukewarm evangelical. He was now Professor of Divinity at Edinburgh University and was the most charismatic early-Victorian Christian in Scotland.

Unfortunately, the events of this particular day in 1843 ensured that neither the old Church of Scotland nor the new Free Church, in which Chalmers was to be a leading figure, was able to undertake the necessary outreach to the rapidly growing industrial underclass. Undoubtedly radical in some respects, the evangelicals were often less urbane and more narrowly focused than their opponents; many of them looked back in awe and admiration to the era of the Covenanters. Anyway, the stand-off could not continue, and it was in the beautiful Church of St Andrew in Edinburgh that it finally reached the point of no return.

The walkout has sometimes been represented as an act of amazing heroism. Well, up to a point. A lot of intelligent and devout people gave up their homes and their stipends on a point of principle. The Revd Dr Thomas Brown, in his superb *Annals of the Disruption* (1884), recalled that the children and wives of the ministers who walked out could be seen weeping as they caught sight of a husband or father 'accomplishing an act which was to leave his family homeless and unprovided'. The children and wives cried 'with warm tear drops'; but then 'the hand of faith was in haste to wipe away'.

The grand gesture of the mass walkout was probably inevitable; it followed a decade of increasingly bitter agitation. Some of those who quit the Assembly had expected to be in the majority; indeed, some of them had confidently expected that they would be able to force the Assembly to defy the government of the day, the House of Lords and the Scottish Court of Session, all of whom had refused to end the rights of individual patrons. It did not work out that way.

The Kirk of St Andrew was completely full; and outside, in George Street, thousands waited, expecting drama. They were not to be disappointed. After the convening of the Assembly, and prayers, the retiring Moderator, David Walsh, a Professor of Church History, decided it was time to make some history himself. He left the Kirk, followed by Thomas Chalmers, the leader of the dissidents. It is not certain how many other ministers immediately followed them; probably about 140. Around 70 elders joined them.

In George Street, they were joined by many more dissident ministers and elders who had not been official participants at the Assembly. This large throng managed to gain some kind of order, and it processed northwards, about half a mile down the hill to the Canonmills area, to a building in Tanfield that had previously been a gasworks and was later to be a newspaper office. At this point in its chequered history, it was serving as a public hall. There, amid acclaim, several hundred ministers of the Church of Scotland signed a deed that amounted to their formal resignation from 'the ecclesiastical establishment of Scotland'.

These men did indeed willingly give up their manses, their stipends – and of course their individual parish churches. Thus the new Free Church of Scotland was born. It testified to very considerable self-belief and the potential for even more considerable self-sacrifice, in a significant minority of Scotland's Christians. But was there just a little too much self-belief? Had there not been scope for a sensible compromise? By that I don't mean fudge, but rather a short-term bridging deal that would have given the national Church a little time to mount a final attempt to persuade the temporal powers that patronage was wholly unacceptable.

There had been 1,195 ministers in the national Church; 455 of them joined the new church. Around 40 per cent of the membership of the old church, and as many as 50 per cent of the eldership, joined too. More than 400 teachers, mainly from Church of Scotland parish schools, also signed up to the new church.

There followed a vibrant period of fundraising and building. An entirely new religious organisation had been created, and very soon it had its new churches, schools and a magnificent seminary – New College, the twin-towered building high above Princes Street Gardens. At about the same time, another new church had been created: the smaller United Presbyterian Church. This, however, was the result of a rationalisation rather than a new split: it was the coming together of various small churches and groups that had seceded over several generations.

The energy of the new Free Church in the first few years was focused and prodigious. By the end of the 1840s – that is, within a mere seven years of the walkout – more than 600 new churches had been built. The enthusiasm, the selflessness, the philanthropy: these were all heroic. Eight years after the Disruption, a religious census showed that Scotland's third city, Aberdeen, had 43 'places of Christian Worship'. Of these, the Free Church, which eight years earlier had had none, now had 15. The national Church of Scotland had seven; the Episcopal Church had two; the Roman Catholics had one. The United Presbyterians had five. 'Independents' had six. There were also places of worship for Baptists, Unitarians, Methodists, Congregationalists, Glasites (a sect who followed John Glas of Tealing) and so on.

All this division meant a confusing surfeit of choice. There was a most unfortunate downside. The old model of the parish state of Scotland had been destroyed, while the democratic, egalitarian aspects of Scottish society that had achieved much since the Scottish Reformation were now in tatters, broken for ever. I write 'egalitarian'; but of course it had not been egalitarian enough. The bitter irritant of patronage had not been dealt with; the national Church had been too weak and too deferential to the secular powers, and sometimes far too grovelling to local landowners and grandees. For the time being, the new church held the moral high ground. But at a cost; Scotland's very identity had been torn asunder. And sadly, the splendid model, combining worship, education, social responsibility and social welfare, the model that John Knox and his colleagues had fought so hard for, was suddenly smashed, and it would never be pieced back together.

Meanwhile, in England, many intelligent, liberal people gazed at the events in Scotland with a bemused incomprehension. Their incomprehension could be justified, for Scotland lost a great deal. Indeed, it was never to be the same; something of its soul and spirit was lost. Far too much energy was spent on a Herculean but ultimately frivolous effort to create the physical reality of the new Free Church with all its new buildings – many of them very splendid ones. There was in this a deeply unpleasant element of competitive ostentation. At first, the dissidents worshipped in 'barns and stables, old mills and granaries, wool stores and malt barns, cart sheds and saw pits, and tents', according to Dr Brown. 'All kinds of accommodation were welcome anywhere, under a roof that could give shelter; when everything else failed, then the open air, among the green fields and glens. Amid such strange surroundings hundreds of thousands of the most earnest minds in Scotland came together for the worship of God!'

This was, according to the ever-enthusiastic Dr Brown, 'a spectacle such as no country in modern times has witnessed'. But soon most of these 'earnest minds' had their fine new church buildings and manses, schools and colleges. It was a great time to be an ecclesiastical architect.

There can be little doubt that those who had walked away from the old Church excelled in building; not just churches, but also other spectacular creations such as David Bryce's great Assembly Hall (1858–60) and, much later, at the beginning of the twentieth century, the grandiose office block that housed the United Free Church offices. Both these buildings were reclaimed by the national Church after the great reunion of 1929.

In the early Victorian era, when the Disruption occurred, Scotland was on the brink of social catastrophe, and it urgently needed a wise and organised Christian response to cope. The response never came.

Already, the danger signs were there for the socially aware to see. In the years immediately before the Disruption, there had been a major strike by cotton-spinners, and serious riots in Paisley – as well as the hellish ongoing saga of the Clearances in the Highlands. As early as 1832, and then again in the 1840s, Glasgow was ravaged by appalling outbreaks of both typhus and cholera. Opium was sometimes used to mitigate the symptoms of cholera, but many thousands died horrible deaths from the acute effects of dehydration. Lack of proper sanitation, and the grievous exploitation of young child workers – some of them as young as 5 – by cynical, greedy 'masters' were perhaps the worst of the many specific social ills.

The rise of the new industrial city or town was an incredibly rapid and almost inadvertent process. A colossal new urban population was created in a couple of generations. Any notion of effective planning or regulation was almost entirely absent. Even worse, any proper sense of organised social responsibility, which you would have expected the Christian churches to sustain, was also absent.

This left a rapidly growing population of acutely impoverished folk, many of them permanently ill, who were unchurched and largely uneducated. Many of these human beings, including, worst of all, very young children, had to work in appalling conditions and live – in the little time they had left each week – in even worse conditions.

Efforts were made, of course they were: there were bursts of revivalist evangelism; the growing temperance movement made some inroads into places where others couldn't or wouldn't reach; there were, here and there, 'mission schools'. Slowly it dawned that the missionary effort in distant lands was perhaps somewhat irrelevant; the work was required back home. But the main Scottish churches could not sustain in the face of the challenge, and it was often the smaller, less fashionable churches and minor denominations and groups, like the Baptists or the Band of Hope, that dealt more effectively and more charitably with the rise of an ill-treated and cynically exploited proletariat. The middle classes became the guardians of both the old national Church and the new Free Church; the growing working class had to look elsewhere for both spiritual and practical succour.

Later, there was some focused effort, channelled through the likes of 'parish societies' and organised parish visitations. Interdenominational town missions – notably the Glasgow City Mission – were established, and they employed and organised home missionaries. These missionaries were rightly concerned with much more than mission worship; they engaged in practical support, especially for the destitute. But the scale of the ongoing housing and health crisis and the systematic exploitation of workers (thousands upon thousands of them children) rendered such commendable effort as almost irrelevant. The social crisis was colossal and continuing.

At last, the state, erratically, belatedly and bureaucratically, swung into action. After Edwin Chadwick's seminal report on *The Sanitary Condition of the Labouring Population of Great*

Britain in 1842, public health became a matter of pressing concern for UK governments; and legislation followed. In education, where the reformed Church of Scotland had done such magnificent work over almost three centuries, the state took longer to intervene effectively. Education was becoming the prerogative of the middle classes.

At last, in 1872, the Education (Scotland) Act gave the country an organised national system of schooling. Schools were now to be financed by both taxation and local rates. If church schools did not transfer into the new bureaucracy, then neither the national government nor the local rates would support them. A new and quaintly named 'Scotch Education Department' was created to oversee all this. Ludicrously, it was situated in London. Meanwhile, with one or two exceptions, education for Roman Catholic boys and girls remained outside the state's orbit – for another 46 years. The Church of Scotland managed to ensure that there was a reasonable input of Christian education in the schools, but the essential fact was that education had been transferred from the Kirk to the state.

The continuing inadequacy of the practical Christian response to the exploitation of labour, grievously inadequate housing, and much else, left a gap that only a political as opposed to a religious creed – socialism – seemed able to fill.

If the national Church had not split in two in 1843, would things have been as bad? Prior to 1843, the parish model was already under strain and might well have been unable to cope. The notion of one blessed nation uniquely covenanted with God was also under strain. Ironically, what rendered matters much worse than they need have been was the sustained energy and enterprise that went into the creation of the new Free Church. For a brief period, this enormous release of focused financial and building effort made Scotland look as if Christianity was still strong; according to the census in 1851, a third of the population attended church each Sunday. There was even a revival in the 1860s. But an insidious general decline had set in despite, or perhaps more likely because of, the huge diverting outpouring of effort that was lavished on the creation and sustenance of the Free Church.

At times, there seemed to be an unseemly rivalry between the old and new churches; who had the best buildings, the biggest manses? Scotland now had not one but two great Protestant organisations, rivals and competitors in terms of bricks and mortar. Had this exceptional energy, over a couple of generations, been devoted instead to practical Christian work among the ever-growing numbers of the impoverished, unchurched and exploited poor, then things might have been rather different and rather better.

⬦

I am a member of the church where the Disruption started; now it is called the parish church of St Andrew and St George. It houses a 'gathered' congregation; that is, people come to the services from all over Edinburgh, and indeed beyond, implying a certain consumerism. This beautiful building in George Street, Edinburgh (designed by Major Andrew Frazer, Scottish Engineer-in-chief of the Royal Engineers) is much used. There are three services each Sunday – the first, at 9am, is a simple communion service with no music, just prayer, a short but challenging sermon, a Bible reading and the always moving ceremony of the communion itself. During this service, I always feel that the church is at its best: the worship is plain, straightforward and very much to the point.

The church is also used for concerts, debates, talks and other events; and it is the site of an enormously successful annual fundraising event for Christian Aid that harnesses the very varied talents and abilities of the congregation (and many others) to excellent effect. Over £100,000 is raised each year.

This is one of the loveliest churches in all Scotland (it has actually been described as the most beautiful church in Europe) – but, although it was recently refurbished and refreshed, there is still no plaque, outside or in, to signify that this is where the Great Disruption commenced.

Three exceptional Victorians

Thomas Carlyle, David Livingstone and Keir Hardie

Thomas Carlyle

Thomas Carlyle, probably the greatest Scottish writer of the nine-teenth century, was, like Hugh MacDiarmid – who is arguably the greatest Scottish writer of the twentieth century – born very near the border with England. This rendered them both strongly Scottish, more conscious of their Scottishness than they might otherwise have been. Carlyle, however, spent most of his career in London, while MacDiarmid stayed in Scotland.

Carlyle could well have chosen religion, but he chose literature instead. But he wrote with a great moral force which was in its own way religious, if not overtly Christian. One of his first coher-ent pieces of writing was a sermon, composed when he was 14. Carlyle enjoyed immense intellectual status in London; his cerebral eminence was colossal but is difficult to categorise. He was often referred to as a 'sage', which will do. He was a thinker, historian, commentator and polemicist. For a time, he was the darling of the early Victorian intelligentsia. Of course, 'darling' is in some ways an inappropriate word; in persona, Carlyle was craggy, grim and dyspeptic. Nothing about him was easy.

He was born in 1795 in Ecclefechan, a village in eastern Dumfriesshire. His parents were deeply committed Christians; and although Carlyle, as his enormous intellect developed, lost his belief in their belief, he retained immense respect for it. His father, James, was a stonemason and small-time farmer, and a member of the Burgher Secessionists – one of the many minor churches that seceded from the Church of Scotland in the eight-eenth century.

Thomas was brought up in a happy (if very earnest and very hard-working) household where a rigorous Calvinism was practised. J. A. Froude, who wrote a celebrated four-volume biography of Carlyle, described him as 'a Calvinist without the theology' – whereas his father had imbibed the theology, perhaps excessively.

Carlyle benefited greatly from the rigorous and democratic education system that had been bequeathed to his country by the Scottish Reformation in the 1560s. He went to the local school in Ecclefechan, and then on to the nearby Annan Grammar School, and from there to Edinburgh University when he was just 13; he was always intellectually precocious. He walked to Edinburgh, a distance of almost 100 miles. He studied, among other things, physics, maths, logic, Greek and Latin.

James hoped and expected that his son would duly become a minister of his church. Carlyle did undertake a part-time course in divinity but decided to become a teacher, though he soon rejected the profession – and also his father's religion. He had in part been influenced by the Enlightenment and its scepticism about religion. Yet he was deeply spiritual, and he could not reject religion totally. His spiritual needs pulled him one way, his intellectual brilliance another. This tension produced some agonised writing, and he remained a tormented, anguished man. Indeed, some of his writing was more than tormented; it was downright sinister, and he has been seen as an intellectual precursor of fascism.

He found at least some fulfilment in his marriage; his wife, Jane Welsh of Haddington, was a warm and intelligent woman, though she was never her husband's intellectual equal. Their marriage was sexually sterile, and there were no children, but in many ways it was very happy. For a time, they lived in Comely Bank, Edinburgh; then in a rather grim farmhouse at Craigenputtock near Corsock in Dumfriesshire; then they moved to London, where Carlyle, through his copious writing and lecturing, rapidly became a celebrity. Jane was convivial, and their house in Chelsea became famous for what might be called salons; Jane was a warm hostess, while Carlyle played the role of the great thinker delivering memorable table talk.

Meanwhile, he wrote history – notably *The French Revolution* – and biography – notably *Frederick the Great* – but it was as a critic of his times that he excelled. The Industrial Revolution had brought in its wake wretchedness and social fragmentation – as well as prosperity for some. Carlyle was brilliant in his onslaughts against the wreckage of the first industrial society, though he was less effective, in the long term, than his contemporaries Engels and Marx. But despite, or possibly because of, his earnest and hectoring style, he had a vast range of admirers. Some of those who claimed he had influenced them were unexpected figures such as the Catholic poet Gerard Manley Hopkins and the pioneering socialist Keir Hardie.

Yet Carlyle was never involved in practical politics; he was a thinker rather than a doer. He was enormously angry at the inability of the Christian churches to respond to the bitter economic and social crisis of the times. In his quest for a renewed social morality, he almost invented a new kind of religion. He awoke the Victorian conscience – a profound moral force. He was a deeply serious man who detested what he called 'expatriated spiritualism' and 'prurient imbecilities'. His tone could be impossibly lofty. In his portentous way, he both patronised the huge new working class, visiting on the massed ranks of workers a cerebral seriousness rather than a direct political route to betterment, while at the same time alerting the middle classes to their plight. But he continued to reject conventional Christianity, whereas the likes of John Wesley tried to make Christianity relevant to and for the workers.

Gradually, Victorian England, which had fêted Carlyle, began to ignore if not to reject him. He no longer enjoyed the status of an unassailable guru. It had been proposed that he should be buried in Westminster Abbey; instead, he was quietly buried in the churchyard at Ecclefechan. He is hardly remembered now. Even so, he is probably better remembered than he would have been had he, as his father had hoped, become a great Protestant cleric.

David Livingstone

If Carlyle's life was one of titanic intellectual effort, David Livingstone's was one of titanic physical effort. He was, supremely, a man of action, a boys' hero in the traditional mould; a man who would never flinch from a journey, however arduous, into the unknown.

Born in Blantyre on Clydeside 18 years after the birth of Carlyle, Livingstone was to become a very distinguished explorer and a somewhat less distinguished missionary. Like Carlyle, he gained Victorian celebrity status. (Sometimes the notion of 'celebrity' is regarded as a modern phenomenon. Far from it.) And his celebrity has proved to be far more durable than Carlyle's. Intellectually, Livingstone was the lesser man; but in terms of personal dynamism, physical resolution and the ability to create a cult, he was infinitely superior. He was genuinely if straightforwardly religious; unlike Carlyle, he never rejected his inherited religion, though he adapted it for his own ends.

His belief in Jesus Christ was simple, sincere and steadfast. He dedicated his life and work to 'My Jesus, my King, my Life, my All'. Despite this, he was by no means a saint. He married Mary Moffat, the daughter of a prominent missionary, but proved to be a somewhat neglectful husband and father. He was capable of both vindictiveness and duplicity.

He is still fêted in many parts of Africa, not least for his persistent and noble opposition to the slave trade. He was supremely a man of action, but he did have his cerebral side; as a boy, he was capable of studying hard while working very long shifts in the local cotton mill. His father, Neil, was a stern Calvinist of Highland stock; his mother came from a Lowland, Covenanting background.

Neil was something of a domestic bully, and his Calvinism verged on the brutish; but, while the young Livingstone would occasionally weep privately (by his own account) because he could not believe that he was one of the Elect, these early traumas do not seem to have affected his adult faith. Altogether, David was an industrious and earnest adolescent, though he tested himself against his very stern father, and he did rebel directly against Neil on the matter of religion. He and his father became much closer after they went to hear a revivalist Congregationalist preacher, Ralph Wardlaw from Dalkeith, preach in Hamilton. They both joined the Independent church there, and this meant that they were reconciled.

Neil had first rejected his son's early interest in science as ungodly, but Livingstone persevered on his own path; perseverance was his hallmark characteristic. His wide reading as an adolescent, in particular the works of Dr Thomas Dick, enabled him to reconcile science and religion; and eventually his father accepted this.

David studied medicine in Glasgow and then trained as a missionary with the London Missionary Society. He was ordained in 1840, and he first set foot in Africa in 1841. His huge fame was based primarily on three magnificent and very long journeys (totalling over 30,000 miles) in which he showed enormous resilience and almost superhuman determination. He relished exploring in difficult conditions, noting that 'the sheer animal pleasure of travelling in a wild unexplored country is very great'.

He was a determined self-publicist, but we should not be too sceptical about his accounts of his adventures. His celebrated book *Missionary Travels and Researches in South Africa* is notable for its detailed scientific observations. His expeditions were characterised by careful note-taking. He was also a skilled navigator, though he did make some serious errors. Above all, he empathised with the Africans he met and worked with; he seems to have been a man totally devoid of racist prejudice. There can be little doubt that his faith underpinned his rejection of slavery and his empathy for the people of Africa.

He has been accused of being a kind of proxy agent for British colonialisation; but, if there is any truth in this, it is simply because he sometimes thought, rightly or wrongly, that colonisation would aid the spread of Christianity. The case against colonisation was that it was part of a wider and arrogant imperial project. It would dilute native culture, if not destroy it. To be fair to Livingstone, he wanted to work with the grain of native culture, not against it; he also thought, perhaps naïvely, that commerce and Christianity could work together to create a better Africa. He may have formally converted surprisingly few Africans to Christianity; but, in his approach to Africa and Africans, he showed himself to be a strong and consistent foe of racist oppression. His fellow explorer H. M. Stanley noted how he saw in Africans virtue where others saw only savagery.

Like Thomas Carlyle, Livingstone was acclaimed in London. Unlike Carlyle, his fame lasted, and indeed grew, after his death – and even now he retains the cult status of an authentic Scottish hero. His life, and in particular his heroic exploits in Africa, helped to refute any notion that Scotland was an introverted, self-obsessed nation. Of course, Scots migrated right across the globe, and played their part as builders and maintainers of the Empire; but in Livingstone the nation could claim a single iconic figure whose expansive life spoke constantly of questing outwards and beyond, of ever-widening horizons.

Livingstone also possessed an empathy for Africa and Africans that was the exact antithesis of the worst kind of colonialism, which was marred by a racist scorn for the colonised. He defended the rights of native Africans to fight for their own territories, and he attacked British colonial policy when he believed that it was misguided. One twentieth-century African statesman, Kenneth Kaunda, described him as a 'freedom fighter'. In Scotland's preferred idea of itself, Livingstone's life and work became, and remain, a key component.

Keir Hardie

Keir Hardie, the most significant of the founding fathers of the movement that was to become the British Labour Party, has probably attracted more myths, and possibly more downright invention, than any other Scottish political figure. What is indisputable is that he became a man of strong Christian convictions, which in turn had a great influence on his burgeoning socialist ideology.

Yet he was never a man for organised, conventional Christianity. His Christianity was never consensual or conciliatory. He was happy to attack other Christians if he thought they were hypocrites, as he often did. He grew up in an environment where most workers disliked or even despised ministers, who were identified with the boss class.

Churches were not welcoming places for the poor, who were often weary to the point of exhaustion and demoralised after long shifts in appalling conditions. The pernicious system of pew rents, which were only gradually phased out through the nineteenth century, made some churches especially unwelcoming. And his Christianity was very personal; some objected to it as being too romantic, humane and inclusive. Hardie had little time for doctrinal disputation or theological semantics.

Keir Hardie was born in 1858 out of wedlock and was always an outsider, both in religion and in politics. In persona, he was something of a loner. He said that 'companionship is good, but solitude is best'. Unlike Livingstone and Carlyle, he was not brought up in a Christian home. His mother, Mary Keir, worked sporadically as a maid in the Holytown–Newhouse area. She was a strong, industrious woman; she married David Hardie, a carpenter, and the family moved to Glasgow.

Keir's early life – the childhood he never had, as he later put it – was one of unremitting toil. From a very young age, he worked at various menial jobs. Eventually, he became a pit boy at Newarthill, working 75 hours a week underground. He worked in the mines from the age of ten, finally quitting when he was 23. At that time, safety in the pits was a sick joke. Hardie saw men and boys injured, maimed and occasionally killed.

In his teens, Keir became a devout Christian and also a convinced advocate of temperance. The two were closely linked; he joined the Good Templars temperance movement and took the pledge. This was when he began to mingle with evangelical Christians. The Good Templars were broad-minded; their Christianity was not sectarian. They had a huge influence on the adolescent Hardie.

The temperance movement was not filled with grim killjoys; far from it. Hardie gained from its fellowship, though he always had something of the puritan in his make-up; and, although he was a warm and at times fiery man, he could behave like a prig. He hated smutty jokes; and colleagues sometimes found him self-righteous.

He tried to form a miners' union but was blacklisted by the Lanarkshire pit-owners. Then he worked, sporadically, as a journalist and a labour organiser. In his early political career, Hardie was a Liberal. (After all, Karl Marx – no less – had called the Liberals the most progressive party in the world.) But he rapidly became disillusioned. Pit-owners, who exploited their men without mercy or restraint, were often prominent Liberals. Hardie eventually stood for election in the constituency of mid-Lanarkshire – not for the Liberals but for 'Independent Labour'. He did not win very many votes. His response was to found, formally, the Scottish Labour Party. He was now a committed and fierce socialist.

The former prime minister, Gordon Brown, once noted that Hardie's socialism owed far more to religion than to economics. Hardie himself wrote: 'Socialism is a handmaiden of religion and as such is entitled to the support of all who pray for the coming of Christ on Earth'. That is a very significant quotation. Hardie's Christianity fused with his socialism in a most potent way as he became a relentless, driven agitator. He never advocated violence, and he rejected any notion of class warfare. As he said, he was fighting a system, not a class. He was a heroic, relentless foe of the existing order, but he was never a revolutionary. He believed passionately in the efficacy of strikes and industrial militancy.

Some regarded him as a fanatic, some as a mere rabble-rouser; more discerning observers saw in this fervent man, with his rugged, bearded appearance and his challenging, revivalist oratory, a man who was much deeper and far more dangerous to the established order. He worked with enormous persistence for Labour representation in Parliament. His career took him to England, and in 1892 he was elected to represent the constituency of West Ham as an independent Labour MP. The following year saw the formal formation of the Independent Labour Party, the parent of the present-day Labour Party.

Hardie's Christian legacy may be seen in the work of great socialist ministers such as James Barr, who eventually became a Labour MP. Before that, as a Free Church minister in various Glasgow parishes, he sought to evangelise the unchurched working class; he campaigned for socialism, pacifism and Home Rule for Scotland. He deeply disapproved of the national Church of Scotland's close links with the upper middle classes.

Others who were influenced by Hardie included the great Glasgow teacher and revolutionary John Maclean, who was appointed by Lenin as the Bolshevik Consul for Scotland. Sometimes, he invoked

Jesus Christ when addressing mass meetings of workers. When a group of ten newly elected 'Red Clydeside' Independent Labour MPs set off from Glasgow for the House of Commons, the scene at St Enoch Station was more like a revivalist Christian meeting. Psalms were sung heartily by the socialist crowd.

As far back as 1884, Hardie had been involved in angry arguments with the Cumnock Congregational Church in Ayrshire; he was always disputatious. From that point on, his Christianity, like his politics, was marked by a defiant individualism. He was, supremely, an independent spirit. His religion was idiosyncratic and personal. He criticised almost all the Christian denominations of his day for their timidity and time-serving.

Hardie died of pneumonia when he was only 59, angry and appalled by the First World War, and utterly spent after a noble life of constant agitation and struggle. He had little time for economic theory, and indeed he tended to scorn academic learning; he preferred an evangelical, almost messianic, approach to politics. He utterly detested unemployment and social injustice, and denounced them with consistent, powerful passion. He also embraced the nascent women's movement and became a supporter and friend of leading suffragettes. In the way he combined Christianity and socialism, he was an enormously influential, even symbolic, figure; his life was one of protest, of anger, of constant, almost divine outrage. Compromise was alien to him.

Hardie could hardly comprehend the idea of living a life without religion. As for his approach to politics, it now seems curiously old-fashioned – possibly because it was essentially religious in its fervour, and we live in secular times. He is not given his due in modern Scotland, despite the colossal hold that the Labour Party held for so long in parts of the country, particularly west central Scotland. He does not have a place in the general pantheon of Scottish heroes, as Livingstone undoubtedly does and Carlyle possibly does. Perhaps this is because some have felt that he was too quick to 'move on' from Scotland when he took his political fight to London.

In the 1980s, the eminent Scottish writer and savant Allan Massie produced a series of brilliant essays on the 101 greatest Scots (his choice). His reflections were insightful and sharp. Sadly, he did not include Keir Hardie among the 101; a grievous omission, in my opinion.

⌧

There is a paradox in these three lives. Carlyle, who early on lost his faith, was in some ways the traditional firebrand preacher, telling (with considerable pertinence) his society exactly where it was going wrong. He did this when the Victorians were struggling, collectively, with their Christian faith; doubts were rapidly growing in intellectual circles, not least because of the increasing popularity of science.

Yet Livingstone, who was much more of a practical scientist than Carlyle ever was, stuck doggedly to his straightforward Christian beliefs. He, like his father, had quit the Church of Scotland for an independent congregation; that journey, very common in Scottish religious life, was the nearest he ever came to religious revolt. His Christianity was serene and confident; some might say complacent. It was of a piece with his head-on approach to life; he was not one for extended internal soul-searching, though he did occasionally suffer from depression.

In other respects, Carlyle and Livingstone were very similar. They were driven men, full of self-belief, the one an authentic prophet, the other a heroic man of action; and their undoubted strength and resolution were rooted in the stern Calvinism of their formative years in Scotland. Both of them left Scotland, as did Keir Hardie, eventually; but the departures of Carlyle and Livingstone were more connected with personal ambition.

Hardie, who was ultimately a far more significant figure than either Carlyle or Livingstone, was not only *not* brought up as a Christian; he came to politics and Christianity at about the same time, and each massively influenced the other in his development. This fusion of politics and Christianity was a very Scottish process. But his Christianity was never soft or complacent: he detested the smugness of much middle-class Christianity in Scotland. Indeed, Hardie was the agitator supreme, the man who wanted to lead the exploited and the bereft to the Promised Land. He was sometimes compared with Jesus Christ; and I'm pretty certain that neither Carlyle nor Livingstone ever had that particular honour. Hardie sometimes invoked the Garden of Gethsemane, and also Christ's crucifixion, in his impromptu public speeches.

The man who followed him as leader of the Labour movement, another Scot, Ramsay MacDonald, described him, perhaps more realistically, as a latter-day Moses. His actual quote was: 'Hardie will stand out forever as the Moses who led the children of labour in our country out of their bondage'.

Jesus, Moses, whoever; Hardie undoubtedly possessed a charged and vital Christian fervour. He was driven by his passion to change lives and to change society; a passion that was Biblical in its intensity and went beyond anything Carlyle or Livingstone sought to do. Hardie apparently read Carlyle's writings with admiration; but Carlyle was essentially an aloof figure, happiest in the study or the reading room, whereas Hardie's natural habitat was the street corner or the community hall or the pithead – or even the moors.

Indeed, he greatly admired the Covenanters and empathised with their bravery and resolution as they were hunted and harried across the wild uplands of Lanarkshire and Ayrshire. At least once he addressed a miners' meeting on open moorland; the atmosphere was no doubt reminiscent of a seventeenth-century conventicle. As for Livingstone, his quintessential territory was probably some hitherto unexplored part of Africa.

Hardie remained much more of an outsider than either Carlyle or Livingstone, and in that particular respect it is not in any way blasphemous to compare him to Jesus Christ. And it cannot be stressed enough that his Christianity was the bedrock of his socialism. He was one of the very greatest Scots, and a fine, prophetic Christian man.

PART 4

Literature

Scotland as hell

George Douglas Brown and John MacDougall Hay

In the later Victorian era, Scottish literature was besmirched – I use the word advisedly – by a group of writers who produced what came to be known as 'Kailyard' fiction. It was unashamedly saccharine and, as far as I'm concerned, virtually unreadable. In its favour was the fact that the writers tried to look benevolently on the world, whereas some of the best Scottish fiction of the following century was to be characterised by an almost malevolent ferocity. In part, Kailyard was a reaction against the rapid industrialisation of much of Scotland, and the appalling social consequences. The Kailyarders were doggedly determined to look on the sunny side of the street, however grim the street might really be.

The two most successful exponents of Kailyard, S. R. Crockett and Ian Maclaren, were both Free Church ministers. The Free Church of Scotland was not always known for sickly sentimentality, but these gentlemen did their best to redress the balance. They preferred to look on the softer side of life, and their fiction often dealt with the mundane lives of rural ministers. Crockett was undoubtedly the better of the two; and, as I write, he is undergoing something of a critical revival.

The principal patron of the Kailyard writers was a cleric from north-east Scotland, the Revd William Nicoll, who made good in London as the founder and editor of the *British Weekly*. Nicoll had inherited from his father, also a Free Kirk minister, an impressive library, which Nicoll cherished. There can be no doubting his interest in books and his encouragement of writers. Also connected with the Kailyard school – half in, half out – was a writer of authentic substance, J. M. Barrie. Meanwhile, it is important to note that a great benefit of the Kailyard was that it produced a reaction – and what a reaction!

Two novels in particular led the ferocious response: *The House with the Green Shutters* by George Douglas Brown, and John MacDougall Hay's masterpiece, *Gillespie*. These two novels, both redoubtable pieces of fiction, were nothing like as popular as the effusions of the Kailyard ministers. Indeed, *Gillespie* has always struggled to find any readers, while the Kailyard writers were adored by the public and still have many enthusiastic readers. Maclaren's *Beside the Bonnie Brier Bush* (the title says a lot) sold over 750,000 copies in the UK and the USA.

Meanwhile, it diminishes both *The House with the Green Shutters* and *Gillespie*, superb novels as they are, to present them as mere reactions – for some, over-reactions – to the Kailyard school. Brown and Hay were undoubtedly reacting against excessive literary sentimentality; on the other hand, they would, I'm certain, have written novels full of gloom and doom whether or not the Kailyarders had preceded them.

George Douglas Brown

George Douglas Brown's early life was very similar to that of Keir Hardie. He was the illegitimate son of a small farmer and a dairy maid in rural Ayrshire. As a wee boy, he was known as 'Smudden's bastard', Smudden being his father's nickname. Brown left school too soon and went off to work in the pit at Tarbolton, Ayrshire. His old teacher managed to save him from life as a miner: he went to Ayr Academy and on to Glasgow and Oxford universities. He was by all accounts a brilliant scholar, but he was uneasy at Oxford and could only manage a third-class degree. He then, with difficulty, earned his living as a literary journalist while writing his masterpiece.

The House with the Green Shutters is beautifully structured. If anything, it is too short. Brown's life was certainly too short: he died of pneumonia at the age of 32. At least he was able to enjoy the success of his one novel; it was very well received. Indeed, the warmth of its reception indicated that Scotland, at the close of the Victorian era, was sick of sentimentality.

The House with the Green Shutters is a relentless story of a self-made entrepreneur called John Gourlay. Brutish as Gourlay is, he towers above the simpering wretches who monitor his doings with spite and malice. Brown's portrait of the sheer nastiness that could fester in small-town Scotland is devastating. Gourlay's wife and son are locked in conflict with him; the novel builds to a violent climax when, emboldened by drink, Gourlay's son kills his father. The son then takes his own life; and Gourlay's wife and daughter also commit suicide, having first consoled themselves by reading St Paul.

John MacDougall Hay

If *The House with the Green Shutters*, Brown's one novel, was grim and melodramatic, it is none the less the gentlest of aperitifs before the perhaps excessively strong meat that is John MacDougall Hay's *Gillespie*. This is my favourite Scottish novel – though, for reasons I've never been able to fathom, *Gillespie* has the unfortunate status of an ignored and shamefully neglected masterpiece. It did not help, certainly, that it was published in 1914, just before the calamitous First World War broke out – and so, although the contemporary reviews were very positive, it was unsurprising that it did not make the impact it was due then.

Almost 50 years later, the distinguished dramatist and man of letters Robert Kemp attempted to build interest in this forgotten masterwork; he arranged for it to be reissued in 1963. This, sadly, again made little impact, but it was the edition I read a year or so later as a teenager. By then, the book was once again disappearing into obscurity.

A few years later, in 1972, when I was working on the *Scotsman*, I persuaded the sympathetic deputy editor Arnold Kemp (son of Robert) to let me go to Tarbert, Loch Fyne, where the novel is set, to investigate its genesis. My first point of call was the Church of Scotland minister, a Mr Eadie, who could not have been more helpful. Within a few hours, he had rounded up some of the town's more elderly worthies who could just about remember the Hay family (MacDougall Hay's father had been the local steamship agent).

Most of them were ladies who admitted that their memories were failing, but some thought that Hay had used various local characters – and incidents – in his narrative. It was clear that some of them did not particularly like the novel, though not all of them had read it. This was not surprising, for its treatment of Brieston – Hay's name for Tarbert – was hardly flattering.

I also visited Hay's widow, Catherine Campbell Hay, who was still alive in Edinburgh. Her memories of her husband were fond but vague; after all, he had died 53 years earlier. Her son, George Campbell Hay, himself a distinguished Gaelic poet, was also present; but he had been seriously ill, and he was embarrassed by his mother's inability to recall fairly elementary things. He had inherited his father's library, and he talked with some enthusiasm about that. I hope I was sensitive and sympathetic; but, although Mrs Campbell Hay could not have been more kind and courteous, it was not a particularly fruitful interview.

The article – a kind of clarion call for Scotland to rediscover this lost novel – was published on the front page of *Weekend Scotsman*, and it did cause a certain stir; but, yet again, the interest in *Gillespie* proved short-lived. There was, however, useful residue in that two prominent Scottish intellectuals – the husband-and-wife team of Isobel Murray and Bob Tait – took up the cause. A couple of years later, they managed to persuade Stephanie Wolfe-Murray of Canongate to publish another edition of the novel, which eventually came out in 1977. They wrote a most perceptive introduction; the novel was well produced, with a strong cover; but yet again it did not make the impact that it deserved, despite – or maybe because of – its public rejection by the Church of Scotland, which refused to stock it in its Edinburgh bookshop.

I think the neglect of *Gillespie* is almost tragic, for it is an enormously ambitious novel of almost demonic power. It is, at least in part, a lofty attack on capitalism. It is no doubt too long, and too melodramatic, and far too violent for some tastes, even today. At times, it reads like the anguished cry of a very tormented and despairing man who is close to madness; but, as a narrative, it is sustained by its rich, relentless style, which has been compared to Herman Melville's in *Moby Dick*.

Gillespie Strang, the eponymous anti-hero who dominates the book, is a brilliant entrepreneur, similar to John Gourlay but on a far grander scale. He starts with a few rabbit snares and becomes the owner of a vast emporium, several farms and an entire fishing fleet. Hay describes all his financial manoeuvres, and the craft with which he cheats people as he builds up his businesses (indeed, all his many scams and rackets), with such relish that you begin to wonder if he is not so much condemning greed as enlightening us as to how to go about making a lot of money. Certainly, *Gillespie* is a world-class primer on how to make enemies and cheat people.

With fluent assurance, Hay shows us just how subtly and stealthily Gillespie builds his commercial pre-eminence until he has the entire community of Brieston in his grasp. There is a large cast of characters; most of them are unpleasant, and those who are good are treated with an unlikely sentimentality. Surprisingly, the local minister hardly features at all. Perhaps this is because Hay himself is preaching at us through the long narrative – which is fitting, because he himself was a Church of Scotland minister.

There can be few great novels that cite the Bible so regularly and determinedly. At one point, Hay uses the phrase 'in spite of Christianity'. A terrible judgement has befallen the folk of Brieston; at the same time, Christ cannot save them. This is a very personal kind of Calvinism; indeed, it is not really any kind of theology but rather just wrath, pure and simple. The most religious – in the orthodox sense – character in the book, Mrs Galbraith, goes mad, such is her hatred of Gillespie, who has cheated her out of her property and has indirectly killed her husband. She becomes crazy for revenge. She imagines herself to be standing at the bar of the Last Judgement. Hay presents her as a 'vicar of the wrath of God'.

The novel has some brilliantly realised, almost cinematic set-pieces – in particular when Gillespie's fishing fleet, supposedly safe in the harbour, is set on fire by angry, defeated men who have been cheated and deceived by Gillespie. The most spectacular scene, indeed the climax of this very long novel, comes when Gillespie's wife – broken by him, and now reduced to drunken whoredom – utters the words 'Gillespie Strang is hell' and then, with the 'savage strength of the demoniac', slashes the throat of her second son, Eoghan, and kills him. This is a spectacularly gruesome scene; Hay's presentation of this 'damnable abyss of horror' is exceptionally graphic and is not recommended for nervous readers. But then, Gillespie Strang is indeed hell.

All this might suggest that the novel is an overwritten Grand Guignol bloodfest; but of course it is much more than that. Gillespie Strang is cunning and devious, but he is also incredibly energetic and almost visionary in his ability to detect trends and capitalise on them. As an entrepreneur, he is touched by genius as he drives his small town forward, and modernises it, with commendable energy and resolution. Gillespie Strang is a bigger man than his neighbours. But, of course, he is laying up his treasure on earth. He will pay for his 'success'.

Despite all the violence, there are many comic passages in the book, while the breaking of a community as it is exposed to over-rapid capitalist change is described in almost documentary style. One of the most amazing features of this great novel is how poetic and Biblical scenes are intermingled with the prosaic chronicling of economic advancement. There are also some very sentimental episodes, such as the one in which the lonely widow Topsail Janet, one of the few really good characters, rescues a wounded solan goose and nurses it back to strength. I find it impossible to read this passage without weeping.

The book is full of sermonising, but it is also a closely observed account of a small Scottish town in the midst of breakneck change. And the agent of change is the titular anti-hero, a pernicious, thieving businessman 'without bowels of pity'.

John Buchan often wrote with a sense that evil was not too far away. MacDougall Hay wrote with an all-consuming sense that evil was everywhere. As an attack on capitalism, *Gillespie* is superlative; as a Christian tract (which I'm sure it's meant to be), it is confusing. Hay's style was apocalyptic rather than theological, although he has been called a neo-Calvinist prophet. Perhaps; what is indisputable is that he produced a Gothic vision of Scotland as hell.

So, *Gillespie* is an intensely Scottish novel, not least in its superb descriptions of Tarbert, of Loch Fyne and of the land of Knapdale. It is also an intensely Christian novel, albeit in a very eldritch way. Its treatment of both Scotland and Christianity is emphatically not, as the cliché goes, for the faint-hearted. Timorous readers should beware.

In a couple of footnotes to this discussion, it is worth noting first that Hay was not 'called' to be the Church of Scotland minister at Grantown-on-Spey in 1914, because an influential local worthy, Lady Seton, found his novel repugnant; and that, almost 60 years later, the Church of Scotland officially designated the novel 'un-Christian'.

Hay was born in Tarbert in 1881, the son of the local steamship agent. He was a brilliant student at Glasgow University – although Glasgow is presented in a most negative way in a long passage towards the end of *Gillespie*. He worked as a journalist, and then taught for a time in Ullapool.

He had to quit teaching when he became seriously ill. He then trained for the ministry at Divinity Hall, Glasgow University (there is a scathing aside about the hall in *Gillespie*). His first and only charge was at Elderslie, a little south of Glasgow; he would have preferred a Highland parish. After *Gillespie*, which was a critical success but emphatically not a commercial one, he wrote a less impressive novel, *Barnacles*; and, when he died in 1919, he was about to embark on his third novel. Too little is known about him; let me conclude this section by saying that I would have loved to hear him preach. And, while he may have been obsessed with the devil, he wrote like an angel.

The big four

Muriel Spark, George Mackay Brown, Compton Mackenzie and Fionn MacColla

In any roll-call of the greatest Scottish creative writers of the twentieth century, the quartet of Muriel Spark, George Mackay Brown, Compton Mackenzie and Fionn MacColla would undoubtedly feature. The first three remain well established in the literary pantheon, and exceedingly popular. Spark was the most subtle of twentieth-century Scottish novelists; Mackay Brown was a fecund writer of both poetry and prose, and in some ways the most seriously Christian creative writer of the century; while Mackenzie was a gloriously life-enhancing, over-the-top figure who should not be taken over-seriously but should not be underestimated either. The fourth, MacColla, is much more obscure – and altogether more difficult, and I shall leave him until last. He was an exceptionally important Scottish novelist, and deserves to be much better known.

I have linked the four of them for one reason: they all became Roman Catholics in adulthood. (There was no significant literary movement in the opposite direction.) There were others, too, who moved to the Catholic faith, respected writers like Bruce Marshall and George Scott-Moncrieff; but the four discussed here were the key ones. Each of them, though in different ways, found something in Catholic Christianity that sustained and unleashed their creativity. For Muriel Spark and George Mackay Brown, the process of joining the Catholic Church had in it an element of liberation. Compton Mackenzie hardly needed liberation, such was his gargantuan self-confidence and love of life; but being admitted to the Catholic Church was of a piece with his exuberant, expansive persona.

When we come to Fionn MacColla, matters get darker; he was a fierce man and a fiercer writer, and his move to Catholicism perhaps more than anything reflected his disgust with Scottish Presbyterianism, something he came to detest with unremitting and ferocious relish.

Muriel Spark

Muriel Spark, born and brought up in Edinburgh, came from English and Jewish stock. Her witty, marginally macabre novels have an ability to disturb the reader because she is the mistress of abruptness. She teases her readers with elegant jolts; she has a refined sense of moral ambiguity. Everything seems to be going smoothly – and then, without warning, the reader is shocked.

The novels continue to be enormously popular. Yet she insisted that she could not have written them had she not become a Catholic. Although she had already written poetry and short stories, she found that she was unable to write the novels she wanted to write until her conversion, when she was in her mid-30s.

In the 1950s, in London, she had flirted with the 'smells and bells' branch of the Church of England, regularly attending a very 'high' Anglican church in Kensington. But she could not satisfy her spiritual – and creative – needs. She was finally drawn to Catholicism when she studied the writings of John Henry Newman, the Victorian spiritual sage who was himself a Catholic convert. Newly a Catholic, Spark retreated to a Carmelite monastery in Kent, where she started to write her first novel, *The Comforters*. Although only one of the many splendid novels that followed was set in Scotland – *The Prime of Miss Jean Brodie* – it is fair to claim that Spark is a very Scottish writer. *Jean Brodie* is, incidentally, a novel that is, among very many other things, a discreet assault on Calvinism. It can be read as an investigation into the tension between the Catholic and Calvinist mindsets.

So, without doubt her conversion set her free to embark on her novel-writing career; after it she was confident and fecund. She suggested that what happened was that she had at last found a location for the religious feelings – at once vague and strong – that she had nurtured through most of her early life. Her one overtly religious novel – though this most subtle of writers was never really 'overtly' anything – was *The Mandelbaum Gate*.

Her life and work progressed geographically – almost 20 years in Presbyterian Edinburgh; a significant period in cosmopolitan London; and a very long coda in Catholic Italy. She once claimed that her formative years in Edinburgh had bred in her a sense of 'exiledom'. Her good friend Derek Stanford, who was, incidentally, a very distinguished book reviewer for the *Scotsman* through the 1960s and 1970s, believed that nonetheless – and, for Spark, 'nonetheless' was a pivotal term – Spark's creative journey amounted to a sustained, imaginative denial of her roots.

She died in 2006 in Florence. She was and is the most delicate of writers; for example, to compare her with her contemporary and fellow convert Fionn MacColla is well-nigh impossible, so completely different are they.

George Mackay Brown

George Mackay Brown was a prolific poet, novelist and short-story writer born in 1921 in Stromness, Orkney. He was to spend most of his life in the little fishing and ferry port. His father was the town's postman; and Brown was brought up as a Presbyterian, though without any great fervour on his or his parents' part. He found the Sunday services drab and uninspiring.

You sometimes sense that, for many Scots, religion needs to be something brighter, more sensual and more aware of physical beauty than anything they believe that they can find in their native Presbyterianism, which can be perceived as grim to the point of dourness. This is the stuff of cliché, and should not be used to undermine the merits and strengths of Presbyterianism, which has a growing involvement in Fresh Expressions of the Church; but I cannot help concluding that so many twentieth-century writers – not just the four discussed here, but also other notable converts to Catholicism, such as Graham Greene and Evelyn Waugh – were looking for a religious context that could assist their creativity, something that they felt they just could not find in Protestantism.

Brown's conversion to Catholicism when he was 40 has been analysed with great sympathy and insight by his friend and biographer, Ron Ferguson (*George Mackay Brown: The Wound and the Gift*, Saint Andrew Press, 2011). Ferguson makes it clear that Brown's conversion was essentially aesthetic and intuitive. Brown was not a writer who was likely to overdo the cerebral hard work; he was a painstaking literary craftsman, but, when it came to Christianity, 'beauty and literature hooked him and reeled him in', in Ferguson's splendid phrase.

I remember being exceptionally impressed by the religious insights in a piece Brown wrote in the late 1960s, several years after his conversion. This was not a poem or a piece of prose fiction. Rather, it was an essay about aspects of Scottish life. In it, Brown achieved something very special. He managed to write with anger (about the legacy of the Scottish Reformation) and at exactly the same time with lyrical awe about pre-Reformation Orkney and the relationship of the ordinary Orcadians with Christianity – the meaning of God in their everyday toil on the land or the sea; the close intermingling of daily work and Biblical revelation. Some might have regarded this as romantic fantasising, an indulgent piece of sentiment about his forebears. Possibly there was indeed an element of that in it. But what impressed me so powerfully was not just the beauty of the prose; it was that here was a piece of overtly religious writing of a kind that very few twentieth-century Scots had attempted, let alone achieved.

That was a relatively obscure essay. Brown's novels, stories and poems are very popular, and are much enjoyed by Scots of all ages and backgrounds. He is a seriously literary writer with a very broad audience. In his relatively short but deceptively complex first novel, *Greenvoe*, one of the characters is a woman with an illegitimate child. She converts to Catholicism, but an aunt then opines that this is 'worse' than the illegitimate bairn. This is gentle mockery of certain pervasive Scottish attitudes that Brown grew up among, but he probably found it easier to reject Presbyterianism than to embrace Catholicism. His slow, careful conversion was agonised. He was lucky to have the process anatomised retrospectively with great sensitivity by Ron Ferguson.

Literary folk feed off one another, and Brown's spiritual journey was partly influenced by another literary convert, Graham Greene. Brown found the 'whisky priest' in Greene's novel *The Power and the Glory* – a worthless man who nonetheless kept the faith – moving and impressive. Ironically, Brown was received into the Catholic Church at around the time Greene was going through a severe crisis of faith.

Brown was reared in a community that encouraged a distinct suspicion, if not actual fear, of Catholicism. Yet, in Ferguson's view, what finally clinched Brown's move were the authority, unity and very long history of the Catholic Church. He reckons that Brown was disturbed by Protestantism's constant divisions – and who in Scotland could not be disturbed, if not angered, by them? Ferguson suggests that Brown found in the continuing Catholic Church 'a resolution for the problem of competing assertions'.

This is very insightful, even if the Catholic Church too has suffered plenty of its own divisions and splits and breakaways. But somehow, over the centuries, it has managed to cope better. (I remember Cardinal Tom Winning once telling me, with a mischievous grin: 'You Protestants have never learned what to do with your troublemakers. When we have a particularly difficult bunch of troublemakers, we just create a new Order and stick them all in it.')

Compton Mackenzie

Compton Mackenzie, still popular but less read today than when he was in his long and splendid pomp between 1910 and 1970, was blessed with enormous literary talent, a keen inductive brain and a theatrical, larger-than-life persona. His father was a distinguished actor – and, although Mackenzie originally set out to be a lawyer, many thought that he should have been an actor–director. Instead, he became a journalist, novelist, short-story writer, politician and a romantic Scottish patriot. He excelled in all these roles, and also found time to be an agent for British intelligence.

Already a brilliant, glittering star when he was an undergraduate at Oxford at the very end of the nineteenth century, he could have picked and mixed 100 different careers. He wrote fluently and maybe just a little glibly, but some of his novels, such as *Sinister Street*, can justifiably be called masterpieces. His last novel, which was much shorter than usual – he should have edited his writing more than he did – was a sensitive study of a homosexual politician, based loosely on Tom Driberg, called *Thin Ice*.

Today, Mackenzie is best known for his entertainments, set in Scotland – comic novels such as *Whisky Galore*, *Hunting the Fairies* and *Monarch of the Glen*. There is in these Highland fantasies a slight tendency to caricature, and he could patronise the Scotland he genuinely adored; but for goodness' sake – Scotland has a surfeit of grimness and sternness, and Mackenzie was to the end a fervent foe of over-seriousness, a constant light in the glaur.

He was received into the Catholic Church when he was 31, and this served to endorse his already positive view of Jacobitism. He wrote several books about the rebellions and Bonnie Prince Charlie, but these are largely forgotten now. His Catholicism was of a piece with the rest of his life – flamboyant and enthusiastic.

He was a distinguished broadcaster, he maintained an unlikely but lasting friendship with Hugh MacDiarmid, and he was a founding member of the Scottish National Party and a high-profile rector of Glasgow University. His life was full of ploys, adventures and schemes. One of his fictive heroes nurtured a grand plan to create a federation of small Celtic Catholic nations. This was exactly the kind of project that Mackenzie would talk about starting in real life – starting, if not finishing.

He nurtured an unrealistic and over-romantic view of Scotland, but he was largely concerned with life's potential rather than the more dreich quotidian realities. He lived for a time in Barra, being enormously fond of the Hebrides. He was perhaps a little less fond of Edinburgh, though he stayed in the city for much of the evening of his long and superbly fecund life. He did not write a one-volume biography; he needed ten volumes to cram in all that he had done.

He remains an unlikely, bright, happy, stylish and fitfully brilliant figure rolling across Scotland's twentieth-century history. He died in 1972, just short of his ninetieth birthday. His funeral on Barra was of a piece with his life – theatrical to a degree. His body was carried to Barra on a small plane that landed on a beach. It was a wet, bleak day – but, undaunted, the octogenarian piper Calum Johnston (a member of an eminent Hebridean Catholic family, famous for their skills at piping, singing and dancing) accompanied the coffin as it was carried uphill to Eoligarry Cemetery, playing a series of laments. Father Aeneas MacQueen then conducted the service; just as it was ending, Calum Johnston collapsed and died alongside the grave. Some thought that this very sad yet theatrical episode was completely appropriate; it was as if Mackenzie was already orchestrating drama from the next world.

Fionn MacColla

Where Compton Mackenzie was a winsome and expansive figure, Fionn MacColla was a writer who was fierce, harsh and bitter. He spent a fair amount of his life in a condition of both cerebral and physical agony; although a successful schoolmaster, he endured periods of homelessness and extreme poverty.

Fionn MacColla was the pseudonym of Tom Douglas MacDonald, a Montrose man who was born in 1906, the son of a fluent Gaelic-speaker. He was brought up in the Plymouth Brethren, an extreme Calvinist sect; and his creative life was an extended and very forceful response to this experience. Although his childhood was not unhappy, he came to detest Calvinism and its influence on Scotland. He was a patriotic Scot who thought his country had been usurped and vitiated by a pernicious creed. His novels are angry, exceedingly angry, yet they are redeemed by their imaginative intensity and honesty; he can write with sympathy about characters he seems to despise. Even so, his fiction is not for the faint-hearted.

He trained as a teacher and, when he was only 19, was appointed headmaster of a small school near Gairloch in Wester Ross. He went on to teach elsewhere in the Highlands, and for a time in Palestine; but his teaching career was intermittent. Later, he studied Gaelic at Glasgow University so that he could at last become fully proficient in the language, and then he returned to the Highlands to serve as headmaster at various schools in the Western Isles. But, in between his stints as a headmaster, he had various crises; for a time, he was sleeping rough. He was received into the Roman Catholic Church in 1935; he had been introduced to Thomist philosophy by a priest in South Uist. He was impressed by Catholic Christianity's emphasis on renewal. His fiction is characterised by great bitterness about evangelical Protestantism, but this was apparently prompted not so much by his adopted Catholic faith as by his extreme hatred of the Calvinism of his youth.

He was much praised by Hugh MacDiarmid but largely ignored by most of the rest of Scotland's literary elite, although he was assisted in times of personal crisis by George Scott-Moncrieff, himself a convert to Catholicism, and by the poet Helen B. Cruickshank. He died in Edinburgh in 1975, unsung and already forgotten.

I admit that I find his three principal and very powerful novels, *The Albannach* (1932), *And the Cock Crew* (1945) and *The Ministers* (published posthumously with the assistance of the Scottish writer John Herdman), difficult to read. They are brilliantly written, but they possess a cerebral force and a furious discontented tension which, combined, are daunting. At times, they might remind readers of MacDougall Hay's splendid novel *Gillespie*; but Hay has more sweep, a wider range, than MacColla; he orchestrates a larger cast of characters and presents a much more textured and nuanced portrait of a Scottish community.

MacColla used his fiction for a specific purpose: to attack Scottish Presbyterianism, hard and head-on. Believing that Scotland's Calvinist inheritance had twisted and even destroyed the lives of many Scots, he used his novels to condemn what he regarded as its extremely repressive and baneful assault on the Scottish nation. So, his novels amount to a sustained polemic; they are unremittingly, brutally contentious. Yet, for all his force, he cannot quite reach that perfectly pitched condemnation achieved by John Buchan in his masterpiece, *Witch Wood*.

In *The Albannach*, Calvinism is presented as nothing less than a denial of life. There is a similar theme in *And the Cock Crew*, which is by far the most powerful novel written about the Highland Clearances; in it, MacColla suggests that pagans and Catholics can appreciate the realities of the world, but Calvinists are concerned only to destroy the context in which people live. The narrative, while very complex, is essentially about a minister who betrays his flock. The novel is also shot through with a distaste for England and the English. For MacColla, the Highland Clearances were about a double dispossession: of the land, and of the soul.

In his times of personal crisis, MacColla was sustained by his Catholicism and by his passionate Scottish nationalism. Both of these 'homes', spiritual and political, helped him to champion, in his extremely intemperate way, the Gaelic language and Highland Scotland.

The Ministers, the final novel of this extraordinary triptych, is more reflective; it is a little gentler, and less bitter. It describes the peculiar events after a new minister, Ewen MacRury, something of an innocent, arrives to serve the people of a Highland community called Mellonudrigill. The minister preaches in English rather than Gaelic. In this and other ways, he soon earns the condemnation and even hatred of his flock, and so he has to be judged by his colleague ministers, who are an unpleasant, mean bunch of hypocrites. In that sense, the novel reflects Buchan's masterpiece *Witch Wood*.

The story is essentially about the persecution of a man who dares to deviate from the hardness of Calvinism, and it has a certain subtlety, not MacColla's customary characteristic. Here, he shows that he can write with kindness about a man who dares to preach in English. It commences with a spellbinding tour de force in which MacRury is placed not just in a limited, precise context but also as a tiny consciousness in the full immensity of the universe, a mere moment in the great longness of time. MacColla was a writer who played for very big stakes; his ambition almost, but not quite, triumphed over his hatred. I suspect that his Catholicism played a benign part in this tentative process.

He found it very hard to get his work published, which is not surprising. Hugh MacDiarmid, often vituperative and nasty but also capable of generosity and kindness, was very positive about MacColla's work; but even his endorsement did little good. When MacColla died in 1975, few noticed; but MacDiarmid, controversial as ever, thundered that his death was a greater loss to Scotland than the deaths of Compton Mackenzie, Neil Gunn and Eric Linklater put together.

The paradox in MacColla is that he was so extremely bitter and eloquent about the alleged negative effects of Calvinism – as he saw it, its spiritual destruction of Scotland, its hatred of what was natural and good in human life, its glorying in the bleak and the mean, its denial of genuine religion, its constant killjoy repression – that he himself seemed to be indulging in a positive orgy of negativity.

He was a mysterious man. I sometimes ask literary scholars and Scottish writers about him; most of them shrug their shoulders or shake their heads sadly. He was elusive and shadowy, despite the force and harshness of his writing. There was something awkward and difficult about him. He was the ultimate outsider.

Novelists do not have to be polite, and they certainly do not have to be charmers, but need they be quite as intellectually brutish as MacColla was? In *The Ministers*, he seemed finally to find a new spirit and a gentler tone. As I indicated, I reckon that this might have been the final creative result of his acquired Catholic faith; but that is sheer speculation.

The only picture of him that I've seen shows a handsome man with a high forehead and a long nose; he is moustachioed and neatly groomed. He looks pensive, even wistful; there is nothing of the brute or the wild man in that face. When he wrote, did some demons take over? I confess to being confused by his writing, which is undoubtedly touched by genuine genius. Whatever his mission was, it was certainly not to cheer us up.

Four texts

Robert Burns, Sir Walter Scott, James Hogg and John Galt

In all the vast and rich treasure-house of Scottish literature, four particular texts are often cited as encapsulating the best of the Scottish literary response to Christianity. These are Robert Burns's satire, *Holy Willie's Prayer*; Sir Walter Scott's novel, *Old Mortality*; James Hogg's novel, *The Private Memoirs and Confessions of a Justified Sinner*; and John Galt's novel, *Ringan Gilhaize*. The first three are not particularly sympathetic to Christianity, or at least to the Scottish experience of the religion. *Ringan Gilhaize* is very different, being an enthusiastic celebration of the Covenanters.

I'm not really sure about the status of the first two; I think Burns and Scott both wrote a great deal that was much better. The Hogg novel is deeper, but problematic. Galt's novel, which is very readable and very partisan, seems to me to be the best of the four as a creative work of literature. But Galt, like Hogg, does not appear to have a place at the top table of the most revered Scottish writers. Those sitting round that table are Burns, Scott, Stevenson and two more recent arrivals, Grassic Gibbon and Hugh MacDiarmid.

Robert Burns

Robert Burns is by far Scotland's most popular writer. Indeed, he is one of the *world*'s most popular writers. Few other poets, anywhere, have attracted so much genuine, straightforward enthusiasm. Part of the reason for his phenomenal worldwide success is, funnily enough, that he is so very Scottish. By this, I mean that he somehow manages to embody in one literary personality, in one body of work, so many apparent opposites; as his fellow Scottish poet, Lord Byron, put it – tenderness, roughness; delicacy, coarseness; soaring, grovelling . . . and so on. You get the picture.

The 'Holy Willie' who is so devastatingly lampooned in *Holy Willie's Prayer* was Willie Fisher, an Ayrshire farmer and kirk elder – and an appalling hypocrite. Fisher's big mistake was to get embroiled in a long dispute with the poet's good friend, Gavin Hamilton. Although Hamilton eventually triumphed, Burns still wanted to take his literary revenge on his friend's enemy.

Holy Willie's Prayer is a clever and very sharp satire on Calvinism, but not much more: I'm certain that Burns wrote many finer poems. For me, a superior satire is his *Holy Fair*, a savage yet subtle commentary on the annual fair at Mauchline, Ayrshire, which was a rowdy and ribald extended open-air picnic masquerading as a supposed preparation for Holy Communion. Drunkenness and lechery were just as prevalent at the event as religious zeal. This was the perfect subject for Burns, who loved to puncture the Scottish propensity for behaviour that was at best contradictory, at worst grievously hypocritical.

Sir Walter Scott

As for Sir Walter Scott, he is an enigma. A genuinely great novelist who is now much less popular in his own country than the poet Burns, Scott was obsessed with his nation's past, far more so than Burns was, and he virtually reinvented Scotland for his own creative purposes. His cultural legacy remains potent, even if relatively few Scots bother to read his novels or his poems – he was a fine poet before he was a novelist.

In his novels, Scott often wrote dialogue in Scots and linked these passages with elegant English prose. So, he was at least in part responsible for the cultural split that has divided Scotland ever since – a split that has not been kind to Scotland psychologically or culturally. The literary critic Alan Bold, the distinguished biographer of Hugh MacDiarmid, once told me that this essentially negative legacy was why MacDiarmid hated Scott.

John Buchan, who revered Scott, claimed that his hero loved 'freaks and oddities' but had 'a clean palate and avoided the rancid'. That is peculiar phraseology; what I think he meant is that Scott tended to sanitise Scotland. He retreated from anything nasty or extreme or too challenging. Well, yes and no. When it came to religion, Scott made it clear that he had a strong distaste for Protestant excess. His father was a stern Edinburgh Presbyterian; Scott was, by temperament and inclination, a much gentler and softer Christian. He became a cautious Episcopalian, though he maintained his links with Scotland's national Church.

Scott was a prolific writer, and socially ambitious. He bought the unfortunately named property of Clarty Hole on the banks of the Tweed, and, Gatsby-like, built a fine country house, Abbotsford, on the land. This project was a testament to his vanity. Then he suddenly faced financial calamity; he tried to write his way out of the crisis, writing far too fast, yet without doubt heroically. Although his writing could understandably, in these circumstances, be slapdash, he was essentially a fastidious, conservative and rather sentimental man, not least when it came to religion.

I noted that, in Scotland today, the popularity of Burns grows ever more strong while that of Scott diminishes. The reason for this may lie in Walter Scott's style. The English writer E. M. Forster sneered that Scott had a trivial mind and a heavy style. I think the first part is unfair – Scott was not usually trivial, though there is triviality in *Old Mortality* – but, sadly, the second part may be just.

Rereading his novel *Old Mortality*, which deals with the Covenanters, I was struck by how many stodgy passages there are in what is supposed to be one of his most compact, readable and action-packed novels. Admittedly, there are also several scenes of enormous vividness and excitement. The novel occasionally threatens to become a fictive rant against the later Covenanters. John Buchan characterised it as 'a grim tale moving among ungenial folk on the highroad of national destiny'.

It is without doubt unkind to the Covenanters, with the exception of one or two characters, including the moderate Morton and the preacher MacBriar, who, although only a minor player, is given the most moving – and I reckon historically valid – set-piece in the novel, when he delivers a superbly powerful and eloquent open-air sermon.

Scott presents MacBriar as a youth more than a man; he is barely 20, very thin, worn out, wasted by vigils, fasts, imprisonment and the fugitive life. Yet, when he starts to preach, 'religious zeal triumphed over bodily weakness and infirmity'. Scott seems to get carried away as he pens this magnificent sermon. Perhaps there was a Covenanting preacher lurking somewhere deep inside his sceptical soul.

Later, in chapter 36 of the novel, when MacBriar is tortured and then executed, there is a peculiar mixture of the comic, the melodramatic and the horrific. First, the interrogation of a doubting Covenanter, one Cuddie, is handled in a couthy, almost frivolous manner; but the tone becomes much darker when MacBriar is questioned. He behaves with dignity and discipline, to the annoyance of his interrogators.

Then the lead interrogator, the Duke of Lauderdale, rings a small bell; and a crimson curtain, covering a 'Gothic recess', whatever that may be, draws back to reveal the Executioner, who is described as 'tall, grim and hideous'. (This scene is typical Scott.) On a table before him are his implements of torture. MacBriar views this 'horrible apparatus' with composure. Scott goes on to describe the preacher's torture with something approaching relish.

MacBriar remains brave and dignified, refusing to incriminate his colleagues, and so the death sentence is announced. MacBriar then delivers his slightly over-pious last words; he forgives his interrogators, announces that he is being sent from darkness to the company of angels and the spirits of the just, and tells his tormentors that he hopes their last moments might be as happy as his. He speaks, Scott tells us, with a countenance radiant with joy and triumph. The scene is over-dramatic, but it does not lack subtlety; the superhuman composure of MacBriar, and indeed his 'joy and triumph', do insinuate that here indeed was a fanatic, if an amazingly heroic one.

So, MacBriar is a caricature, if a generous one. Elsewhere in the novel, Scott's tendency to emphasise the grotesque (while not always avoiding the rancid, *pace* Buchan) does not make him the most sensitive chronicler of the religious divisions that wracked Scotland in the late seventeenth century. He presents, in the form of the egregious Covenanter Habakkuk Mucklewrath, a preacher given to horrible excess: 'I say, take the infants and dash them against the stones; take the daughters and mothers of the house and hurl them from the battlements, that the dogs may fatten on them as they did on Jezebel, the spouse of Ahab'. This is obviously grotesque, yet there may be just a hint of historical validity in it. Thank goodness that Scott balances it with MacBriar's noble eloquence.

Towards the end of the novel, it transpires that MacBriar's background is, surprisingly, in the Church of England. This may be significant, given Scott's own slightly devious preference for Episcopalian Christianity.

Scott, according to his friend James Hogg, 'seldom or never went to church'. Further, he 'dreaded religion as a machine by which the good government of the country might be deranged'. His own worship arrangements verged on the dishonest. I suspect that, deep down, he had a real disdain for the Church of Scotland. In Edinburgh, he eventually chose to worship at an Episcopal church, although in the Borders he sent his children to the Church of Scotland. His father, as we noted, was a strict Presbyterian of the old school; often, in Scottish life, such fathers have produced rebellious reactions. Scott certainly admitted in later life that he had not enjoyed the kirk services he endured when he was young. He once quipped that the only good thing about going into a Presbyterian church was that you knew you would come out of it.

For all that, he was a sincere Christian man. He claimed that, if called to die as a martyr for Christianity (which was of course extremely unlikely), then he would do so. An empathetic and sensitive writer, he had probably tried to imagine how he would behave in hideous circumstances such as those faced by MacBriar. Scott's personal Christianity was certainly not extreme; it was cautious and essentially social rather than evangelical. In his fiction (not just in *Old Mortality*), religion is sometimes presented as a source of discord and division. In his rather bourgeois way, he had distaste for zealots: he once wrote that, in Scotland, 'Presbyterians of the more violent kind became as illiberal as the Papists'.

James Hogg

James Hogg's life was almost as remarkable as his literary output. The son of a struggling Borders farmer, he had a tough childhood.

His father's farm finally failed when he was just 6, and James was never properly schooled. He worked as a shepherd and taught himself how to read and write. And he taught himself well, for he became a superb writer. Before he wrote his masterpiece, *The Private Memoirs and Confessions of a Justified Sinner* (1824), Hogg had already written *The Brownie of Bodsbeck*, which some have interpreted as a riposte to his friend Scott's *Old Mortality*. It was certainly published after *Old Mortality*, though Hogg claimed it had been written earlier.

Hogg has often been regarded as a literary freak. 'I do not understand the man', wrote Thomas Carlyle. 'His poetic talent is authentic, yet his intellect seems weak.' (Most people's intellects were weak when compared with the juggernaut that was Carlyle's.) This was typical of the way Hogg was often patronised. Sometimes he played the part of the rustic buffoon, which of course encouraged condescension. His sociability was excessive, and he was very vain.

The Private Memoirs and Confessions (originally published anonymously) is very much a one-off. It is short but profound, and leaves readers with a deep and lingering sense of unease, as if we have just encountered something that suggests pure, undistilled evil. Indeed, this is probably the most frightening novel ever written by a Scot, and quite possibly the most frightening novel ever written in English (and it is written in English, not Scots). There is a murky malignancy hanging over and around it, something that is almost impossible to analyse.

It is a tale of murder and suicide, and it comes in two parts. The first, by the so-called editor, narrates the grisly events of the story; the second part is the 'Confession' of the sinner, supposedly recovered from his grave. There is a rather coy endpiece which is convoluted and out of keeping with the rest of the novel. It brings in Hogg himself, in a rather tricksy and self-regarding way.

The devastating religious element in the book concerns the way that the anti-hero, Wringham, is supposedly 'justified' – that is, saved – because he is one of the Elect. His salvation is assured and unconditional. Whatever he does in this life, no matter how evil or reprehensible, does not really matter, for he is one of the Elect and will not be punished in the next life. It is a novel in which the

Devil, in the person of the mysterious Gil-Martin (who appears as Wringham's sinister alter ego), plays a leading role.

Hogg had imbibed the folk culture of the Borders, in which the Devil regularly featured. The dualism between the 'real' Wringham and the 'evil' Wringham – the latter taken over, as it were, by the Devil – is a variation on the theme of split personality.

Hogg is confronting a perversion of Christian doctrine and attempting to analyse religious delusion. His novel is not an explicit condemnation of Calvinism; it is too subtle for that. It undoubtedly raises deep and disturbing questions about the theology of predestination in its extreme form. Is it possible that good works and faith in this world, much praised and encouraged in most versions of Christianity, are merely a way for the unelected or unjustified to try to buy a place in heaven in the next life? Again, could it be that the various sins committed by the justified, the Elect, are all part of God's grand plan?

There has been, over the generations, a long, and for me rather obscure, literary debate about whether the novel was intended as a satire, almost as a darker prose version of *Holy Willie's Prayer*. Early on in it, we have a stark presentation of what was required by the 'arbitrary and unyielding creed' of a Scottish Calvinist minister: prayer twice every day, and seven times on the Sabbath. But you were to pray for the Elect only, and to doom all who were alien from God to destruction. That is devastating, but it is not satire. Perhaps Hogg embarked on his novel with satirical intent; but I suggest that both its psychological subtlety, and the power of its presentation of sheer evil, take it far beyond mere satire.

There are further questions, involving the controversial notion of national identity. Is Hogg suggesting that Scots are, as a people, peculiarly two-faced? Do we have a propensity to hypocrisy predicated on our Christian inheritance? Are we struggling with twin identities? Has the Calvinist background of many of us disposed us to have two different personalities at the same time? This train of thought inevitably leads towards a later and more popular novel, R. L. Stevenson's *Strange Case of Dr Jekyll and Mr Hyde*, which, while set in London, was really about Edinburgh. Dr Jekyll was a man 'committed to a profound duplicity of life'.

All I can say is that, for me at any rate, the latter is a somewhat crude and unsophisticated work when compared to *The Private Memoirs and Confessions of a Justified Sinner*.

John Galt

And then there is John Galt's magnificent *Ringan Gilhaize*, this very fine author's firm favourite among his many novels. It was written as a forceful response to *Old Mortality* – Galt was infuriated by Scott's fictive treatment of the Covenanters.

The distinguished writer and critic Paul Henderson Scott claims that it was because Galt reacted against Walter Scott's novel so forcefully that he was inspired to write this very special and unusual story – a novel that was different from anything Galt had written before. It is also unlike anything written by any other authors according to Paul Scott. Galt himself was to claim, without any false modesty, that it was 'unique'. I cannot comment on that, but I have found nothing else like it in Scottish fiction. It is the most profoundly Scottish book that I have ever read; it romps through a problematic time in Scottish history in a way that manages to be intelligent, sensitive and very partisan, all at once.

Galt was very annoyed that Walter Scott had 'treated the defenders of the Presbyterian church with too much levity'. He recalled that his own ancestor, John Galt of Gateside, had been deported to America for refusing to renounce the Covenant. And so, *Ringan Gilhaize* is in a sense a glorious act of literary revenge, a bold artistic attempt to set the record straight. It is almost a freak, an audacious personal narrative, a remarkable, rollicking story that belts along at breakneck speed, so much so that its subtlety is not always apparent.

It is a fictitious autobiography, and is written by the fictive Ringan Gilhaize entirely in the first person. This presents various technical difficulties, not least because it covers around 150 years of history, which is obviously well over Ringan's own lifespan. Galt surmounts this problem with great skill. Ringan is a Scottish patriot, a fervent Presbyterian, a Covenanter and a murderer – he kills Claverhouse, one of the generals who hunted down the Covenanters, and who was generously treated by Walter Scott.

Appended at the end of the novel is the entire text of the Declaration of Arbroath, which of course was drafted by a Catholic many generations before the Covenant was even thought of. Galt writes from a blatantly Presbyterian and patriotic viewpoint; he regarded the Covenanters as rebels with right on their side, freedom fighters giving their all for a great Scottish cause against the agents and soldiers of the English state, in the same heroic tradition of fourteenth-century Scots fighting for Robert the Bruce. He mixes the psychology of hardline Presbyterianism into a heady brew of action and adventure, all in the context of a very skilfully realised historical background, and the result is a challenging text that is very far indeed from being a conventional literary novel.

Galt presents a chancy, dangerous Scotland that is violent and uncertain; treachery is constant, and there seems to be no such place as a safe house or indeed any kind of refuge for desperate fugitives. Real historical events are stitched into the narrative seamlessly. *Ringan Gilhaize* is largely about what Ringan himself terms 'the divine right of resistance'. It is about extreme political action taken for a religious cause. It is a very 'committed' novel in its aggressive sympathy for a certain kind of Scottish Christianity. It is also a very political novel in its strong, implicit endorsement of political action against tyranny.

Galt's enormous enthusiasm for both the Covenant itself and the Covenanters was perhaps unlikely in that he was, intellectually, very much a product of the Enlightenment. The stock notion of the Enlightenment is that it nurtured a fastidious distaste for organised Christianity. Its leading lights were generally sceptical about, if not downright antipathetic to, supposed religious fanatics such as the Covenanters. It is to Galt's colossal credit that he, a sophisticated man of the world – businessman, entrepreneur, newspaper editor, distinguished colonist as well as novelist – could spring to the defence of the Covenanting cause with all the narrative gusto and literary subtlety that he evinces in this heroic narrative. Too much gusto for some, of course; in sophisticated Edinburgh (Galt himself was always very much aloof from the Edinburgh literati), the pundit Francis Jeffrey sneered that the novel was 'tiresome' and that the narrative was 'neither pleasing nor probable'.

Galt, unlike many great writers, lived a very full and active life. He was born in Ayrshire, the son of a shipowner and sea captain, and spent his teenage years in Greenock by the Clyde. He read widely as a child and youth, and decided that he was a Tory, if an unlikely one. He once suggested that he had been born to be radical, and that his Toryism was partly born of a mischievous contrariness. He worked for a merchant company in Greenock, and then in his mid-twenties left for London, where he tried to establish himself as a writer, penning, among many other works, a biography of Cardinal Wolsey – a somewhat unlikely choice.

Indeed, there was always a slightly antic perversity about John Galt. He was a restless man of enormous energy, though he was plagued by bad health. He went on a long journey around the Mediterranean, meeting and befriending the Scottish poet Lord Byron along the way. When he returned to London, he studied to become a lawyer – but he still could not settle and make a success of his life. He started to write novels, which he was to do intermittently for the rest of his life. He usually chose Scottish subjects. He wrote quickly and well, and soon became a literary star.

Always rootless, he then changed tack and acted as the legal agent for some Canadian colonists who had been spurned by the British government when they claimed damages after the US invasion of Canada in 1812. This work made him decide to try out his own luck in Canada. He proved to be an energetic and resourceful colonial entrepreneur. He acted as the secretary of a land-development company and founded the town of Guelph. The smaller community of Galt, Ontario, was named after him.

He is perhaps the most underestimated of all Scottish novelists. His output was uneven, which is hardly surprising given that he was such a busy lawyer, journalist and man of business. At periods in his hectic life, he seemed to regard writing as a second-rate activity; he certainly did not despise the life of business. But he had a writer's sensitivity. In Canada, he clashed with a senior British mandarin, Sir Peregrine Maitland, and came off worse. The dispute was complicated, and Galt's entrepreneurial career went badly off course. He became indebted and was eventually briefly imprisoned back in England. His three sons all made considerable contributions to the development of Canada, and he is perhaps better remembered in Canada than in his native Scotland.

His pawky, occasionally sentimental yet never over-nostalgic novels, such as *Annals of the Parish*, chronicled changes in Ayrshire communities that were dealing with the growing onslaught of early industrialisation. In the *Annals*, the action is viewed through the eyes of an old kirk minister, Micah Balwhidder. Galt's writing was always imaginative, yet it had its documentary side. He could write with poetic power (though he was actually a poor poet), but he was always well aware of what was going on in the world around him, and there is little that is dreamy or fanciful in his fiction. Galt's last years were marked by serious illness and depression. He died, disappointed and spent, when he was 59.

He understood the small towns of Scotland as few others have. A realist, he was by no means resistant to the huge changes that were stirring and that were to bring about massive social upheaval. He was also one of those rare novelists who have a genuine insider's understanding of the world of entrepreneurial business. And he nurtured deep, even profound, insights into the quiddity of Scottish Protestantism.

Ringan Gilhaize, as a novel, is very strong meat; and Ringan himself, as a character, is even stronger meat. Galt gives Ringan these words: 'I have taken up the avenging pen of history, and dipped it in the blood of martyrs'. That Galt could write with profound sympathy about a man many would regard as a bloodthirsty fanatic and assassin, and also write with gentle humour about the social changes in the Scotland of his own time, shows him to have been a novelist of very considerable range and sensitivity.

Ringan Gilhaize is an exceptional work of fiction. Sir George Douglas regarded it as an 'epic' that 'compels the reader to sympathise with the best of the Covenanters . . . in their most earnest and loftiest ideals'. The novel explains, with depth and power, what happens when a patriotic Scot is driven to extreme political action because his state outlaws the version of Christianity he cherishes – indeed, as it seems to him, when his state declares war on his God. Above all, the novel more than makes up for the whimsical frivolity of Walter Scott's treatment of the Covenanters in *Old Mortality*.

Two Thomsons

The first Thomson and the second Thomson

There have been two distinguished Scottish poets called James Thomson. The first was the son of a Borders manse who went south to England to seek his literary fortune, which he duly achieved. He was phenomenally successful. The second was far less successful, but for me he is the better poet, if only because of his very fine poem *The City of Dreadful Night*.

The first Thomson

The first (eighteenth-century) Thomson was not a particularly impressive pupil at school in Jedburgh, but, encouraged by a farmer-minister called Robert Riccaltoun, he imbued himself in the lore of the Borders ballads and songs. He went on to Edinburgh University to study divinity, where he was told that his prose style, as he composed sermons, was 'too ornate' for him to follow his father into the ministry.

So, Thomson considered his options. This was in the period immediately after the signing of the Union between Scotland and England, and he decided to sail south from Leith and try his luck in London. He was ambitious, he knew he had considerable literary talent, and he had a sunny, optimistic disposition. He settled in Richmond, by the Thames, and made the acquaintance of the leading literary men of the day, including Dr Johnson, who described him as gross and uninviting in appearance. Coleridge, more positively, noted that 'the love of nature led him to a cheerful religion'.

He wrote many poems that were exceedingly successful. Just two of them remain well known. *The Seasons* is an eccentric but highly popular long poem celebrating the four seasons but also encompassing matters botanical, political, ecological and goodness knows what else. The other poem is the dreadful *Rule Britannia*, that bombastic celebration of British patriotism which, I suspect, many genuine British patriots regard as deeply embarrassing.

Whatever; Thomson was, in his own time, one of the most successful (in terms of sales) British poets there has ever been. He had escaped what would perhaps have been a dreary and frustrating career as a Scottish divine, unsuited to his upbeat persona; instead, he managed to establish himself as the darling of literary England.

The second Thomson

The second James Thomson, a tormented drunken Scot, never achieved popular success. He produced one true masterpiece, which is notable for its defiant rejection of God. Not even the prose of Dickens in his descriptions of Victorian London by night could equal the brooding horror of the huge nocturnal city that Thomson evoked in his long poem *The City of Dreadful Night*. (Of course, the city is not necessarily London, the city that Thomson drank and suffered in; it could be any great Victorian city – indeed, any nightmare city.) Thomson's city is presented in a clever, insidious way; it is not the physical, silent city itself that repels, but the loneliness and despair of the lost soul, bereft of hope or solace, wandering through its dark desolation.

Thomson was born in 1834 in Port Glasgow, the son of a seaman. His mother was a staunch Christian. He was educated at the Royal Military School in Chelsea, where he trained to be a teacher. The early death of his wife led to a more or less permanent crisis, though he continued his career as an itinerant army schoolmaster until his alcoholism led to his dismissal. He then worked sporadically as a journalist, penning articles for publications such as *Cope's Tobacco Plant*, in which he had to plug (!) tobacco products wherever possible.

His last years were degraded and desperate. He managed to make a living of sorts as a (very irascible) literary journalist. He had his admirers, including Karl Marx, but his life fell into the pit. He was wracked by extreme melancholy and persistent insomnia. He was eventually imprisoned after setting fire to his landlord's kitchen.

The City of Dreadful Night presents a gloomy, yet in its way epic, portrait of a vast dark indifferent hell, both external and internal. The physical city is the external context for the terrible internal horrors within the narrator's soul: 'The City is of Night, but not of Sleep . . . The pitiless hours like years and ages creep, A night seems termless hell.'

Thomson presents man as an isolated and bereft figure, wandering around a gloomy metropolis in which God is conspicuously absent. 'There is no God; no Fiend with names Divine, made us and tortures us; if we must pine, it is to satiate no Being's gall . . .'

This is hard, bitter atheism of almost horrifying intensity, and I find it astonishing that Thomson's great poem has been anthologised in a compendium of Scottish Religious Verse.

Biographies and novels

*John Gibson Lockhart, Margaret Oliphant
and Robin Jenkins*

John Gibson Lockhart

John Gibson Lockhart is remembered as the first and best biographer of Sir Walter Scott, his father-in-law. This is a pity, for he was a man of very many parts, and he excelled in several roles. Educated in Glasgow and in Oxford (which he loved), he became a lawyer and then made his name as a prolific journalist (he eventually served as editor of the *Quarterly Review* in London) and satirist. He wrote a biography of Burns that was not particularly impressive; and his huge biography of Scott is slightly tainted by his dislike of James Hogg. He was a type; very good-looking yet cold in persona, and in his dealings with others he could be aloof, proud and opinionated. When James Hogg first met him, he found Lockhart 'a mischievous Oxford puppy'. Through his prolific career, Lockhart seems to have been feared more than liked.

He wrote four novels; and the best of the quartet is *Adam Blair*. First published in 1822, but set about 75 years earlier, it is far ahead of its time as a study of the personal life of a Church of Scotland minister that concentrates on his – for the most part repressed – sexuality. It is a bleak novel that teeters on the brink of bitterness but ends on a redemptive, upbeat note.

Lockhart was the son of the minister of Cambusnethan, and he understood the constant stresses in the almost impossible life of a Scottish rural minister – a man expected to provide consistent support and frequent admonition to other people; a man who had to set a high public example while always being aware that his every deed and statement would be scrutinised and analysed, not necessarily sympathetically. The minister might well have been very well educated, yet could be mired in a claustrophobic, limited community where he could easily find himself lonely and even isolated.

The novel's narrative is straightforward. A young minister, recently widowed, becomes very fond of his relative, the unhappily married Charlotte Campbell. They begin to depend on each other for emotional support. Eventually the inevitable happens; they commit adultery, although in a joyless, bleak way. The minister is disgraced; he serves a long, self-imposed penance; at the very end of the novel, after his extended 'purification', he is asked to return to his parish, where he resumes his ministry, an old and – in most respects – defeated man.

The novel oscillates between melodrama and excessive introspection, and is by no means a masterpiece, but it has power and considerable narrative drive. It deals with the constant pressures of a Scottish minister's life in a way that is both sensitive and profound. It is not a subtle story, save in one respect: Lockhart shows that it is the minister himself, far more than his parishioners, who finds forgiveness almost impossible.

Margaret Oliphant

Another Scottish novelist who wrote sympathetically about ministers was Margaret Oliphant, who was born in Wallyford, just east of Edinburgh, in 1828 and brought up in Glasgow. Most of her adult life was spent in England. Almost wholly neglected now, in the Victorian era she was enormously popular, although somehow she contrived to make little money from her writing. Her work was sometimes compared with that of Trollope, though she lacked his worldly wisdom and his shrewd kindness towards most of his characters.

She wrote novels about both Scottish and English provincial life, often dealing sympathetically and realistically with stresses or strains in the manse or vicarage. But her most celebrated book was a study of Edward Irving, a colourful and controversial religious figure in early nineteenth-century Britain. Irving was born in Annan in 1792; he studied divinity at Edinburgh University and eventually became minister of Hatton Garden Presbyterian Church in London. He was a charismatic figure, and his rhetorical powers were extraordinary. Many eminent metropolitan figures, including politicians and writers, were spellbound by his preaching.

A new church had to be built specially for him, so vast were his audiences. However, he tended to get carried away when dealing with what he regarded as the essential humanity of Jesus Christ; and in effect he developed his own version of Christianity. His excessively emotional performances in his pulpit give the lie to the notion that, in nineteenth-century Britain, people were scared to express emotion and were generally inhibited and buttoned up in public. On the contrary; it was a time of brazen sentiment and over-the-top public performance, although such behaviour was often disdained by the ecclesiastical authorities. Irving's theatrical preaching and the later public readings of Charles Dickens – almost orgies of melodramatic and sentimental manipulation – were typical of the age.

Irving may now be seen as a pioneer of the Pentecostal movement. His success was spectacular but short-lived. His overblown rhetoric and pulpit histrionics led to his condemnation and expulsion by the Presbytery of London. With his most loyal followers, the Irvingites, he formed a sect that soon fizzled out. He returned to Scotland, where he died in Glasgow, aged just 42, a forlorn and forgotten man. For a brief, heady period, he had been by far the most popular preacher in Britain.

Robin Jenkins

Robin Jenkins was one of the most respected and prolific Scottish novelists of the second half of the twentieth century; like Mrs Oliphant a century earlier, he was a thoughtful and scrupulous novelist. In persona, he was introverted and perhaps excessively sensitive. In the early 1980s, he continued writing novels but did not submit them for publication. In a profile of the author for the *Herald*, Jack Webster revealed that these typescripts were lying, literally, in a bottom drawer in the novelist's house at Toward, above his beloved Clyde estuary. Jack's revelation prompted a minor outcry. There was indignation in Scotland's literary community and beyond. Why was this distinguished Scottish author writing just for himself and not for the wider public?

Rather presumptuously, I decided that the *Herald* (of which I was deputy editor at the time) should play its part in bringing at least one of these unpublished novels to the light of day. After some hesitation, Jenkins agreed. We found a willing publisher, and the novel Jenkins chose was *The Awakening of George Darroch*, a sympathetic study of a kirk minister in the mid-nineteenth century. In part, it was also about the Disruption, although that event does not take place until the end of the action and is little discussed.

The book was launched, in some style, at the George Hotel in Edinburgh. This venue was chosen not because it was one of Edinburgh's more swanky hotels, but because it was adjacent to the church where the ministers had walked out at the start of the Disruption. It was a lively event attended by many folk – not just literati, but people from all walks of life. But the author himself seemed rather ill-at-ease. It was obvious that he was slightly embarrassed. He was a very private man, and, although he was courteous and gracious, he said very little, although he did emphasise that he didn't think that his book should be regarded as 'a Disruption novel' – rather, he saw it as more a sympathetic look at the life of a Victorian minister.

Jenkins obviously could not regard himself as any kind of celebrity, and indeed I began to wonder if we had done him a disservice by arranging for the novel to be published . . . yet good did come out of this stunt, if stunt it was, for Jenkins seemed to recover confidence; and, in the later 1980s and into the 1990s, he wrote some fine novels – which he wanted to see the light of day!

Meanwhile, I must admit that, for a novelist who produced superb novels such as *Fergus Lamont* (very long) and *The Cone Gatherers* (very short), *George Darroch* is a slightly disappointing work. It certainly had nothing of the intensity of what, for me, is Jenkins's finest novel, *The Thistle and The Grail*. Ostensibly a novel about that great Scottish obsession, football, it really treats football as a surrogate for religion.

The hero, a decent but weak and almost broken man called Andrew Rutherford, finds more pride and pleasure in football than in religion. Rutherford sees Scotland as a country of dying faith, likening it to the neglect of rotting roses, and bemoaning the loss of the secret at the heart of the resurrection. So, Rutherford, an excessively sensitive man who lived a life that was close to despair, probably had quite a lot of the author, his inventor, in him. Jenkins, in a creative way, blessed him through the understated, slightly ironic reverence of his writing. It is highly significant, in the Scottish context, that his love of football is presented as a compensation for the loss of religion.

Lewis Grassic Gibbon

Growing up in the north-east of Scotland in the 1950s and 1960s, I was vaguely aware of a book by that often dreaded and elusive spirit, 'the local author': a novel that seemed to be talked about a lot, but rarely read. There was supposedly something subversive and disreputable about it. The writer, apparently a man of pronounced left-wing views, had been a journalist in Aberdeen. He'd been supposedly fired for fiddling his expenses; he'd then disappeared off to England, and on to a career as a soldier. This turned out to be, more or less, correct.

When I eventually read the novel, in adolescence, I was gobsmacked. It was wonderful, and I'd read nothing like it before. At this time, more people were reading it, not just vaguely talking about it. It gradually 'took off' and eventually became widely popular, helped by a notable television adaptation. Now it is regularly acclaimed as the greatest Scottish novel of the twentieth century; and one poll actually suggested that it is the best Scottish book of all time.

The book is, of course, Lewis Grassic Gibbon's *Sunset Song*. It is the first part of a three-novel trilogy but is usually read on its own. *Cloud Howe* and *Grey Granite*, the other two novels, are considerably shorter and much less impressive. Gibbon did intend that the three books should be read as one great novel; and that may well be the correct literary way to approach them. But *Sunset Song* remains far more popular than the other two. It is written in a magnificent rollicking style that is unique; neither English nor Scots, it has a rhythm all of its own, and incorporates many Scots words that are obscure and forgotten. Despite this, it is gloriously readable.

Rereading *Sunset Song* after many years, I was immediately struck by how concerned, indeed obsessed, Gibbon was with Christianity in the small community of Kinraddie. (It is obviously a fictive community; but, in terms of its physicality and locality, it is very much set in the Mearns, the area of farming country south of Stonehaven and north of Laurencekirk, where Gibbon – real name James Leslie Mitchell – grew up.) *Sunset Song* is peppered, right from the start, with sly and mocking references to the religious life of the parish. The minister, the Revd Gibbon (no doubt this was intended as a joke), is an absurd man, a womanising hypocrite. Yet, at the end, the young heroine, Chris Guthrie, newly widowed, marries the Revd Gibbon's successor.

Chris Guthrie is the principal character: a complex, confused, ardent and sensual woman of considerable resource, but to some extent trapped by her limited rural environment. Her father, John Guthrie, a small farmer who works in his fields with inhuman intensity, is almost a pastiche of the Scottish hard man: an unimaginative, brutal, God-fearing boor. His tragedy, if tragedy it is, is that 'he loved the land better than God or his soul'. The most sympathetic of the minor characters, Long Rob of the Mill, is very hostile to Christianity.

Early in the novel, Gibbon describes what happens when three ministers come to Kinraddie to compete for the vacant pulpit and indeed the vacant manse. (Often, in Scotland, manses were fine big houses, sometimes bigger than the actual church.) The first preacher 'wore a brave gown with a purple hood on it, like a Catholic creature'; the second was 'an old bit man from Banff'. Some of the parishioners thought he'd be best, as he wouldn't be always on the lookout for a bigger kirk and a bigger stipend.

Stuart Gibbon, the third preacher, won 'by a thumping majority'. The author has some sport with his fictive namesake's attempt to ingratiate himself with the congregation: 'It was fair tickling to hear about things like that read out from a pulpit . . . a woman's breast and thighs . . . in that voice like the mooing of a holy bull'. The congregation soon find that they've made a grievous mistake: the man is pitiful, a hypocrite and a buffoon. When the First World War breaks out, towards the end of the novel, he preaches a ridiculous sermon praising the Germans; when he realises how unpopular this is, he glibly changes tack and whips his congregation to a war-mongering fervour (reminiscent of the real-life poet, Jessie Pope).

Gibbon describes the custom in the Church of Scotland whereby ministers applying for a vacant parish have to preach a sample sermon. The congregation, having heard two or three guest preachers, then vote for their choice. This practice, cruel as it could be, was better than that of having the local laird appoint his nominee – this happened all too frequently, and was a grievous continuing nonsense in a supposedly democratic church. (Over the years, I have witnessed several ministers 'trying for the pulpit', and I've been struck how nervous they all were, despite the fact that they were accomplished clerics, used to preaching.)

The novel ends with a brilliant series of set-pieces showing how the community of Kinraddie is affected by the faraway war; and then Chris, who is still young, having lost her first husband – shot as a deserter – decides to marry the new minister, one Robert Colquhoun, Gibbon's replacement and the son of the 'old bit man from Banff'. In truth, the novel ends in rather a hurry.

Gibbon is devastating about the national Church in *Sunset Song*, mainly because he does not take it seriously. He certainly does not respect it. Indeed, the Church of Scotland is presented as a joke, a comical counterpoint to the hard life of a rural community – and this in what has become the most generally venerated Scottish novel of the twentieth century.

The second part of the trilogy, *Cloud Howe*, describes Chris's life as the minister's wife in the mill town of Seggett. The minister is an idealist, but he soon falls into an obscure mysticism. He is mocked by his parishioners, while his wife is seen as an aloof snob. In the third novel, *Grey Granite*, Chris, once more a widow, runs a boarding house in a big port. The focus is now on her son Ewan, who becomes a communist agitator. Chris, after three failed marriages, is no longer at the centre of the action. Ewan has become the main character, but he is not presented with the same subtlety as Chris. The trilogy peters out.

But *Sunset Song* is utterly magnificent, a one-off rapture of a novel.

'Mac the great' and others

Hugh MacDiarmid, Alan Bold and Andrew Young

Hugh MacDiarmid

Hugh MacDiarmid (the pseudonym of Chris Grieve) was the contentious colossus who towered over creative and cultural Scotland for much of the twentieth century. 'Mac the great' was brought up in a rich Christian context, with a Presbyterian father and a very talented (and poetic) minister as key early influences, and in his teens he was an enthusiastic and formidable Sunday School teacher; but his religious zeal soon evaporated, and he became instead a determined, if erratic, foe of all organised religion in Scotland. Even so, he could never shake off the legacy of the Christianity in which he was steeped as a boy and an adolescent. Christian references abound in his poetry.

MacDiarmid was a considerable Scottish patriot, a relentlessly cerebral, combative, heroic writer and altogether a literary titan. He certainly thought so himself; as he said, he was vain but had much to be vain about. He could sneer spitefully at other Scottish writers, past and present – yet, in just about everything he wrote, there is something that is life-enhancing and worthy of deep reflection. The word 'genius' is much overused; but he was, without doubt, a writer of compelling, glorious genius. He was lucky in that he had a formidable disciple, the poet and journalist Alan Bold, who was 50 years younger but served, in the evening years of MacDiarmid's long and fecund life, in the roles of minder, propagandist, apologist and indefatigable champion.

MacDiarmid was brought up in the final years of the nineteenth century in Langholm, near the border with England, which possibly accounts for his intensive and sometimes showy awareness of his Scottishness throughout his long and very fecund creative life. His father, like George Mackay Brown's, was a postman, and was an elder in the United Free Church. The young MacDiarmid was greatly influenced by the local Free Church minister, the Revd Thomas Cairncross, who was a distinguished poet as well as a preacher of very long and stirring sermons. Cairncross wrote many lyric poems and a book of popular Christianity called *The Making of a Minister*. He wrote thus of the Langholm in which he ministered: 'It lies by the heather slopes/Where God spilt the wine of the moorland/Brimming the beaker of hills'.

This kind of invocation of Langholm in its own holy land probably influenced the young MacDiarmid more than he cared to admit in later life, although – never the most charitable of men – he was eventually to condemn Cairncross as a hypocrite and a careerist. Had the poet been born a little further north, perhaps in the coalfields of Ayrshire or the industrial badlands of Lanarkshire, it is quite possible that he might not have experienced Christianity at all in his youth. In that case, he could of course not have rejected it as a young man; he might even have embraced it, with that persistent ardent contrariness that was his defining characteristic.

As it was, from his late teens, MacDiarmid was a consistent (and consistency was not usually one of his virtues) atheist: his son Michael Grieve assured me of this more than once in conversations I had with him much later. But that does not mean that MacDiarmid should not have a place in this esoteric survey. He never wholly shook off the shadow of the Revd Thomas Cairncross, despite appearing to resent it bitterly. In his maturity, he could praise what he called the 'tremendous' message of Christ's Sermon on the Mount, and at the time of his nervous and physical crisis in the mid-1930s he referred to the 'certainty' of the Resurrection.

I think his avowed atheism should be seen as of a piece with his intermittent communism and consistent socialism; he saw it as an organised and effective way of dealing with the 'interdependencies of life'. Although a lot of his writing was self-consciously cerebral and political, much of it was also infused with mystical and spiritual depth. Despite this, he was an engaged, practical citizen, rooted in everyday matters; he did not eschew civic life. For a time, he was an industrious if somewhat wayward newspaper reporter; he served as a town councillor in Montrose; and he was also a Justice of the Peace. He was a very committed, if somewhat erratic, Scottish nationalist. (He managed to get expelled from both the Communist Party of Great Britain and the Scottish National Party, though not at the same time.) He had periods of retreat, especially in Shetland, but for most of his life he was committed to intensive public activity. He was on an eccentric and often vituperative mission to revitalise, and even to reinvent, not just Scots literature and the Scots language, but the nation itself.

In the First World War, he served as a sergeant in the RAMC in Salonika and France; in the Second World War, he contributed resolutely to the national effort by working – very hard, for a man who was almost 50 – daily ten-hour shifts as a fitter at Mechan's Engineering Yard at Scotstoun on Clydeside. The work was physically exhausting, and he was transferred to the copper shell shop. Here he suffered a serious industrial accident when a heavy pile of copper plate collapsed on him, injuring both his legs and one of his arms, and almost killing him. (This is not the kind of thing that happens to many middle-aged poets in the workplace.)

At this time, he was staying with his brother, Andrew. Their relations were hardly fraternal; indeed, they loathed each other. MacDiarmid was very good at making, and keeping, enemies, and he treated his long-suffering brother as an enemy rather than a host. As soon as he recovered from the accident in the copper shop, he worked briefly as a postal worker further down the Clyde at Greenock, which, at this time of war, was the busiest naval port in Britain. Through contacts he made there, he became a deckhand on a Norwegian vessel that was supporting larger vessels of the US and British navies in the Clyde estuary. (Significantly, these wartime roles he had in the 1940s lacked rank, and were humbler than his service as a senior non-commissioned officer in the First World War.)

A small and not particularly strong man, he drove himself on with an almost crazy zeal for life, for controversy and disputation, for literature and for very hard work. And, above all, for Scotland. He packed an enormous amount of very varied experience into his long life (he was even, for a short time, the headmaster of a tiny school in Easter Ross). Those who criticise or debunk him should always remember how hard he worked and how engaged he was.

Unremittingly combative and ferociously intelligent, he was a much more intellectual poet than Burns, though he does not seem to touch human beings in their millions as Burns can. But he was constantly reaching for his own soul, and for the soul of Scotland at the same time; many of his poems are charged with an undoubted, and very moving, spiritual questing. His rejection of Christianity does not mean that he was without spiritual ardour; far from it.

To paraphrase from his best, longest and most difficult poem, *A Drunk Man Looks at the Thistle*, he could hear eternity dripping drop by drop; and he heard God passing with a policeman's feet, in the long coffin of the street. His drunk man refused to be crushed by 'the echoes of that thundering boot' as he saw a monstrous thistle (an awkward and prickly symbol of Scotland's soul).

So, the thistle in this extraordinary, very long and very ambitious poem – quite possibly the most ambitious poem of the twentieth century – is an ambivalent (and of course very Scottish) sign pointing, in a rather confused but powerful way, to what Scotland is searching for. The eponymous drunk man is a splendid creation. He comes to realise that he can't see Scotland if he can't see what is infinite. His boozed-up contemplation of the complexities of Scotland reaches unlikely if ironic heights as he gradually becomes 'a greater Christ, a greater Burns'. (In today's Scotland, the latter is probably regarded by many as more provocative than the former.)

The poem, which is cerebral and satirical rather than emotive, is at first a paean to inebriation, then a gloriously idiosyncratic celebration of Scotland, and ultimately a complex statement, replete with many literary references, of ethereal and spiritual – if only obscurely Christian – inquiry. The drunk man starts off as a typically tiresome inebriated Scotsman but slowly progresses beyond mere drunkenness into a profoundly spiritual state where he not only identifies with the destiny of Scotland – whatever that might be – but also achieves an unlikely oneness with the entire created universe. From the petty and pathetic worry of having to crawl home to face the wrath of his girning wife (a very Burnsian concern), he soars away from this dreary reality and finds a transforming resurrection. The thistle, which had been 'grisly' and 'Presbyterian', has become, as if by magic, the key to the entire universe – and beyond.

The drunk man does not so much look at the thistle, and all that it represents, as grapple with it.

MacDiarmid was determined to write in Scots for literary and political purposes; *A Drunk Man* is in Scots, sometimes difficult and recondite Scots. He tried, and failed, to reinvent Scots as a living language, used routinely in everyday life. But he succeeded in reinventing it as a literary language. He also, later in his career, wrote sublimely in English. Some of his early Scots lyrics are particularly beautiful. They were published in the *Glasgow Herald*, which supported him when he was making his way in the literary world. To the paper's great credit, it also published extracts from *A Drunk Man*, a difficult and very controversial poem; this showed real editorial confidence and vision.

MacDiarmid was an enormously complicated man; he often contradicted himself. Well aware of this, he suggested that his 'job' was to erupt like a volcano, emitting not only flame but also a lot of rubbish. Even at the various times when his body was weak and ill, he remained truculent and fierce. With considerable self-knowledge, he once said that he would fight hard for a communist state, and, once that was achieved, fight hard to get rid of it. He strove relentlessly, without any concern for his mental or physical condition. His literary output was huge, especially if his prolific journalism is also taken into account.

It's not surprising that he suffered a very serious mental and physical crisis in 1935. But he recovered fully, and continued on his contrary and disputatious way until he died in 1978, aged 86, a brave and feisty battler for so many causes, lost and won. For me, he was by far the greatest Scot of the twentieth century. A case could be made for him being the greatest Scottish writer of all, bar none. If his political diversions and polemical ramblings could sometimes be tedious, there is no denying his literary integrity. Few, if any, other Scottish writers have been so devoted to their art.

He was a true and fervent Scottish patriot. Throughout his life, he was hostile to the English – sometimes vehemently so. He saw Calvinism as being associated with an Anglicising tendency, and actually came to believe that the English had used Calvinism to subjugate Scotland. (Certainly, it is true that many of the keenest Scots reformers, including Knox himself, were very Anglocentric; and the man who vanquished Scotland with more ferocity than any other, England's great general Oliver Cromwell, was a fervid Calvinist. But maybe MacDiarmid was contemplating more insidious uses of Calvinism.)

He certainly detested Scots whom he regarded as toadying to the English 'ascendancy'. He could write with extraordinary venom about other Scottish writers. Take Edwin Muir, for many Scots an almost saintly literary figure. MacDiarmid saw him as anything but saintly; he had utter contempt for the Orcadian writer, and cuttingly dismissed him as part of the 'Anglo-Scottish literati'. He could also be very nasty about the great John Buchan, despite the fact that Buchan had, with typical insight, understood the gargantuan literary task that MacDiarmid had set for himself. In 1925, Buchan commended what he called MacDiarmid's 'revolutionary' attempt to reinvent Scots as a living, working language. For this perception and generosity, Buchan was to receive a lot of uncalled-for abuse from the man he had praised.

Even Burns did not escape MacDiarmid's withering scorn. He felt that the Scottish adulation of Burns was a 'mystery'. He thought that, in his general behaviour, Burns had been so far removed from the generally accepted moral standards of the Scottish people that he could not understand why the Ayrshire poet was so adulated – unless it was all a giant exercise in hypocrisy.

But, as well as the constant backbiting, there was constant celebration of Scotland, its people, its potential and, perhaps above all, its magnificent landscape. He took an enormous, detailed delight in the glories of physical Scotland, from the raised beach of a Shetland island and the magnificent Torridon mountains in Wester Ross to the gentler hills by Montrose where his 'drunk man' finds his own Calvary, right down to the beautiful Border country he roamed in his youth. He did not, however, appreciate Scotland's cities, and he detested Glasgow; referring to the Bible, he would note that Cain was the first city-builder.

At the same time, he apprehended the universe and its many mysteries with a philosopher's curiosity; and, always, he was aware of the sheer mystery of life. There are many references to God in his poetry; and some of these are scathing. He wrote two controversial 'hymns'; both were addressed to Lenin, not God. Yet, along with his own creation, the questing 'drunk man', he believed that 'the thistle', that great and unlikely symbol of Scotland, could in time 'unite Man and the Infinite'.

MacDiarmid believed that the Church of Scotland had utterly betrayed its potential as a positive force in the wider Scotland. In his grand maturity, in 1976, he wrote that, even with all their education and brainpower, the ranks of hundreds upon hundreds of Church of Scotland ministers had contributed little or nothing to the literature of their country. (This was not quite true; think, for example, of John MacDougall Hay.) Even the most prominent of them, he opined, had not produced anything of note that would outlive them.

He was, above all, a free spirit, and he wanted Scots to think for themselves. Even as he pursued his erratic political allegiances, he came to reject all 'handed-down' ideologies. And he hated any maudlin, creepy notion of Scottishness, such as that peddled by his contemporary and enemy, the enormously popular entertainer Sir Harry Lauder, who not only presented Scotland as a kind of cloying wonderland peopled by egregious dolts, but also ended his shows with a sick-making, schmaltzy religiosity.

MacDiarmid rejected any parochial, cosy view of Scottishness. He was ambitious for his country. He always looked for the context, the big picture. His mature refusal to allow any religious explanation for the mysteries of life and the universe (the mysteries he was so well aware of and evoked so brilliantly) was very strong, and in a way his genius came to symbolise Scotland's lost Christianity.

Alan Bold

I find it impossible to write about MacDiarmid without invoking the spirit of Alan Bold, an exceptional literary journalist. Bold died, aged just 54, in 1998 – 20 years after his great hero MacDiarmid.

Bold, a huge man who was an amateur boxer in his youth in Leith, was obsessed with MacDiarmid. He did not conform to the stereotype of the literary figure. He was softly spoken, but his sheer size made him physically intimidating. He insisted to me and to others that he was the gentlest of men, a big softie. Sometimes, on pub crawls, he took with him a Leith hard man as his 'minder' in case he got into trouble he couldn't get out of. Indeed, he was not as conciliatory as he often claimed to be. He was brainy, boozy and belligerent. He once told a well-known female Scottish writer (Jessie Kesson) that she was really a man. To her irritation, he insisted he was serious. He often got into 'scrapes'; once, at a big private party in Edinburgh's Queen's Hall, he managed to lock himself in the ladies' toilet. Mayhem ensued.

Alan was a man of great kindness and spectacular literary productivity (he once wrote a novel in three days). His output was splendidly diverse: not only did he write excellent poetry and copious literary journalism, he was also a distinguished painter. He was very helpful to many writers and journalists, and immensely professional; if a book review or a literary essay was needed at short notice, he thought nothing of getting up at 4am, hungover or not, to get on with the work. He had a huge range of, and eclectic, cultural tastes: he could talk with equal authority about Elvis Presley and William Gerhardie and Eddie Turnbull.

He was MacDiarmid's most distinguished disciple; MacDiarmid encouraged Alan and admired (some of) his poetry. Alan made it his mission to explain MacDiarmid to the rest of Scotland. He worked scrupulously at understanding and explaining the great poet's sometimes obscure and often complex mental processes. After MacDiarmid died, Alan did an enormous service to Scottish literature by writing a thorough biography of the poet, which was eventually published in 1988. He also produced a huge edition of the poet's letters, and a very fine critical study, *The Terrible Crystal*.

Alan was consistently intrigued by what he saw as immensely strong Christian symbolism in MacDiarmid's finest work. He accepted what MacDiarmid regularly and insistently told him: that he was in no way a Christian writer. Alan understood this, but he remained certain that there was a deep layer of subliminal Christian imagery in much of the best poetry. I stress that I am not suggesting that Alan Bold was determined to claim MacDiarmid as some kind of covert Christian; that would most certainly not have accorded with his own cherished roles as a literary devotee and a serious critic. On the other hand, his determination to explore the deep roots of the poet's genius undoubtedly led him to believe that his hero's work was very strongly infused with authentic Christian imagery.

I got to know Alan in the late 1970s, when my job on the *Scotsman* meant that, among many other things, I had to commission the paper's book reviews. Alan proved to be an exceptional reviewer. This was just when MacDiarmid was dying of cancer. Alan some-times suggested that, along with my friend Julie Davidson, who was to become my wife, we should visit the poet at his cottage near Biggar. But I knew that MacDiarmid was seriously ill, and thought this might be intrusive.

As far as I know, MacDiarmid's last published work was a letter in the *Scotsman* in the early summer of 1978, praising Alan Bold's very controversial football verse. In my role as features editor of the paper, I had decided to publish some of Alan's (soon to be notori-ous) World Cup poems from his book *Scotland Yes!* – a selection of light new verse including some poems ingenuously anticipating Scotland's successes in the World Cup finals in Argentina.

Various intellectuals have suggested that football has replaced Christianity as modern Scotland's preferred, if surrogate, religion. (This is one of the themes of the fine novel by Robin Jenkins, *The Thistle and the Grail*.) Many Scots are undoubtedly obsessed with the game, and it inspires devotion, controversy and, occasionally, something close to salvation.

Anyway, my selection of Bold's poems was presented on the front page of the *Weekend Scotsman*. This created an enormous stooshie. The readers' reaction was virulently hostile. The switchboard may not have been jammed, but the editor, Eric Mackay, received many calls and letters of complaint. At best, the poems were characterised as childish doggerel; at worst, as infantile insults to the readers, the Scottish nation and also its proud football team (which was duly to perform calamitously in Argentina just a month later). What aston-ished me most about this excessive and visceral reaction was the sheer indignation of so many who complained to the editor: his paper had dared not to take football seriously. I remember reflect-ing that there might have been far less controversy had the poems been about religion.

As a young newspaper executive, I was quite worried by this eruption of pompous reader fury, and I was also aware that Alan was, unusually for him, rattled. Nobody of any significance seemed prepared to defend the poems and their presentation. The pitiful Scottish literary world was, at worst, sniggering gleefully on the sidelines; at best, it was silent.

Then, with a gesture of immense kindness, Hugh MacDiarmid, Scotland's finest living poet and a figure of world reputation, rallied from his sickbed and sent in a letter supporting the poems. Not only did he support them; he also made it clear that he had a very high regard for them. MacDiarmid acknowledged that high intelligence and football fanaticism seldom went together. In that respect, Bold had given his subject an unwonted dignity. But his poems were written with fine directness and economy. MacDiarmid went on to note that Scotland had in Burns a grand popular poet, and that he – MacDiarmid – had thought it was high time for a great unpopular one. He had reckoned the role might be his, but now it seemed that it would instead be Alan Bold's.

He proceeded to congratulate Bold on his 'splendid achievement', and he also congratulated the *Weekend Scotsman* on the 'splendid spread'. He concluded by writing, with gentle false modesty, that he thought he could recognise good poetry when he saw it. So, he applauded Bold's work.

This letter, intelligent, considered and perhaps just a tad mischievous, was a magnificent gesture; it certainly meant a great deal to both Alan and myself. Written by a man who was very close to death, it was a gesture of high charity, one that I would regard as essentially Christian.

✠

In the months and years that followed MacDiarmid's death a few weeks later, I had several conversations with Alan about the great man. The younger poet revered MacDiarmid, his memory and his huge corpus of poetry, literary journalism and letters. We did not often talk about religion, but Alan did tell me he was absolutely convinced that much of the complicated symbolism in MacDiarmid's work was without doubt Christian in origin. He also thought that there was a distinct mystic side to MacDiarmid, who sincerely believed that individual human beings could be transfigured.

Alan Bold also believed, more controversially, that MacDiarmid's intellectual elitism and exclusivity, and his frequently expressed contempt for so many other writers, were in part a Calvinist position: MacDiarmid regarded himself as one of the Literary Elect. Whether or not this was the case, it is indisputable that MacDiarmid had an unusually grand conceit of himself and was always confidently and aggressively conscious of his superiority to other Scottish writers. He called them, among other things, mucky mucks, fatheads, old wives of both sexes, lookers under beds, creeping Jesuses and commercial Calvinists. He had a great way with insults.

Like so many Scots, MacDiarmid had soaked up Calvinist Christianity when he was young, only to reject it in early adulthood – yet there lingered for him, and for so many other twentieth-century Scots, such as the prophetic educationist R. F. Mackenzie, some residual and enduring message that had been received and could never be totally, inexorably rejected.

Andrew Young

An altogether gentler and far less celebrated poet than MacDiarmid was Andrew Young. Born six years before MacDiarmid, Young never rejected the Christianity of his youth. Indeed, he became a clergyman: first in the United Free Church, and then – perhaps surprisingly – in the Church of England.

Young was born in Moray, where his father was a stationmaster. He received his tertiary education in Edinburgh, where he studied theology at New College. His first collection of poems was published shortly before the First World War; it attracted little notice. Indeed, it was not until much later, in 1950, when his *Revised Collected Poems* was published, that he at last received serious and deserved critical praise.

He had earlier ministered in Temple, Midlothian, but he found the place too cold. He moved to a Presbyterian church at Hove, on the Sussex coast; and then, in the 1930s, he became an Anglican. His last 19 years of full-time ministry were spent very happily in rural

Sussex as the vicar of Stonegate, a village near Royal Tunbridge Wells. Later, he was a part-time canon at Chichester Cathedral.

Utterly unlike the unruly MacDiarmid, with his constant, bludgeoning zeal for controversy, Young was a quiet – you might almost say furtive – poet. Indeed, his verse has a deceptive innocence, closely observing the natural world and sometimes possessing a suggestion of darkness that reminds the reader of Thomas Hardy.

Young occasionally lets slip a kind of Calvinist fear; indeed, one of his most haunting poems is called 'The Fear': out walking, he senses that he is being followed by some unpleasant beast. When he turns to find what is pursuing him, he sees only a bough heaving in the wind, and a bird raking through the leaves. Young adored flowers; and few have written about them better.

In his later years, he thought long and hard about death, and indeed started to write poetry about his own death. He became both more visionary and more mystical. He was without doubt one of the very greatest British poets of the twentieth century, and possibly the most subtle religious poet, but in persona he remained excessively private and modest.

Even so, his neglect amounts to a minor literary scandal. In recent years, his work has at last become somewhat better known, partly because he has been resolutely championed by the distinguished Scottish anthologist and poet Lesley Duncan.

John Buchan

John Buchan was a man of extraordinary precocity. He excelled in many areas, but he achieved most as a writer. Indeed, I would suggest that his magnificent novel *Witch Wood* is not just the finest Scottish religious novel of the twentieth century, but quite possibly the finest Scottish novel of the century. Buchan's father was a committed Calvinist – and Buchan imbibed his values, yet *Witch Wood* excels as a critique of the distortions of Calvinism that have blighted Scotland over the years.

John Buchan was an intensely devout Christian; of that there can be no doubt. Born the son of a Free Church minister, he learned to say his prayers every day – a habit he never dropped during his years of intensive public service. He could quote long passages from Bunyan's *Pilgrim's Progress*, as well as the Bible, by heart. In the evening of his life, he produced a powerful clarion call for the revival of Christianity:

> The quality of our religion is being put to the test . . . I am of Blake's view: *Man must and will have some religion; if he has not the religion of Jesus he will have the religion of Satan* . . . I believe that civilisation must have a Christian basis, and must ultimately rest on the Christian church. Today the Faith is being attacked, and the attack is succeeding. Thirty years ago, Europe was nominally a Christian continent. It is no longer so.

These words were written in 1939. He was obviously thinking of Nazism, but he was also penning what he believed was a wider truth: that the true richness in our world is the gospel of Christ. John Buchan strongly believed that if we lose Christ, we lose all.

In our secular times, many Scots would regard the passage quoted above as the ranting of a fanatic or the haverings of a zealot. Buchan was neither of these; he was a multi-faceted and able man of the world, one who excelled in many fields. When Buchan died, the editor of *The Times* said that the newspaper had never received so many unsolicited tributes to a public figure, pouring in from people of all walks of life.

There was nothing narrow or repressive in Buchan's disposition. He moved in many circles, and he crammed an amazing amount of life-enhancing effort into his 64 years. He was a man who achieved much success in the secular world. But to say that he was successful begs various questions. He had his critics; one of the more perceptive was the great Catholic novelist and critic Graham Greene, who accused him of worshipping success and materialism. The radical Scottish educationist R. F. Mackenzie – the closest to a genuine prophet I've ever met – despised Buchan. Mackenzie believed that he condescended to ordinary folk, consistently chased the mighty or the influential, and hankered after the life of a landed gent. Mackenzie reckoned that, from his schoolboy years, Buchan was determined on one thing: advancement, but advancement in England, not Scotland.

Hugh MacDiarmid, the greatest Scottish writer of the twentieth century, was more ambivalent. He could be very caustic about Buchan, but he was generous enough to appreciate that Buchan wrote well. Like many others, he thought Buchan wasted his true potential as a Scots writer because he resided in Oxfordshire and lived the life of a rural squire. MacDiarmid cared enough about Buchan and his talent to want him to return to Scotland.

Buchan himself once let slip that he thought Scotland produced more very good second-class people than any other country – but very few of the first class. His own career, while superficially one of enormous public success, did not really satisfy him. He inherited much from his father, who, although easy-going in persona, was deep down a hardline, driven Calvinist. Buchan's personal Calvinism manifested itself in a pressing sense of duty – and a constant awareness of evil, lurking everywhere, often where least expected.

※

John Buchan was born in Perth in 1875 on the day of his mother's eighteenth birthday. The next year, the family moved to Kirkcaldy in Fife, where he had a splendid childhood. Always a great walker –

he once strode across country for 63 miles without any significant break – as a wee boy he walked every day over 3 miles to his school, and 3 miles back. John belonged to a local gang who could be quite wild in an innocent kind of way: they once set some barrels on fire and rolled them into a derelict quarry.

His summer holidays were spent in the Borders at his grandparents' farm at Broughton, where his grandfather was an elder in the Free Kirk. Buchan was particularly proud that he came from Borders stock. During these long, fondly remembered summers, he befriended shepherds and tramped the hills. He became acquainted with poachers working the River Tweed. He learned about the country, its ways and its demands, and he developed a superb eye for the natural world. No-one has ever written better about the Scottish landscape than John Buchan. The Scottish Borders gave him, as he later recalled, happiness, security, adventure and nostalgia.

His father became minister of the John Knox Church in the Gorbals, just south of the Clyde in the heart of industrial Glasgow. Unlike his novelist son, the Revd John Buchan was not driven or ambitious. In his spare time, he would quietly arrange flowers or read Walter Scott. Although he was a dreamer, he was a committed minister, and he sometimes preached in impromptu style outside his church.

John Buchan went to school and university in Glasgow, and thence to Brasenose College, Oxford. Later, he wrote that he must have been 'an intolerable prig' at Oxford. He was older than most of his college contemporaries, and disapproved of many of them; he thought he had been 'pitchforked into a kindergarten' – he always had a superb turn of phrase. The revels of 'the alcoholic children' among his fellow undergraduates offended him. A plain speaker, he was unpopular with the 'emancipated schoolboys' he found himself among.

Whatever; if he was a prig, he was a very industrious one. He was president of the Oxford Union, he won the Newdigate Prize for poetry, and he wrote a history of his college. By the time he left Oxford, he was already listed in *Who's Who*. This frenetic activity continued as he made his way in the wider world.

He had written his first novel in 1895 when he was 20; another seven books were produced before he left Oxford. In London, he produced much fluent journalism, and read manuscripts for a publisher. He also read for the Bar, then left to become a colonial administrator in South Africa, and then returned to London to work as a specialist in tax law. He married Susan, the daughter of Norman de l'Aigle Grosvenor, a distant descendant of the Duke of Wellington. Although he sometimes patronised his wife, calling her 'my dear child', the marriage was successful and happy. At this time, Buchan was something of a dabbler, if a high-end one: he worked as a novelist, journalist, lawyer and publisher. In the First World War, he was a war correspondent; in 1917, he became the government's Director of Information.

Shortly after the war, he bought Elsfield Manor, about 5 miles north-east of Oxford, on the fringe of Otmoor; he had grown to love the (surprisingly wild) country around Otmoor during his student days, and Elsfield was to be the place where he was happiest. (I got to know Otmoor quite well during the late 1960s when I was at Oxford; and even then it was, though close to the city, a strange and bereft area, with an isolated feel. Most of the so-called 'seven towns of Otmoor' were in fact tiny and rather unprepossessing villages in which time stood still.)

So, Buchan had found a place to love and cherish; significantly perhaps, not in Scotland. He set his Saturdays aside for rambles across Otmoor or further afield, to places like 'Brill on the hill', although the hill was tiny by Scottish standards. He claimed that Otmoor was 'as remote from man as Knoydart or Barra'. He loved wandering through this mysterious 'waste', with its pitted and ribbed mud tracks. His biographer Janet Adam Smith, who as a young woman would sometimes visit the Buchans at Elsfield on Sundays, described Otmoor as 'surprising and untamed'.

But I reckon Buchan protested too much when he compared Otmoor to wild and lonely parts of the Scottish Highlands and Islands. He had settled into the life of an Oxfordshire squire; to some extent, as he must have realised, he had turned his back on Scotland. In his most popular story, *The Thirty-Nine Steps*, there is a passage that I think is psychologically revealing. After his – brilliantly described – adventures in the uplands of Galloway, the plot requires the book's hero, Richard Hannay, to rendezvous with a Foreign Office mandarin by the banks of the River Kennet, deep in Berkshire. We are told: 'After Scotland, the air smelt heavy and flat, but infinitely sweet'.

Although he could write beautifully, with both precision and awe, about the Scottish landscape, I suspect that it was the Oxfordshire landscape that he came to love the most. One of his critics, the Scottish writer and educationist R. F. Mackenzie, insisted that Buchan always wanted to live not like a Scottish laird but like an English lord of the manor.

On Sundays, he would worship at the local Anglican church, though he assured his mother that he would 'never' be an Episcopalian. (He claimed that Scottish Presbyterianism was 'in his bones'.) This ambivalence was reminiscent of Sir Walter Scott. Sometimes, letting his guard slip a little, he disclosed a dislike of Scottish clerics. In a brief but significant passage in *The Thirty-Nine Steps*, he gives a hilarious account of a political meeting in the Borders. It is a fast-moving narrative, and there was no need at all to even mention the chairman of the meeting. But Buchan succumbed to temptation, describing him as 'a weaselly minister with a reddish nose' who 'soliloquised on his influenza'.

In truth, his approach to Christianity was broad-minded; his personal religion was deep and sincere but inclusive; he was not one for bigotry or sectarianism of any kind. But, in religion, as much else, he had a tendency to succumb to snobbery. The only real flaw was an undercurrent of anti-Semitism, which sometimes stains his novels.

When he was young, he was strongly influenced by R. L. Stevenson; but he came to dislike Stevenson's work. One of his friends, the young Oxford historian A. L. Rowse, said that Buchan came to feel that Stevenson had 'altogether too much artifice' as a writer; Buchan felt that Stevenson's optimism and masculinity were essentially a pose.

He was elected MP for the Scottish Universities – which he represented in the Tory interest in the House of Commons, where there was some sneering about his voice: remarks were made about his 'Free Kirk whine', his 'manse intonation', his 'mincing tones'. Despite his Toryism, he liked and admired Ramsay MacDonald, his fellow Scot, who as Labour leader was reviled as a traitor by his own party for forming a National government.

Buchan too was treated with suspicion by some on his own side. He was never offered the Cabinet post he thought he deserved. Some regarded him as a dilettante. He told the Tory leader and prime minister Stanley Baldwin that politics had always been his chief interest (which was certainly not true). In his frustration, there was just a whiff of what that other prominent and sometimes peevish Scot, John Reith, was also to suffer.

Buchan had been 'bitterly disappointed' when he was not elected to a Fellowship at Oxford's most prestigious college, All Souls, in 1899. That rankled for many years, as did his failure to gain a significant honour for his work during the First World War. (He enlisted the support of many of the great and good to lobby on his behalf, but to no avail.) Later, he became embroiled in an unedifying dispute with Nelsons, the firm that published his books and where he worked part-time. The squabble was about money, pure and simple: Buchan felt he was underpaid. Before his wedding, he collapsed from excessive nervous tension. His progress through life was by no means as smooth as has sometimes been suggested.

He was delighted when, in 1933 and again in 1934, he was asked to serve as Lord High Commissioner to the Kirk's General Assembly. He was not first choice, but he took to the post with aplomb. He had a profound sense of Scottish religious history; he adored ceremony; and he knew that his mother, in particular, would be delighted.

Then he was appointed Governor General of Canada, his last prominent public post, and ennobled as Lord Tweedsmuir of (significantly) Elsfield. His time in Canada was a great success, though he did not warm to the Canadian premier, Mackenzie King; he had a much warmer relationship with the outstanding US politician of the time, Franklin Roosevelt. King was a Calvinist of the old school, and was shocked when Buchan told him that he did not believe in predestination.

✠

John Buchan died in 1940. Superficially, it had been a glittering career. But was it? He crammed too many tasks, too many offices, into his relatively brief life. He took all his posts seriously, but the world did not always respond to him as he expected it to; as a young man, he had been talked of as a future prime minister; he never came close to that. And, while his novels were enormously successful, now he is remembered for what he called his 'shockers' – particularly the Richard Hannay stories – rather than his more serious fiction. (He also wrote various biographies, full of insights but sometimes too hastily written, of great men such as Montrose, Walter Scott and Cromwell. And he worked on a history of the Church of Scotland.)

Where he excelled was as a writer of serious fiction. He wrote two genuinely great novels, which I discuss below. He was never a fashionable man, and certainly never became a real insider, a pillar of the Establishment. There was something elusive about him: as has been said, a Scotsman when in England, and an honorary Englishman when in Scotland.

In physique, he was lean and wiry; this helped him in his youth, when he would roam over the Border hills for mile after mile. But, as he became more and more prone to illness in the second half of his life, he found that he lacked physical strength. His mind remained strong, but his body became very weak. His poor health was matched by a certain unease with himself and the world. His Christian faith, while strong and sincere, was not of the kind to provide easy comfort.

In part, these tensions made him the fine writer that he was. His many years of public service allowed him to understand how the world worked, but he was not kidded; his essential Calvinism kept him aware that darkness was always there or thereabouts. He understood that civilisation was fragile; man's capacity for barbarism was never conquered. He had a real sense of the evil that stalked, and stalks, the world. His best biographer, Andrew Lownie, ends his excellent study of Buchan by quoting some acute words from his subject: 'A writer must invariably keep the best of himself for his own secret creative world'. And we should be grateful that he did just that.

As I suggested above, Buchan wrote too many books, fiction and non-fiction. And he wrote some of them too quickly, in rushed interludes between his many public duties. The best two are both outstanding novels, one set in seventeenth-century Scotland – *Witch Wood* – and the other set in twentieth-century Canada, *Sick Heart River*.

Witch Wood was his own favourite among his novels. He thought it was 'historically true'; he incorporated in the story much of the research for his biography of Montrose, who actually appears in the novel, though not as a major figure. He had written in his youth a rather slapdash biography of Montrose; he rewrote it between 1926 and 1928, and he mined this work to provide the superbly realised background in his fictive masterpiece.

Witch Wood is a novel of many merits. Among these are its sense of place: Buchan was writing about the country around Broughton that he knew and loved as a boy and a youth, but he was imagining it as it had been 250 years earlier, when it was far more wooded. His use of Scots is remarkable; he had a wonderful feel for the language. Unlike almost all writers, including Scott, who have written in both Scots and English in the same novel, Buchan's use of the two languages never jars, is never strained. He wrote many of his novels as entertainments, but *Witch Wood* is a work of deadly and deep seriousness. It amounts to a full-frontal assault on the excesses of Calvinism.

My good friend, the journalist and writer Arnold Kemp, was always convinced that this most powerful book is essentially a morality tale with a simple theme: if you repress men and women with an unduly grim religion, then you will drive them to perverted delights. Fair enough; but the theme is broader. Buchan wanted to assault the sheer hypocrisy, the degraded perversion that Scottish Calvinist extremists brought to Christianity: if you were of the Elect, you could do as you wished.

The barbaric activities that the young and ingenuous minister, David Sempill, slowly realises are taking place in his parish were no doubt, to some extent, a revolt against religious repression. But it was a revolt that was inexcusable in its excess. Meanwhile, over-zealous Calvinism is represented in particular by two of Sempill's fellow ministers, a couple of odious creeps whose oily religiosity is presented, with both subtlety and force, as nothing less than an abomination. These are strong words, but it is an extraordinarily strong novel.

When he arrives in his parish, Sempill is an innocent. He is at first enchanted with the great wood; slowly, bitterly, he understands that it has become a hateful place of fear and evil, a vast gloom-laden setting for devilry. In the heart of it, there is a pagan altar where women and men wearing grotesque masks celebrate a perverted version of the Christian sacrament.

Sempill bravely confronts this devilry – but, with almost unbelievable cynicism, his own Presbytery excommunicates him for his pains. One of Sempill's few supporters, a decent but drunken farmer, suggests to the minister that the excesses of the new Presbyterianism merely drove the parishioners back to their bad old ways (devil-worship) and indeed made them hypocrites as well as sinners. Similar views are held by the one local minister who supports Sempill – significantly, a man who is weak both in courage and in physique. His insight is that if innocence and joy are purged, religion will be soured and the result will be degradation and serious sin. But again, this man is not really sufficiently appalled by the perversion of Christianity that Buchan assails. David Sempill himself becomes crazed in his zeal to exterminate the evil around him: one of his enemies, an 'unco guid' elder, the ultimate justified sinner, is directly driven by Sempill to madness.

All this is very strong meat. *Witch Wood* is possibly the most deep novel about Scotland ever written; what makes it yet more compelling is the scrupulous care with which Buchan fills in the historical background. The novel also anticipates Grassic Gibbon's marvellous *Sunset Song*, which was written a year or so later, in Buchan's understanding of the rhythms of the farming year: lambing, sowing, harvest, and then the blackness of winter.

There are some magnificent set-pieces in this (relatively short) novel: they include a witch-hunt and Sempill's trial before his Presbytery, when the hypocrisy overflows; and there are some romantic interludes that Buchan just about carries off. The heroine, Katrine Yester, is not presented realistically but rather as a symbol of beauty and goodness amid all the darkness and doom.

Montrose makes only a brief appearance in the story; his colleague, Mark Kerr, has a bigger part, and at one point is secretly sheltered by Sempill. R. F. Mackenzie, always a mordant commentator on Buchan's writing, described the idea of Montrose travelling in disguise through Covenanter country as being like a well-spoken SAS officer trying to move incognito through the Republican heartlands of Northern Ireland.

Buchan subtly decided to suggest rather than graphically describe evil and depravity, but some of his scenes are direct and vivid and even brutal. His description of a hunted, tortured 'witch', delirious and squirming on the ground, is harrowing. Scene after scene builds to a grand critique of the 'demented twist' of Calvin's doctrines that could 'blast and rob a man's heart'. Another powerful set-piece occurs when Sempill comes across a group of drunken Covenanters who, like a pack of terriers, have chased and cornered a cat – except that the cat in this case is a poor Irish woman, a wretched creature lying in the lane, her clothes torn, her feet raw and bloody, her neck wounded. She dies before Sempill's eyes.

As he researched his revised biography of Montrose, Buchan become psychologically immersed in mid-seventeenth-century Scotland, one of the most terrible periods in Scotland's history, yet also a time of greatness. Here we have the paradox of the Covenanters. In writing this book, I confess I simply could not make up my mind about them: there is so much to admire, so much to detest. Buchan's novel sums up the best of the Covenanting position thus: you are faithful to your king so long as the king is faithful to law and religion. Your loyalty to the Kirk is the same.

And indeed, Buchan himself was ambivalent about the Covenanters, and certainly alert to the complexities of Calvinism; his great novel is by no means a one-dimensional attack on the doctrines of John Calvin. At the same time, the excesses of the Covenanters, their fanatical belief in an extreme, bent Christianity, are presented with enormous zest.

Witch Wood is without doubt a literary masterpiece; in the long progress of Scottish fiction, it is the ultimate antidote to Kailyard sentimentality, more forceful even than great earlier works like *Gillespie* or *The House with the Green Shutters*.

I believe it also has a significance way beyond literary history. The novel explores Scottish Christianity and its terrible under-belly with insight and even horror; you are forced to question, very seriously, just what kind of people we Scots are. *Witch Wood* is a deeply disturbing book, written by a Christian who understands the Devil. It is also a suffocating story because of the vileness of many of the characters, the weakness of the good folk who support Sempill and, in particular, the claustrophobic, stifling intensity of the setting.

As I reread it, a subversive thought occurred: is Sempill's par-ish really a metaphor for Scotland as a whole? Is Buchan indicting not just the more extreme Covenanters and a group of odiously hypocritical Calvinists – but Scotland itself? Is he writing an angry lament for Scotland's doomed relationship with Christianity? He might well be.

❖

After the dark power of *Witch Wood*, *Sick Heart River* is a gent-ler and more redemptive novel. Written when Buchan was himself dying, it is the story of a dying man on a peculiar mission in the remote wilderness of far North-West Canada. The book's hero, Edward Leithen, is searching for another man who has vanished in the wilderness; in doing so, he is in effect searching for his own soul, with death imminent.

It is a much kinder book than *Witch Wood*, but there is one great similarity: *Sick Heart River* is imbued with an intense sense of place, and Buchan does not hold back in his description of the harshness of the 'bleak immensities'. He describes a vast, hostile landscape 'where Man is nothing and God is all'.

Leithen had once been a straightforward Calvinist; he has mel-lowed, although in this great wilderness he is ever more aware of the strength of God. He rejects 'the glib little humanism' of his times. He is seeking to find, rescue and save a tormented man, a distinguished New York banker. This man's abrupt rejection of his apparently successful life, and his flight to the wilds, is never properly explained. And, indeed, the nature of Leithen's own journey is also mysterious. There is in the whole novel the sense of an extended and rather vague parable. Yet there is nothing wispy about it; the writing is clear and diamond-hard.

At the very moving conclusion, Leithen is in an encampment of Hare Indians, who are partly of Scottish descent and whose bereft and isolated community has been wracked by illness and privation. They have given up, mired in despair and disease. Leithen has recovered a little in the wilderness, having finally found the banker; he now finds the strength to encourage the Indians to find strength too. Somehow, almost Christ-like, the spent Leithen rallies them, and in so doing exhausts himself but finds true peace. This man, who had deliberately gone into the vast, lonely wasteland to save another man, now saves a community. Leithen gives the Indians the will to live, and then prepares for his own death. 'In sympathy with others, he lost all care for himself.'

Sick Heart River is not a particularly Scottish book in the sense that *Witch Wood* is. But Leithen's long and harrowing journey across the – superbly described – wilderness is obviously not just a physical one; it is, in the best sense, a Christian quest. This is Buchan's most profoundly religious work, for it is redemptive in a way that *Witch Wood* isn't. R. F. Mackenzie's slightly sour slant on this was that Buchan was trying to expiate all his own faults by sending one of his more sympathetic characters into a bitterly bleak territory to try to find salvation.

The conclusion to this most rewarding of novels is gentle and full of hope, yet it is earlier that Leithen senses that 'a great mercifulness' is breaking on him 'like a sunrise'. This anticipates the religious nature of Leithen's recovery and renewal. He realises that he had always hoped to die in April, when 'the surge of returning life would be a kind of earnest of immortality'. At that moment, he recovers the 'tenderness' he had lost. Tenderness is a peculiar word to use of a successful, worldly man, struggling in a hostile environment. But then, it was no doubt his worldly success that had made him lose his human tenderness.

Buchan himself, like his hero, is finally turning away from the quest for worldly success and reaching out to the ultimate Christian verity.

The Elie declaration

The Church of Scotland is in no state to be shedding good ministers, but that is what is currently happening over the vexed issue of gay clergy.

Slowly but surely through the early years of the twenty-first century, the Kirk's General Assembly has moved towards fully accepting gay clergy. I predicted that this would become a serious and increasingly divisive issue in my book *Outside Verdict* (Saint Andrew Press, 2002). Writing ten years later, Professor Walter Humes kindly noted that I had been 'uncannily prescient'. I appreciated the compliment, but I'm sure the signs were clearly there, even in the final years of the previous century. The liberals were gaining ascendancy over the evangelicals, and the issue of gay clergy would almost certainly become the key, defining issue that would ensure their triumph. And so it proved. Except that it must be a dangerous and hollow triumph if it entails the loss of good ministers.

What I failed to understand or predict at the start of the new century was the very deep pain, anguished heart-searching and intense spiritual grief that would be suffered by a growing number of ministers – and in some cases their congregations also – as they agonised about whether or not to quit the Church that they had served well and loved deeply. Indeed, I sometimes wonder if it is actually worse for the ministers who have decided to struggle on in a Church they no longer really trust or respect. This is just one of many acute problems the Church of Scotland currently faces; it is the one that brings with it the most pain, the most heartbreak.

It was at the General Assembly of 2011 that the crisis came to a head. The commissioners voted by 351 to 294 to move towards the acceptance for ordination of candidates in same-sex relationships. The Moderator, the Rt Revd David Arnott, declared: 'As the national Church, we shall continue to provide guidance and spiritual leadership for the Scottish people'. At the time, I noted that it was Mr Arnott's remarks rather than the actual Assembly decision that really infuriated the evangelical wing in the Kirk. They regarded his comments as provocative. They believed that their Church was abandoning its traditions and values and its commitment to Biblical truth. This was the year 2011, when an exodus of individuals, and also some entire congregations, became inevitable.

I believe that, as Christians, we have to listen to those on the outside as well as the insiders with their power and patronage, even when they seem to attack or assail their own church. Sometimes in times of crisis, comments can be off-puttingly vitriolic and sometimes they can be gentle and quiet but the Church has the task of listening and understanding the root of each message.

The Revd Brian McDowell, a man I know to be a conscientious, industrious and compassionate pastor, as well as a fine preacher, moved to the congregation of Elie and two adjacent linked parishes in 2007, after serving for over a decade as a full-time private-school chaplain in Edinburgh. I was a governor of the school for ten years, and I worked closely with Brian on various pastoral issues. I was always impressed by his empathy with young people and his tireless commitment to his job. After he moved, he and his wife Mary were very happy in the manse at Elie, a prosperous community on the littoral of the East Neuk of Fife. There, Brian was a success; he grew the three linked congregations at a time of general decline, and was a popular and effective minister.

Then, after four years of successful ministry, he stood in the pulpit at Elie and made a dramatic declaration. He announced that he had reached a decision that weighed very heavily with him. He was giving up his work among people he had come to love. He believed that the Church of Scotland, through the decisions of its sovereign body, the General Assembly, had challenged the very authority of God.

Brian's resignation declaration may seem old-fashioned in its Biblical strength, and possibly more resonant of the Old Testament than the New; but, to me, his words remain enormously moving (and I write that as someone who would have no personal objection to being in a congregation with an openly gay minister). Brian stood steadfast as he announced his decision. Here is the peroration at the conclusion of his magnificent declaration:

> God values nothing in a nation, a church or a human heart but his truth. The present schemes and designs of the Church of Scotland will be of no profit in the coming days. A thousand woes will one day fall upon those who have sneered at the Word of God and substituted a human philosophy that is neither good nor true . . . There are many who regard truth and error as matters of small consequence. If a man lives rightly, they say – what does it matter his beliefs? Such statements should not surprise us. Night and day are alike to a blind man. Truth and error are alike to an ignorant man.
>
> But remember: God will have his truth glorified . . . This is the day for us all to make the truth of God our chief interest and the object of our prayers. All else will pass away: the grass withereth, the flower fadeth, but the Word of God shall stand for ever.
>
> Mary joins me in saying that the four years we have spent here have been among the happiest and most blessed of our lives. We are deeply sad at the circumstances that have brought us to this present pass. We would be sadder still if any of you should feel that anything you have done or said had in any way been the cause of our present situation. You have not.
>
> Please pray for us, as we shall pray for you.

Endnote

by the Very Revd Lorna Hood, Moderator of the
General Assembly of the Church of Scotland 2013–14

The information spread like wildfire round the town that Renfrew North Church had called their new minister – and she was a 'wumman'. There was a question on everyone's lips: 'Wis there naebudy else?'

It was 1979, and women had been ordained for some ten years, but only a handful of these 'strange creatures' had been inducted into parish churches. I recalled that time with some affection when I was installed as Moderator of the General Assembly in 2013 – and, listening in the packed gallery, were members of that same congregation where I have ministered for some 35 years. I also recalled that it was 50 years almost to the day when the pioneering Mary Levison had petitioned the General Assembly to be ordained.

Now over a quarter of the parishes are served by ministers who just happen to be female. But, perhaps more significantly, if you look at the wider Church you'll see that women not only make up the majority worshipping in many congregations but also serve in positions of leadership locally and nationally. Although, for some, the change has been too slow, there are still some areas in Scotland with no female ministers and all-male kirk sessions. These are, however, small pockets, reflecting perhaps as much a cultural position on the place of women as a theological one.

The place of women in the Church, now simply taken for granted, reflects not only a society in Scotland that strives to be welcoming and inclusive but also a Church that is committed to demonstrate, in its life, an openness and equality that is the hallmark of the gospel. The changing attitude to the place of women in the Kirk is but one example of a renewed confidence, willing to let go of the past, and finding new ways of worshipping and serving.

For several years, the Church did not appear at ease with itself, was afraid to engage with the media, and was often unable to speak with one voice on the major issues affecting the people of Scotland. A past Moderator, seeking to issue a statement on an important issue, was told simply to keep his head down.

Yet, over my year as Moderator, I have witnessed a Church that is now seeking to live up to its calling as the national Church – a calling based not on privilege but on service, speaking out on the major issues affecting Scotland. A strong voice speaking out on behalf of the poor and the voiceless; being there for people at times of deepest need and showing them the love of God and the power of the risen Christ; standing alongside them whether they have a faith or not.

Wherever I have visited, those in education, industry, social services and hospitals shared their vision and their hopes for a future Scotland. And they did not envisage Scotland without its national Church. There are many challenges ahead, with declining numbers in membership and in the ministry. But the Church is facing up to these challenges with a new determination and a renewed vision. I am confident that we will continue giving service as a national Church that is welcoming and inclusive to all the people of Scotland.

References and further reading

Bold, Alan, 1983, *The Terrible Crystal*, Routledge.

Brown, George Douglas, 1901, *The House with the Green Shutters*, John MacQueen (2005, Polygon).

Buchan, John, 1941, *Sick Heart River* (2007, Polygon).

Buchan, John, 1927, *Witch Wood*, Hodder & Stoughton.

Galt, John, 1821, *Annals of the Parish* (2004, Kessinger).

Gibbon, Grassic, 1932, *Sunset Song* (2006, Polygon).

Hay, John MacDougall, 1914, *Gillespie* (1979, Canongate).

Jenkins, Robin, 1987, *The Awakening of George Darroch*, Penguin.

Lockheart, J. G., 1822, *Some passages in the life of Mr Adam Blair, Minister of the Gospel at Cross-Meikle* (1963, Edinburgh University Press).

Reid, Harry, 2002, *Outside Verdict*, Saint Andrew Press.

Scott, Walter, 1916, *Old Mortality*, John Murray (1993, Edinburgh University Press).

Spark, Muriel, 2009, *The Comforters*, Virago.

Spark, Muriel, 1961, *The Prime of Miss Jean Brodie*, Macmillan.

Wylie, James Aitken, 1870, *History of Protestantism*, Cassell Petter & Galpin.